"After over thirty years in uniform, I hadn't expected to learn something new about leadership from a book—but Tom Gordon proved me wrong. His engaging style brings to life a well-covered topic with insights that are extraordinarily perceptive and informative. If you are going to read one book on the topic of leadership—this is it."

—**Col Andy Milburn, USMC (Ret.)**, former commander, Marine Raider Regiment, author *When the Tempest Gathers: From Mogadishu to the Fight Against ISIS, a Marine Special Operations Commander at War*

"From his first days as a Citadel cadet and during his thirty years of active Marine service, Colonel Gordon studied great leaders and great leadership in order to record best principals, best practices, and best publications. But Colonel Gordon is not just a scholar of leadership but an outstanding practitioner as well. He has used those observations he recorded to great effect as he led Marines in war and peace; during training and operations; and with high achievers and leadership challenges alike at all levels of the Corps. Now he has distilled thirty plus years of study into fifty lessons of leadership applicable to all leaders, military and civilian, who desire to maximize their skills at 'getting things done though people.' A true textbook for all leaders or those who hope to be."

—**LtGen Richard P. Mills, USMC (Ret.)**, president and chief executive officer Marine Corps University Foundation, former commander, Marine Forces Reserve

"Tom Gordon has skillfully compiled a treasure trove of useful leadership lessons in his very compelling narrative. A must read for those focused on becoming better leaders and team builders!"

—**LtGen Mike Dana, USMC (Ret.)**, former deputy commandant, Installations and Logistics

"A great field guide of character and competence, the key components of trust and the core of leadership. A compilation of experiences to help shape your own. Tom sees life as an opportunity to learn and we should take advantage of it."

—**RDML Brian Brakke, USN**, former commander, Navy Expeditionary Combat Command

MARINE

TURNING
LEADERSHIP
PRINCIPLES
INTO PRACTICE

MAXIMS

COL THOMAS J. GORDON, USMC (RET.)

NAVAL INSTITUTE PRESS
ANNAPOLIS, MARYLAND

Naval Institute Press
291 Wood Road
Annapolis, MD 21402

Library of Congress Cataloging-in-Publication Data
Names: Gordon, Thomas J., date, author.
Title: Marine maxims : turning leadership principles into
    practice / Col. Thomas J. Gordon, USMC (Ret.).
Description: Annapolis, Maryland : Naval Institute Press, [2021] |
    Includes bibliographical references and index.
Identifiers: LCCN 2021011621 (print) | LCCN 2021011622
(ebook) | ISBN
    9781682476970 (hardcover) | ISBN 9781682477175 (epub) |
ISBN 9781682477175 (pdf)
Subjects: LCSH: Leadership. | United States. Marine
    Corps—Officers—Training of. | United States Marine
    Corps—Officers—Conduct of life. | Command of troops. |
    Gordon, Thomas J., 1969-
Classification: LCC VB203 .G67 2021 (print) | LCC VB203
    (ebook) | DDC 359.96/33041—dc23
LC record available at https://lccn.loc.gov/2021011621
LC ebook record available at https://lccn.loc.gov/2021011622

♾ Print editions meet the requirements of ANSI/NISO z39.48-
1992 (Permanence of Paper).
Printed in the United States of America.

29 28 27 26 25 24 23 22 21   9 8 7 6 5 4 3 2 1
First printing

"Act only in accordance with that maxim through which you can at the same time will that it become a universal law."
—Immanuel Kant, *Groundwork of the Metaphysics of Morals*

CONTENTS

PREFACE

I am passionate about leadership. Over thirty years in uniform I closely observed my leaders, seniors and subordinates alike, in the hopes of distilling some determinative quality or practice that explained their successes. I wrote down what I saw, and I am sharing these lessons here because leadership can be learned—and is learned best by modeling the behavior of great leaders. Some of these maxims are perhaps a bit clichéd, but I have found them no less true.

I make it a point to learn something about leadership daily. I study great leaders in search of practical cases of exemplary leadership. On my daily commute I listen to leadership podcasts and audiobooks. My bookshelves are filled with the works of the great leaders—military leaders, statesmen and presidents, business leaders, captains of industry and athletic teams, and religious leaders. In my readings on leadership I look for my next book in the cited works of my last, hoping to find the root or primary source of their wisdom. In doing so, I found there are few original thinkers in the field. Contemporary leadership authors borrow from and build on the previous generation's work. So if these maxims are not of value to the reader, I trust that at least the bibliography will be.

After reading about leadership, there are few things I enjoy more than talking about it. I seek out mentors by starting leadership conversations with them to tease out some of their wisdom. I relish the opportunity to gather with junior officers and staff noncommissioned officers (SNCOs) to talk with them about leadership and to test my theories, always looking to glean their feedback and perspectives. As a result, this work is about "paying it forward"—meaning, it is all leaders' responsibility to pass on what they have learned to the next generation so that its members may become better, more effective leaders. It has been said that the true measure of leaders' success can best be found in the success of their successors. In the final analysis of one's career, the only part of your leadership that will endure is the future success (or failure) of those whom you led.

I selected these maxims because they are principle-based and practical. They are a collection of practices and behaviors that can be applied daily. Their value is more demonstrative than a theoretical proclamation about how you should lead. As I enter the final stage of my career in uniform, my response to examples of great leadership has gone from "I hope to do that" to "I wish I had done that." This reality, however, has not dissuaded me from my quest. I will forever seek opportunities to develop future leaders and grow my own leadership skills in the process. If your leadership is not growing, it is dying.

In his book *Developing the Leaders around You*, the leadership guru John Maxwell wrote that the development of great leaders is the highest calling of leadership. Maxwell attempts to answer the first question posed in every military academy or Reserve Officers' Training Corps (ROTC) leadership course curriculum: "Are great leaders born that way . . . or made through work, study and practice?" We share the same answer—that while there are a few naturals out there with inherent leadership qualities, for the vast majority of us leadership skills come through hard work and a lot of practice.

I have benefited greatly from some great coaches and mentors throughout my career. Many of these maxims are direct lifts from their wisdom. If you do not yet have a mentor, find one. Most mentors will not come to you (initially); you have to seek them out. Some of my most influential mentors are known to me only through their written word. Their works line my bookshelves. Therefore, in addition to the "saved rounds" (practical thoughts and tips) at the conclusion of each maxim, I included some recommended readings that have informed my positions and style.

I should say here, as does a recent Marine Corps tactical publication, that "unless otherwise stated, whenever the masculine or feminine gender is used, both men and women are included."[1]

My motives for writing this manuscript were ultimately self-serving—the best way to learn something is to teach it. Pulling these axioms together has been illuminating and has shown me how much I myself need to improve as a leader. As I previously confessed, many of these maxims are not mine, and my application of them has in some cases never advanced beyond the aspirational. Any success I may have had was borrowed. Where I fell short, I have included my missteps here so the reader can benefit from them. Of the reader and the leader of the future, I only ask that you go on to make new and original mistakes.

John Maxwell wrote that leadership is about adding value to people.[2] If these maxims are of value to you, then I have accomplished my mission.

INTRODUCTION

I t has been said that less than 1 percent of the population is capable of an original thought. If this is true, I consider myself a proud member of the majority. Therefore, I must preface this work by stating that these leadership maxims are not mine but an anthology of the truisms I picked up from my leaders, both good and bad, along my nearly thirty-year journey in uniform. If one's leadership approach is analogous to a toolbox, these maxims are the instruments I acquired from some (one way or another) remarkable leaders. Further, I am obliged to add that the views expressed are my own and not to be construed as implied by or representative of positions of the U.S. Marine Corps (USMC) or Department of Defense (DOD).

One of my first mentors, the Marine officer instructor (MOI) at The Citadel, Maj Bill Gerichten, insisted that all aspiring Marine officers at The Citadel carry a "green book." This standard-DOD-issue, green clothbound notebook became my leadership journal. Whenever I observed a leadership practice that I admired, I captured it in my ever-present green book in the hopes that someday I might be in a position to put that example into action myself. Conversely, whenever I had the misfortune to work for or in the proximity of a "tool," one who exhibited less than admirable leadership qualities, I documented their missteps in the back of the book as a reminder of what not to do if ever placed in a similar position.

About ten years ago, after twenty years of service, the book was full. I consider myself blessed to have far more entries in the front of the book than the back. As a gift, I shared these maxims with the officers of 1st Tank Battalion, the unit I was in command of at the time, during a leadership retreat. My intent was to "pay it forward" and provide these leaders with a leadership primer they would, ideally, build on through their own careers.

Though my original green book was filled, I continued to collect and record the great and poor leadership I observed. Interestingly, as I assumed command of larger organizations the primary source for these "best practices" came not from the leaders I worked for but from the subordinates I was serving. Instead of gathering techniques in the hopes of employing them someday, I found myself thinking, "I wish I had done that." Such is the talent of the leaders in today's Marine Corps.

Though I am presenting these maxims as leadership tactics, techniques, and procedures (TTPs), I do not pretend that they alone will make you a good leader—Marines see through insincere ploys and hollow rhetoric. Just as reading a book on golf will not by itself make you a better golfer, just reading about leadership will not make you a better leader. Without authenticity, the application of any leadership maxim will come across as forced or contrived. One of the most important leadership attributes I found is to truly care about those Marines whom you serve. There is nothing Marines will not do to accomplish the mission—including making the ultimate sacrifice—if they believe their leaders genuinely care for them.

Compiling these maxims was an exercise in self-reflection. I discovered significant gaps between what I had intended to do and what I actually accomplished. My own application of these maxims was never as clever, skillful, or deliberate as this manuscript may lead one to believe. The purpose of this work is not to rewrite the history of my various commands or whitewash my many leadership shortfalls. Instead, I offer what I hope will be a practical tool—a primer for the reader's own "green book" of leadership. Please feel free to add and delete as you choose, but whatever you keep, make it your own!

LEADERSHIP DEFINED

Leadership is not a noun; it is a verb. It is not a position or a place; it is a relationship. Leadership is a dialogue between the leader and the led. Marines don't serve their leaders; leaders serve their Marines. Leadership is not a problem to be solved, but it is about solving problems. In fact, if people are not bringing their problems to their leaders, chances are people do not see them as leaders, regardless of their reserved parking space, title, or rank. The Marine Corps uses the word "inseparable" to describe the relationship between the leader and the led. Every Marine will attest that LtGen John A. Lejeune, the thirteenth Commandant of the Marine Corps, said it best:

> The relation between officers and enlisted men should in no sense be that of superior and inferior nor that of master and servant, but rather that of teacher and scholar. In fact, it should partake of the nature of the relation between father and son, to the extent that officers, especially commanding officers, are responsible for the physical, mental, and moral welfare, as well as the discipline and military training of the young men under their command who are serving the nation in the Marine Corps.[1]

Despite what the Marine Corps teaches, leadership is not the sum of one's personal leadership traits. Gen Anthony Zinni, USMC (Ret.), once said, "Adherence to a prescribed list of leadership traits will make you a good person, but not necessarily a good leader."[2] Leadership is about results. You cannot separate leaders from the effects of their leadership. Ineffective leadership is actually the *absence* of leadership and therefore not leadership at all. Your legacy as a leader, however, will be defined not by *what* you accomplished but by *how* you did it. If you lead with integrity, you will be remembered as a leader worth following. Leaders who are in it for themselves are not followed willingly. Dictating is not leading. Leadership, therefore, exists only in the eyes of an organization's members and stakeholders.

The U.S. Marine Corps defines leadership as the "art of getting things done through people." The determinative factor for Marine Corps leadership is mission accomplishment. "Mission first, people always" is a popular refrain within the Corps. We are, however, ever mindful of the sacrifices required to accomplish this mission. We may be required to sacrifice the very thing we swore to protect—Marines under our charge. This paradox is what sets military leadership apart from that of our civilian counterparts.

Writing in the late fifth century BC, the Greek historian Xenophon was perhaps the first to define military leadership as a relationship between the leader and the led. Xenophon defined leadership as "following by free will during times of intense hardship."[3] Plato, Socrates, Cicero, and other ancient philosophers believed coercion was antithetical to leadership; to these ancient thinkers, requiring people to do something against their will was more akin to tyranny. Plato defined leadership as the art of inspiring the soul regardless of external circumstances. Two and a half millennia later, Lord Moran—Winston Churchill's personal physician during World War II and a frontline army surgeon during the Great War—defined leadership as "the capacity to frame plans which will succeed and the faculty of persuading others to carry them out in the face of death."[4]

Though the consequences of military leadership eclipse those in the corporate sector (the loss of human life versus a dent in the bottom line), we can still learn much from leaders not in uniform. The military certainly does not have a monopoly on effective leadership. In fact, the military has more in common with civilian leadership than it has differences. In unpacking these maxims, I borrowed heavily from some civilian leadership heavyweights to provide context that transcends the civilian/military divide. My own leadership style has been greatly influenced by my readings of John Maxwell, Jim Kouzes, Barry Posner, and Jim Collins, to name a few.

John Maxwell distilled his definition of leadership down to a few words—influence, value, and service. Though today's military is still a hierarchical, position-based organization, its leaders can be distinguished by their influence more than by their positions or ranks. In all of Maxwell's many books on leadership, his leadership objective is always to "add value to people." When you take time to get to know your people and appreciate their efforts, you add value to them, and they in turn add value to the organization. Leadership for Maxwell comes down to service. Maxwell knew too well that people overestimate the perks and underestimate the price of leadership.[5] In my personal experience, RHIP (Rank Hath Its Privileges) was always eclipsed by RHIR (Rank Has Its Responsibilities). In command, there are rarely two consecutive good days: the intrinsic benefits of leading Marines outstrip any extrinsic reward.

Jim Kouzes and Barry Posner, in their classic work *The Leadership Challenge*, define leadership as "the art of mobilizing others to want to struggle for shared aspirations."[6] The key to Kouzes' and Posner's definition is two words: "want to." To these authors, leadership is about influence. Simon Sinek, another popular writer in the field, distinguishes leadership from manipulation, focusing on the "why." In his book *Start with Why*, Sinek helps leaders find their "purposes." Once discovered, these purposes provide their inspiration. People do not buy what you do, he writes, but they buy why you do it.[7]

In a 2001 *Harvard Business Review* article that would become the basis for a best-selling book on leadership, *Good to Great*, Jim Collins paints a compelling and counterintuitive portrait of the skills and personality traits required of an effective leader. Collins calls the person who has attained the pinnacle of the art the "Level V leader." Level V leadership consists of a duality—what some would consider a paradoxical combination of professional will and personal humility. This humility, when combined with a ferocious resolve, is revealed in an effective leader's tendency to give credit to others while reserving blame to himself.[8]

From all of these sources, perspectives, and experiences, I developed my own definition of leadership: *the ability to inspire others to find the will and the way to accomplish the mission.* In keeping with Marine Corps doctrine, mission accomplishment remains paramount, though I elevate the ways and means to equal importance. To be effective, a leader must personify the will and skill to persevere in the face of danger or difficulty. Done properly, leadership solves problems while adding value and making everyone on the team better.

Great leadership is more about multiplication than addition. The best leaders set conditions in which subordinate leaders can grow and, therefore, increase their influence. In the Marine Corps, you can trace the genealogy of our great leaders. As the commanding officer of the 7th Marines, Col Buck Bedard's battalion commanders included LtCol Jim Mattis, LtCol Robert Lee, and Maj Bob Neller. All but one of his regimental commanders when he was a division commander as a major general went on to be lieutenant generals, and James Mattis was to become the secretary of defense. One went on to be the Commandant of the Marine Corps and the Chairman of the Joint Chiefs of Staff; his assistant division commander, BGen John Kelly, went on to be the commander of U.S. Southern Command (USSOUTHCOM), secretary of homeland security, and White House chief of staff. I do not know who the next leaders of the Corps will be, but I will bet a disproportionate number will have served together in a battalion led by one of these current paragons of leadership in the Corps.

A distinction I do not find useful is that between leadership and management. The truth is that a good commander needs to be both an effective leader and a proficient manager. Some of the following maxims are leadership techniques, while others are management best practices. Leadership, beyond the obvious responsibilities (a commander leads people and manages things), can be a nebulous concept. Management is a science, however, and its consideration gives form and structure to leadership discussions. It is the leader's job to inculcate a vision in the collective and inspire it to achieve an end state, but he will never get there without properly managing the planning and supervising the execution.

If you are reading this because you aspire to become a greater leader, I ask that you check your motives. This is not a self-help book. You need not read past the second maxim—"It Is Not about You"—to realize that these maxims are not about your ascent to greatness. Servant leaders do not aspire to "be somebody"; they have a passion to *do something*. Leadership is about service and ability to see beyond yourself in the service of others. The first maxim—"Know Thyself"—requires you to check your motivations, calibrate your moral compass, and decide what you are willing to do in order to accomplish the mission. Every maxim thereafter focuses on the mission or the Marines and sailors.

Leadership is easy. Being a leader is hard.

I

———

Leadership Philosophy

1

Know Thyself

This first maxim is neither new nor novel. This ancient Greek aphorism was first inscribed above the entrance of the Temple of Apollo at Delphi. It appears also in Plato's *Protagoras* (written as a "dialogue" between Plato's teacher Socrates and a locally celebrated thinker). Here Socrates praises certain philosophers—remarkably enough—for their use of "pithy and concise sayings" to educate.

A century before, "Master Sun," the ancient Chinese military strategist Sun Tzu, prophetically wrote in the third chapter of his treatise *The Art of War* this axiom: "If you know the enemy and know yourself, you need not fear the result of a hundred battles. If you know yourself but not the enemy, for every victory gained you will also suffer a defeat. If you know neither the enemy nor yourself, you will succumb in every battle."[1]

"Know yourself and seek self-improvement" is the first principle of leadership every Marine is taught at Officer Candidate School. So, why is it first? Because when you know who you are, you will know what to do. Though these maxims are intended for practical use, a certain degree of introspection is required in order to build a parapet behind which you can hold your ground when things get tough as a leader. Thematically, these maxims build on a foundation of character, courage, and will. Without a solid foundation, your leadership will be like the proverbial house built on the sand: it will wash away when put to the test.

In his book *Good Leaders Ask Great Questions*, John Maxwell wrote that "the unexamined leader is not worth following."[2] Maxwell encourages leaders to check their motives daily. People have two reasons for doing everything, he writes, "a good reason and the real reason."[3] Leaders who do not question why they are doing something are unlikely to stay on track, perform at their best, or reach their potential.

Self-awareness is foundational because it is impossible to manage the emotions of others if you are not in tune with your own moods. Yet knowing yourself is not easy. We have all worked for a leader with a highly developed sense of importance and a remarkable lack of self-awareness. In his work *Poor Richard's Almanack*, Benjamin Franklin observed the great difficulty of knowing oneself: "There are three things extremely hard: steel, a diamond, and to know one's self."[4] Leaders who are self-aware—those capable of being honest with themselves about themselves—are perceived as authentic.

Knowing yourself enables you to align your beliefs and your behavior. This alignment produces authenticity. Marines value authentic leaders—leaders they can believe in. Authenticity occurs when there is congruence between stated values and deeds. Integrity means integrating your values into your actions. Identifying and declaring your values is key, and by "walking the talk" and being yourself you build credibility. Conversely, if people do not believe in the messenger, they will never believe the message.

When General Zinni taught leadership after retiring from public service, he would often ask students to respond in writing to the following question: "Who are you?" The students, believing their essays would be collected and reviewed, spent some time polishing their responses. Instead of collecting them, the general asked the students to consider revising their responses, knowing this time that they were for their personal consumption. Many students were taken aback to realize the differences in their public and private responses. When answering the question the first time, students tried to sell themselves. The second time, however, they realized that they defined themselves quite differently to other people than they did to themselves.[5] The discovery of the discontinuity between one's "ideal" and "actual" selves can be the most critical moment in a leader's development. Personal and professional growth as a leader is possible only through deliberate personal discovery. Only then will you know where you need to improve and what you need to reinforce. The best leaders are acutely self-aware. They are honest with themselves about themselves. They know their capabilities and limitations and understand how each is perceived by their people. Pastor Rick Warren once preached that humility is not denying your strengths but being honest about your weaknesses. Self-aware leaders are able to amplify their strengths and mitigate their shortfalls by surrounding themselves with people who balance or compensate for their deficits.

John Maxwell once said, "Leadership is an inside job."[6] When you are bigger on the inside than the outside, the outside cannot control the inside. By taking the time for personal reflection, you calibrate your moral compass. You do not need a compass when the weather is clear and you know where you are going, but when it is dark or foggy or you find yourself in unfamiliar terrain, you turn to your compass. Decisions that are self-evident do not require a moral compass. However, as a commander, you rarely get the opportunity to make easy decisions; your subordinate commanders or staff should have already made those decisions, based on your guidance and intent. You are left, therefore, with only the gut-wrenching, ugly ones. By taking the time to calibrate your compass in advance, you will know what to do when faced with that tough call. Leadership challenges and ethical dilemmas are always pop quizzes—you do not have time to study up beforehand.

An introspective first step in knowing thyself is to take one of the battery of personality assessments on the market today. Such tests as the Enneagram have been around for centuries. Perhaps the best-known modern personality "test" is the Myers-Briggs Type Indicator (MBTI), first published in 1962 by Katharine Cook Briggs and her daughter Isabel Briggs Myers. According to the MBTI, there are sixteen psychological types, identified by four individual type preferences. At the Marine Corps Command and Staff College (CSC), students take a modified version of the MBTI, the Keirsey Temperament II Sorter (KTS II), during their first week of school. The purpose is to provide the students insight into how their personalities can be perceived by others. Knowing your colleagues' personality types may inform how you communicate with subordinates and staff and can reduce misinterpretations.

My wife Candace and I have hosted a "small group" in our home off and on for ten years. Looking to strengthen our faith through a community group gave us the reciprocal benefit of strengthening our marriage. They say adult learners learn best by teaching, so Candace and I learned about ourselves and how to communicate better by mentoring these younger couples. As you might take a personality test, we took a "temperament quiz," as part of a sermon series. Again, there are a battery of these tests on the market. Most associate your temperament with a color: red (sanguine), yellow (choleric), green (melancholic), or blue (phlegmatic). These colors can be traced back to ancient Greek medical theory, which held that the four fundamental bodily "humors" (blood, yellow bile, black bile, and phlegm) could cause illness if out of balance. The Marine Corps Family Services offers similar training to new military spouses, by means of the Shipley Communications "Four Lenses" program. The best personality and temperament tests aid self-coaching by listing the favorable characteristics of your temperament alongside possible negatives. Doing the assessment with your spouse will prevent you from glossing over those less desirable attributes: you need to work on them!

Exercise

- Take the KTS II online assessment: http://keirsey .com (top right-hand corner of web page) to determine your four-letter temperament type.
- Take a temperament test with your spouse: https:// www.temperamentquiz.com.

Saved Rounds—Some Thoughts and Tips

- The toughest person to lead is the one in the mirror.
- Conduct a deliberate self-assessment: if you discover a discontinuity between your "ideal" self and your "actual" self, create a personal training plan to develop your strengths and mitigate your weaknesses.
- "If you don't know who you are, someone will tell you who you are. If they can tell you who you are, they can define you. If they can define you, they can contain you." (Chaplain Madison Carter, U.S. Navy.)
- Check your motives—and your motivations—daily.
- Identify your red lines: What are your "no penetration" lines? (These are things you cannot tolerate regardless of circumstance. These could include integrity violations, fraternization/sexual relations with a subordinate/adultery, drug use, etc.)
- A good friend and Navy chaplain, Ray Stewart, once said, "A warrior without a cause to fight for will find the wrong things to fight against."

Recommended Reading

- For more on self-awareness, see Maxims 22, 23, and 35.
- *Primal Leadership: Unleashing the Power of Emotional Intelligence,* by Dr. Daniel Goleman.
- *What Got You Here Won't Get You There: How Successful People Become Even More Successful,* by Marshall Goldsmith and Mark Reiter.

2

It Is Not about You

As you wrestle with the first maxim internally, recognize the paradox of the second: "It is not about you." Once you are in charge, your personal performance is subsumed by the organization's measures of effectiveness. Your personal aspirations are exchanged for the command's vision, and even your personal well-being is replaced by the needs of your people. It is no longer *you* that matters. Gen Joseph Dunford, then Chairman of the Joint Chiefs of Staff, speaking at the Center for Strategic and International Studies, was asked what advice he would give to the midshipmen in the audience. It was this:

> It's no longer about you. You know, to this point someone cared about your grade-point average. Someone cared about your level of physical fitness. Someone cared about your personal appearance. Someone cared about your accomplishments, your achievements. The day you become commissioned, that's all in the sticker price of being a leader. Nobody cares. You get no credit anymore for any of those things. What you get credit for is the impact that you have on the young men and

women that you'll be . . . fortunate enough to lead. That's actually what you get credit for.[1]

It is difficult for some young officers to grasp this transition. In order to attain their current positions as officers of Marines, they had to be ultracompetitive. Candidates at Officer Candidate School (OCS) today, on average, have a 3.5 college GPA, a Scholastic Aptitude Test score of 1200, and a Physical Fitness Test (PFT) score of 287. Having passed the screening at OCS and completed the additional nine to twelve months of rigorous training at their military occupation specialty (MOS) courses, they are rightfully proud. But once they hit the fleet, none of that matters. From the moment their titles include the word "commander," the only things they are judged by are how well their commands perform and how well they care for their Marines. They immediately become responsible for "everything the unit does or fails to do," regardless of their knowledge of, participation in, or proximity to the event.

In researching his second book, *Leaders Eat Last*, Simon Sinek spent considerable time at Marine Corps Base Quantico, Virginia, observing how the Marine Corps makes its officers. This Marine influence is woven into the book throughout. The title itself is a nod to a Marine Corps custom that we Marines take for granted—that as leaders, we eat last. LtGen George Flynn captured it for Sinek: "The price of leadership is self-interest."[2] Leadership is about taking responsibility for those entrusted to your care and placing their needs above your own. Great leaders truly care about those they are privileged to lead.

One of my favorite Sinek stories, popular on the internet, is that of a nameless former under secretary of defense who, in remarks to a convention in Washington, D.C., paused to reflect upon his Styrofoam coffee cup. He had addressed, he explained, the same audience the previous year, when still in office. He recalled how he had been chauffeured around and greeted at the venue with a cup of coffee in a porcelain cup. When he had arrived that morning, however, he had poured his own coffee, into a Styrofoam cup. "All the perks, all the benefits and advantages you may get for the rank or position you hold; they aren't meant for you," Sinek explains. "They are meant for the role you fill. And when you leave your role, which eventually you will, they will give the ceramic cup to the person who replaces you. Because you only ever deserve a Styrofoam cup."[3]

Gerald Brooks, a renowned leadership speaker and pastor, once said, "When you become a leader, you lose the right to think of yourself."[4] If you are a leader, the sacrifices go up as you move up. I admit, I never dwelled on or even considered the sacrifices while in command. For me, command was not a sacrifice—it was the greatest possible privilege of all.

SERVANT LEADERSHIP

The first line in Pastor Rick Warren's seminal book, *The Purpose Driven Life*, reads, "It is not about you."[5] In what he describes as an "anti-self-help book," Pastor Warren goes on to explain how the quest for personal fulfillment, satisfaction, and meaning can be fulfilled only in understanding and doing what God placed you on earth to do. If you aspire to be a leader—whether you're a Christian or not—that purpose is service.

The contemporary phrase "servant leadership" was coined by Robert K. Greenleaf in his 1970 essay published as *The Servant as Leader*.[6] Since then, many authors have written extensively on the subject. My favorite is Ken Blanchard. If you enjoyed his *The 10-Minute Manager*, you will find his writings on servant leadership equally insightful. Blanchard traces the concept of servant leadership back to the first book ever printed with moveable type, the Bible. Regardless of your religious beliefs, the Bible is a remarkable collection of leadership parables. In the Gospel of Mark, James and John are angling for positions of prominence in Jesus' kingdom to come, having, as the disciples often did, interpreted Jesus' parables literally. In Mark, Jesus rebukes them: "Not so with you. Instead, whoever wants to become great among you must be your servant."[7] Jesus' message to his disciples is as much a lesson in leadership as it is in divinity. Leadership is not about perks. The only privilege we accept as commanders in the Marine Corps is the opportunity to lead the distilled excellence of all that is great in this nation.

"Managers look after numbers, leaders look after us," wrote Simon Sinek. In his *Leaders Eat Last,* Sinek applied the Alcoholics Anonymous "twelfth step" to leadership. Studying the AA program, Sinek found that addicts learned to control their addiction by serving other addicts. The spiritual awakening described in the twelfth step—the key to sobriety—is servant leadership.[8]

Servant leadership does not require altruism, only authenticity. If you are truly in it to serve others, selfless leadership creates a virtuous circle, a feedback loop in which the benefits always outweigh the costs. World-renowned author and motivational speaker Zig Ziglar once said, "If you help everyone get what they want, you will get what you want."[9] I have found in command that the more you care, the more your people will care. The more you give of yourself, the more you will receive in return.

"It is amazing what you can accomplish if you do not care who gets the credit." I remember reading these words of Harry S. Truman on the desk of Col Jim Clark. Clark, a self-effacing logistician, was the first commander of the R4OG, the Retrograde, Redeployment in support of Reset and Reconstitution Operations Group. It was an ad hoc organization formed in Afghanistan in 2012 with the awesome responsibility of "retrograding" (collecting) and redeploying (in this case to the continental United States) all the equipment in the theater, in support of the Corps' "reset and reconstitution" strategy. His task was daunting, his resources were minimal, and his authority was limited. Clark's command was a tenant organization on board Camp Leatherneck in Helmand Province. His mission was in support of the Marine Expeditionary Force (MEF) Forward, with which he had no established command relationships. Clark, in fact, answered to four bosses: the commander of Marine Forces Central Command (COMUSMARCENT), the "component commander"; the commanding general (CG) of MEF (Forward), the "supported commander"; the theater support commander (an Army general answerable to the Joint Task Force commander but doing the Army's bidding in country); and at Headquarters Marine Corps, the Deputy Commandant for Installations and Logistics (the three-star responsible for the Commandant's reset strategy). Anyone familiar with organizational structure theory, the principles of war, command relations, or the personalities involved would know that Clark was being set up for failure. Failure, however, was not in his lexicon.

Clark had at least been sent individuals, "augments," to assist, and adroitly built a team out of them that extended stakeholder relationships throughout the theater and back to the service headquarters in Washington, D.C. He crafted policies and streamlined procedures to expedite the retrograde and redeployment of equipment directly to the stateside depots and executed with tremendous speed and cost savings. He worked with the battalion commanders in the field to ensure they remained focused on the fight while he manipulated the "business rules" to allow them to keep their equipment until the last possible moment, without sacrificing accountability or incurring undue risk to the mission. As a result, the R4OG received the Marine Corps' award for logistics excellence. Clark was not there to receive it. With his work done, he had moved on, never drawing any attention to himself—he who had been the catalyst for a strategy that drew accolades from agencies ranging from Headquarters Marine Corps to the U.S. Government Accountability Office (GAO).

I chose the word "catalyst" to describe Col Jim Clark's leadership after reading *The Starfish and the Spider: The*

Unstoppable Power of Leaderless Organizations, by Ori Brafman and Rod Beckstrom. If you want to learn how to lead
flat, decentralized organizations that are disrupting—that is,
fundamentally changing—the world today, I highly recommend this book. Exploring the implications of the recent rise
of decentralized organizations such as Craigslist and YouTube,
the authors identified a pattern of humility and selflessness
in their leadership cultures. All of these seemingly leaderless
organizations had a catalyst who had started the movement
and then, once it was up and running, turned over all control
to the subordinates. These catalysts exhibited remarkable
people skills. They were emotionally intelligent, with deep
understandings of people and the "mapping" skills necessary
to connect advocates with resources. They all had a desire
to help and a relentless passion to accomplish the mission.
People sign on and follow a catalyst, because they are more
likely to follow someone who "gets me." Above all, these catalysts knew it was never about them.[10]

The evil twin of the catalyst is the egoist. We have all
worked for one before—the "it's all about me" commander.
Their self-confidence is eclipsed only by their amazing lack of
self-awareness. In his book *A Passion for Leadership*, the former
secretary of defense Robert Gates wrote, "The handmaiden of
egotism is arrogance."[11] Arrogant commanders cannot be told
anything they do not already know. Their lack of empathy
is toxic. Far from inspiring, they actually drain energy from
organizations. Eventually, however, their arrogance catches up
with them. Egoists tend to believe the rules do not apply to
them—until the day arrives when they do.

TO BE OR TO DO

In his book *Boyd: The Fighter Pilot Who Changed the Art of
War*, Robert Coram describes Col John Boyd, U.S. Air Force
(USAF), as "the most influential military theorist since Sun
Tzu," a thinker who made "more contributions to fighter
tactics, aircraft design, and the theory of air combat than any

[other] man in Air Force history."[12] That's high praise for a cantankerous, high-flying, field-grade officer the Air Force elected to retire as a colonel. After retiring Boyd became, as perhaps he is best known, the architect of "maneuver warfare." A principle of maneuver warfare, the "OODA" (observe, orient, decide, act) loop, is attributed to him by Gen Al Gray, the twenty-seventh Commandant of the Marine Corps, in *Warfighting,* Fleet Marine Force Manual (FMFM) 1.

In a speech at the U.S. Air Force Academy, Secretary of Defense Bob Gates described Colonel Boyd as a "brilliant, eccentric, stubborn, and frequently profane character who was the bane of the Air Force establishment for decades." Boyd had spent his final years in the Pentagon, vocally dissenting from and bucking his service headquarters. He walked the halls of "the Building" recruiting like-minded junior officers to join in his quest for change. Having been passed over for promotion himself, Boyd took care that they understood the costs of joining his rebellion. He offered each a choice: to be someone—be recognized by the system and promoted—or do something that would be impactful to the service and the nation:

> You're going to have to make a decision about which direction you want to go. *If you go* [one] *way, you can be somebody.* You will have to make compromises and you will have to turn your back on your friends. But you will be a member of the club and you will get promoted and get good assignments. Or you can go [the other] way and *you can do something—something for your country and for your Air Force and for yourself.* . . . If you decide to do something, you may not get promoted and you may not get good assignments and you certainly will not be a favorite of your superiors. *But you won't have to compromise yourself.* . . . To be somebody or to do something. In life there is often a roll call. That's when you have to make a decision. *To be or to do?*[13]

The irony of Colonel Boyd's story today is that no one knows the names of the Air Force generals who ignored his ideas and pushed him out of the service, but countless military theorists credit Boyd with our "maneuver warfare" doctrine, air-to-air combat development, and the design and acquisition of the F-16 and F-15 fighter jets. While not the best exemplar of military bearing and courtesy, Boyd always put the needs of the country, the Air Force, and his fellow airmen (meaning both men and women) above his own personal aspirations and career. I do not believe career prospects in uniform are as binary today as they were for Colonel Boyd; however, his lesson is timeless and speaks directly to your purpose in life. Do you aspire for title and a life of privilege, or are you willing to serve and sacrifice everything for a just cause?

YOUR LEGACY

Inspirational speaker and author Jon Gordon writes that "the best make everyone around them better. They leave a legacy."[14] Jon Gordon's sphere is that of professional athletics and sports psychology, but his Christian faith is a strong undercurrent in his work. Gordon believes God instills in all of us a desire to be great, that we were made to be great to benefit the greater good. Success, fame, and fortune are all temporary. Money, power, and prestige do not fuel the kind of energy it takes to be a great leader. The best, he believes, are driven by a bigger purpose, a purpose beyond themselves. I have come to the realization that the positions with which I have been entrusted were not given to me *for* me but as opportunities to serve for the betterment of others.

Saved Rounds—Some Thoughts and Tips
- "True humility is not thinking less of yourself; it is thinking of yourself less." (C. S. Lewis)
- You bring out the best in your Marines by sharing the best of yourself.

- Leadership coach and author John Maxwell takes Truman's adage a step further: "Great things happen only when you give others credit."[15]
- It's not about you: "It's about Marines."[16]

Recommended Reading

- *Leaders Eat Last: Why Some Teams Pull Together and Others Don't,* by Simon Sinek.
- *The Servant Leader: Transforming Your Heart, Head, Hands & Habits,* by Ken Blanchard and Phil Hodges.

3

Marines Don't Care How Much You Know but Will Know How Much You Care

*Nobody cares how much you know
until they know how much you care.*
ATTRIBUTED TO THEODORE ROOSEVELT

I often begin leadership discussions by asking Marines, "What is the fifteenth leadership trait?" The Marine Corps has published fourteen of them, known to every Marine by the mnemonic *"J J DID TIE BUCKLE"*:[1]

Justice
Judgment
Dependability
Initiative
Decisiveness
Tact
Integrity
Enthusiasm

17

*B*earing
*U*nselfishness
*C*ourage
*K*nowledge
*L*oyalty
*E*ndurance

I would review the above list and ask them what trait was missing. The responses would vary, and the answers were never wrong. The "fifteenth leadership" trait, I would offer, is actually the first—it is *love*. To be a great leader, you must love your people. There is nothing Marines will not do for an organization that they believe truly cares about them. Notice, however, I did not say there is nothing they would not do for "you." We have already established that it is not about you; it is about the mission and the Marines.

This leadership maxim is actually very simple to demonstrate but impossible to fake. Marines can distinguish leaders who are authentic from those who are just out for their own advancement. They will know how much you care.

I found the easiest way to demonstrate to Marines that you care is by taking the time to get to know them. As a group commander (colonel-level command), I made it a point to study the official service biographies of the staff members and the battalion commanders before I arrived. Once in command, I made a point of learning all I could about the battalions' staff members and their company commanders. Whether they were lieutenants or lieutenant colonels, I always knew and referred to them by their first names. Admittedly, my memory is not the best, so I wrote down their first names and the names of their spouses and children in my green book, which I would refer to often until I committed them to memory. I programmed their birthdates into the calendar in my Blackberry (early twenty-first-century smartphone) and made a point of wishing them a happy birthday in person when possible. I knew where they were from, and I learned, more importantly, where they wanted to go. If I was going to write their performance evaluations, be it as a reporting senior or reviewing officer, I got to know them.

Learning the aspirations and concerns of your subordinates should begin on day one. During my initial counseling sessions, I would always ask:

- How will you define success during this tour?
- What are you most excited about?
- What is your biggest challenge?
- Where do you see yourself in five years?

I have learned that there are things that you will never know about your people unless you ask. Everyone has a story, and by taking time to get to know your Marines' stories, you communicate to them that you care about and value their contributions and sacrifices. When people feel they are valued, they commit themselves more strongly to the organization. Conversely, when people feel they are being used, their primary motivation shifts to self-interest or self-preservation.

Taking the time to get to know those who directly report to you is expected. Getting to know their—that is, your—troops takes time and a lot more effort, but the return on this investment is exponential. The further you penetrate into your organization, the less expectation there is that you will personally know the Marines you find. Doing so, however, multiplies their perceived worth within the organization. An easy place to start doing this arises when a member of the command receives a Red Cross message. These messages have visibility up and down the chain of command. Whenever I would read about a young Marine losing a parent or sibling, I would set a calendar reminder to follow up with that Marine in a few weeks and on the anniversary of the death the following year. As Marines, we are good at rushing in to provide immediate aid and comfort when we learn of a death or serious injury, but as professionals in the field will tell you, people most need help after the initial attention has faded away. Ask a Marine, "I bet you're missing Dad today, aren't you?" on the anniversary of his father's death, and you will know you made a difference.

Perhaps my most effective leadership tool in command was a thirty-nine-cent stamp (you'll have to spend a little more today). When trooping the lines, the sergeant major and I would often discover individual Marines or sailors who were outpacing their peers or putting in considerable extra effort. I would often make it a point to record their names in my green book. When we returned to the headquarters, I would ask the adjutant to pull their Records of Emergency Data (REDs), with the names of their parents and their address. I would then take a few moments and pen a short note telling Mom and Dad how well their son or daughter was doing and how much I appreciated their efforts. I would always close by acknowledging their roles as parents in raising "such a fine Marine" and asking for their continued support. I called these my "letter bombs": sending one was akin to lighting a ninety-six-hour time fuse. It would normally take forty-eight hours for the letter to make it home and another twenty-four hours before Mom or Dad read it. That evening the parents would undoubtedly call their Marine and tell them about the letter. The kinetics would occur the next morning when the Marine returned to work. Whatever they had been doing that had caught my eye and that of the sergeant major before the letter, they would now be doing twice as much of it, twice as fast. If they were in leadership positions, they would be pulling their whole teams faster.

The effectiveness of the "letter bomb" was not attributable to the cost (in those days thirty-nine cents) or the time and effort (about ten minutes and a few pen strokes). It was effective because the letter intrinsically connected the "what" with the "why." Marines join the Marine Corps for a variety of reasons, but often it is to make someone proud, usually their parents. By taking a few minutes to recognize what the hard-chargers in the organization are doing and why they are doing it, you get a return that is exponential in terms of productivity and commitment.

I know my letter bombs worked, from observing the performance of the Marine or direct feedback from the parents. Ironically, I never had a Marine himself directly acknowledge to me one of my letters to their next of kin. Furthermore, I doubt the Marines ever shared the letters with their peers. I surmise the only people who knew about the letters were the subjects, his or her parents, and my adjutant. But everyone in the organization witnessed the effects.

If taking a few minutes to acknowledge the efforts of a hardworking Marine can increase performance, the opposite is equally true. It is easy to halt the efforts of Marines who go above and beyond. All you have to do is nothing. "Why should I bust my ass," they ask themselves, "if no one is going to notice?" Regrettably, this refrain is heard too often in the "smoke pits" around the Corps.

Saved Rounds—Some Thoughts and Tips
- Write down the first names of your "first reports'" immediate family members in the back of your commander's notebook and refer back to them until they're memorized.
- Populate your calendar with your Marines' birthdays and make it a point to wish them well personally on their birthdays.
- When you receive a Red Cross message for a Marine in your command who has lost an immediate family member, set a reminder in your calendar to follow up on the anniversary of the loss.
- Reach out to the widows, widowers, and parents of fallen Marines on their birthdays or the anniversaries of their deaths.

Recommended Reading—*Once an Eagle*, by Anton Myrer. When I was a major, an early mentor of mine, Col Jim Casey, gave me a copy of *Once an Eagle*, which was published in 1968 and is now on the Commandant's Professional Reading List. The novel juxtaposes the careers of two Army officers through the world wars and, under another name, Vietnam. The protagonists, Sam Damon and Courtney Massengale, reflect, respectively, the best and the worst of the officer corps. Be Sam Damon!

4

Do Right and Fear No Man

"Do right and fear no man" was the first line of every command philosophy I published, from my first company command on Parris Island, and it was inscribed on the quarterdeck of the II MEF Headquarters Group at Camp Lejeune. My message was clear and simple. Though my philosophy went on to define the values, beliefs, and expectations for my tenure in command, I did not much expect that the junior Marines would read beyond that first line. They did not have to.

By "right" I meant that each Marine should do what he or she "ought to." Our actions would not be defined by situational ethics, but would be judged according to an honor code that transcended legal compliance or social norms. We would lead with character, even when it was hard. We would do what was right, regardless of the cost. Experience has taught me that the right way is rarely the most efficient or expedient. Doing the right thing often requires a halt or redirection of the organization's forward momentum or your own personal aspirations. If continued progress compels you to compromise your integrity, don't proceed.

By declaring that we would do the right thing, I was demanding that we operate with integrity. We would integrate

our values into our actions and would never fear the consequences of well-intentioned failure. Doing the right thing
meant that we would not compromise on standards. The tag-
line of BGen Dave Odom, as commanding officer of 4th, was
always, "The right thing, the right way, every day." Dave knew
integrity requires consistent adherence to espoused values. It is
an absolute. It has been said and is worth repeating: If you have
integrity, that is all that matters; if you do not have integrity,
that is all that matters.

I GOT YOUR BACK

I wanted all members of the command to know that if they
were trying to do the right thing, I had their backs, regardless
of the outcome. My generation scoffs at the contemporary
idea of "safe spaces." The concept itself is anathema to the culture of the Corps. But we all do need a secure environment in
which to develop professionally. Junior leaders need to know
that they will be supported when making difficult decisions or
holding their ground on a matter of principle. If we desire our
future leaders to be bold risk takers and innovative problem
solvers, then we need to set conditions where they are not
afraid to fail. As a commander, it is your responsibility to set
conditions that allow subordinates to learn. If they cannot
learn to make decisions in a peacetime environment, it will be
too late to start in combat.

The "fear no man" clause was intended not to be bellicose
but to distinguish my leadership style. I loathe leadership
by fear and intimidation. Many of the senior leaders I was
exposed to as a lieutenant and junior captain ascribed to a
Machiavellian philosophy of leadership. Since they knew they
could never make all of us love them, they elected instead to
make us fear them. Authoritarian leaders can achieve short-
term gains, but their potential will always be limited to what
they can directly coerce. Ironically, toxic leaders can create
a cohesive command climate. They, however, will never be
inside the circle. The *esprit* they achieve is more a repudiation

than a reflection of their leadership. Cohesion in such units is the antibody to their toxicity.

FEAR NOT

Most of us joined the Marine Corps because we wanted to measure ourselves and prove that we had what it takes. Confident we could overcome our fears, we volunteered to travel the dark alleys of the world to show ourselves worthy successors of the heroes who had gone before us. The truth is that we as leaders of Marines are subject to fear, but our fear is more nuanced. When I was first commissioned, I was afraid of being afraid, of appearing weak. That fear has given way to new trepidations. Today, my fears are more rooted in missed opportunities. I fear surrendering the initiative—failing to make a timely decision—more than the cost of failure. The courageous, it has been said, are not the first to see but first to do.

When the thirty-seventh Commandant, Gen Robert Neller, espoused spiritual fitness as one of the three aspects of overall fitness, along with the mental and physical, he recognized the role faith plays in our resiliency and overall well-being.[1] Publishing in 2016 his All Marine Corps Bulletin (ALMAR) 033/16 within so secular a political climate itself required a degree of resolution to do what was right. Personally, any courage I may muster is derived from my faith and the confidence that I am doing what is right. My faith is inextricably linked to my leadership style. I routinely read books on the spiritual aspects of leadership. Andy Stanley, John Maxwell, Craig Groeschel, and Perry Noble, all of whom are referred to throughout these maxims, began their careers as pastors before expanding their influence into the world of leadership development. As I mentioned earlier, if you are looking for a great book on courageous leadership, try the Bible. If you conduct a simple word search, you will find in it no fewer than 365 "Fear nots" in the Old and New Testaments, each an instance portraying deeply flawed individuals struggling with leadership challenges only to find courage and resolve through their faith.

There is another, more practical reason to advocate spiritual fitness within the Corps. Back in the early 1960s, seeking to explain the complicity of the German army in the Holocaust, Yale University professor Stanley Milgram conducted a controversial experiment. After studying the Nuremberg trials of 1946, Milgram, a psychologist, sought to define the limits of obedience to authority and the claims of personal conscience. The Nazi defendants had based their defense of genocide on "obedience to orders." Milgram wanted to see how far ordinary people would go in obeying an instruction if it involved harming another, innocent person; to do so, he designed an experiment involving pairs of volunteers, playing the roles of "learner" and "teacher." Or so the volunteers thought: the learners, unbeknownst to them, were actually actors.

The "teacher" was told to administer an electric shock every time the "learner" made a mistake, increasing its intensity each time. The shock generator ostensibly provided "stimuli" ranging from fifteen volts (a slight shock) to 450 (a fatally severe shock). The actor-"learners" would respond accordingly. The results were disturbing. Two-thirds of participants continued to the point of administering shocks that, as far as they knew, would kill the "learner." Of this phenomenon Milgram wrote, "The extreme willingness of adults to go to almost any lengths on the command of an authority constitutes the chief finding of the study and the fact most urgently demanding explanation."[2] I, however, find encouragement in the third of the "teachers" who refused. Only those who felt they were accountable to a higher power did not continue with the experiment.[3]

THE CONFIDENCE TO DEVIATE

"Maneuver Warfare," the Marine Corps' warfighting philosophy, is predicated as defined in Marine Corps Doctrinal

Publication (MCDP) 1, on the assumption that the Marine leader closest to the situation is best positioned to seize the initiative through bold and decisive action. Armed with the "commander's intent," subordinates are expected to adhere to its scheme of maneuver until the plan no longer makes sense or a better option presents itself. "Mission-type" orders and decentralized decision making enable subordinate commanders to take advantage of fleeting opportunities. Christopher Kolenda, a former U.S. Army paratrooper, wrote in his book *Leadership: The Warrior's Art* that combat leaders should select their methods of control based on the basis of organizational maturity, not on their own capacity to micromanage subordinates' actions. Trusting and empowering subordinates to deviate from the plan is fundamental to our warfighting philosophy.[4]

As a commander, I aspired to establish a command climate that encouraged aggressive and disciplined risk taking. I wanted the commanders to know that I trusted them to deviate from the plan or policy when the situation dictated. Simon Sinek, after spending some time with LtGen George Flynn, wrote that when people follow rules only because they are afraid of the consequences of not doing so, they will lack the confidence to correct what is wrong. "Rules are for normal operations," said General Flynn.[5] When well-intentioned mistakes are treated as learning experiences, young leaders who make them are more likely later on to make the timely decisions required to retain the initiative in complex and fast-moving environments. If you cannot trust your subordinates to make timely decisions based on what is right, you have the wrong commanders.

Saved Rounds—Some Thoughts and Tips
- Define your leadership philosophy in one sentence.
- Trust your gut and let your commanders know you trust theirs.
- Your integrity buys your Marines' trust. It will take a while to build but can be blown in an instant.

- Retired colonel Mike Killion's command philosophy at Weapons Company, 3rd Battalion, 8th Marines was "do the right thing for the right reasons, and everything else will take care of itself."

Recommended Reading

- *Profiles in Courage,* by John F. Kennedy. In 1954, then-Senator Kennedy wrote this book while recovering from surgery to fix his back, injured during World War II. The book profiles eight U.S. senators who defied public opinion and their parties' positions to do what they felt was right and in the best interest of the country. They all paid dearly for their principled positions. Publishing the book was a bold move for the then–junior senator from Massachusetts. Kennedy was signaling to his party and his constituency that if elected, he would do what he felt was right regardless of the consequences.

- *The Anatomy of Courage,* by Lord Moran. Lord Moran was a British frontline doctor in World War I and Winston Churchill's personal physician in World War II. First published in 1945, Moran's firsthand account of the psychological effects of war and how leadership can overcome it is still widely cited today.

- *Washington's Farewell: The Founding Father's Warning to Future Generations,* by John Avlon. Washington is one of my personal heroes. His farewell address, issued directly to the people of the United States and printed in newspapers around the world, declared his intention to step down as president at the completion of his second term. The address was once mandatory reading in every grade-school civics class and was among the governing principles of this nation until President Woodrow Wilson entered the Great War in 1917. Washington was not a well-educated man; it was his character that drove his achievement.

As an officer, I also found Washington's approach to religion instructive. Washington believed in religious pluralism, viewing organized religion through a utilitarian lens. A practical idealist, Washington believed there could be no happiness without virtue. Responding to Alexander Hamilton, he wrote, "Of all the dispositions and habits which lead to political prosperity, religion and morality are indispensable supports. And let us with caution indulge the supposition that morality can be maintained without religion."[6]

5

Organizations Move at the Speed of Trust

first heard this maxim in 2012 while attending an after-action review facilitated by Gen James Mattis of a large exercise in the Middle East. I do not know whether the general had read Stephen M. R. Covey's book *The Speed of Trust* or if this was an original "Mattisism," but both the author and the general had the same insight. They both realized the operational potential of a culture of trust. Where there is trust—when the members of the organization assume good intent—tremendous efficiency and agility can be achieved. Conversely, where there is a lack of trust, Covey argues, organizations pay a "tax."[1] Its members are slow to act and suspicious of the leadership.

The military implications here are huge. In fast-moving, chaotic environments you need your subordinates to make timely and accurate decisions. Decisions in such environments carry a significant degree of risk. Our warfighting doctrine is predicated on mission-type orders and trust tactics in order to generate operational tempo.[2] To be successful, Marine leaders understand, they must trust subordinates to make timely decisions based upon the expressed "commander's intent." Commander's intent informs the actions and initiative of subordinates by clearly defining the purpose of the task and describing the desired end state. Subordinate commanders in turn, based on the primacy of proximity to the action, are empowered to deviate from the plan should the situation on the ground necessitate a change or a fleeting opportunity presents itself. Equally important is the fact that the subordinates need to trust their leadership in order to be willing to make these decisions. Leadership consultants James Kouzes and Barry Posner write, "Leadership is a relationship founded on trust. Without trust and confidence, people don't take risks. Without risk there can be no change."[3]

THE CIRCLE OF TRUST

Trust is the most determinative quality in building cohesive units, and yet it is often taken for granted by its members. In cohesive teams, members share a sense of belonging. They believe in the team, because they believe the team has their back. Giving a speech in South Korea when he was the secretary of defense, Ash Carter said, "Security is like oxygen. If you have it you don't think about it. If you don't, it's all you can think about."[4] The same could be said of trust. The fact is you do not know the value of trust until you lose it. In both of his best-selling books on leadership, Simon Sinek talks about the "circle of safety." Inside this circle we feel like we belong—we feel secure. In *Leaders Eat Last* Sinek wrote, "Great organizations become great because people within the organization feel protected."[5] In the Peloponnesian Wars the Spartan phalanx was the most effective fighting formation of its time because the interlocking shields protected each infantryman and the hoplite to his left. It was the collective security provided by the shields, not the length of the spears, that made the phalanx so formidable.

Whether the culture is one of trust or suspicion, the commander "owns" it. Andy Stanley, the lead pastor of North Point Community Church, once said that in every relationship there are gaps between what we expect and what occurs.

When a team member fails to deliver as expected, a gap is created. As a leader, you determine what goes into that gap—trust or suspicion.[6] In highly cohesive organizations, members are offered the benefit of the doubt until proven otherwise: "Private Jones is late. Something must have happened." The degree of trust within an organization is directly attributable to the amount of trust the leader extends to its members. I have learned to assume good intent. When an otherwise good Marine drops the ball, I assume there is something going on that I am not aware of.

Stephen R. Covey wrote in his seminal work *The Seven Habits of Highly Effective People* that integrity is the foundation of leadership. If you have integrity, people will trust you.[7] Your integrity is the source of your moral authority. As a leader, you protect your integrity and build trust by owning the gap when the organization comes up short. John Maxwell staked out a similar position in his *The 21 Irrefutable Laws of Leadership*. In defining "The Law of Solid Ground," Maxwell wrote that trust is the foundation of leadership. When you lose trust, you lose influence.[8] Jack Welch, after retiring from General Electric, wrote a book, *The Real-Life MBA*, in which he described the necessity of an atmosphere of truth and trust. "Truth gets you the right answer quickly. You don't get truth without trust."[9]

THE TRANSFERENCE OF TRUST

Your people need to know that you believe in them and that you trust them. Research shows that leaders who are trusting are regarded as trustworthy. The inverse is also true. Micro-managers—those with a propensity to control the smallest details—receive low scores with respect to personal credibility. Simon Sinek addresses this phenomenon in his book *Start with Why*. Sinek argues that you cannot convince someone that you have value, just as you cannot convince someone to trust you. In both cases, you have to earn it.[10]

In the Marine Corps, when we attempt to manage the bottom 2 percent by developing policies that penalize the other 98 percent, the message our junior noncommissioned officers (NCOs) hear is that we do not trust them. The level of trust and responsibility we extend to our NCOs in combat is incomparable, but when we return to home station we strip their authority and subject them to paternalistic policies. For example, why is it that a sergeant who ran countless patrols in Iraq is told how many beers he can store in his barracks refrigerator?

Saved Rounds—Some Thoughts and Tips
- Assume good intent.
- When it comes to earning trust, Craig Groeschel offers a different take: "Trust is not earned, it is extended. Mistrust is earned."[11]
- Loyalty is a result; it is not a requirement.
- LtGen George Flynn once said, "Trust is what makes the magic happen."

Recommended Reading—The Speed of Trust: The One Thing That Changes Everything, by Stephen M. R. Covey.

6

Your Greatest Impact Will Be on the Ends of the Bell Curve

"You'll spend 90 percent of your time on the bottom 10 percent of your people"—we all have heard this maxim. However, if you are in fact spending 90 percent of your time on the bottom 10 percent of your Marines, you are reacting and not leading. I say this recognizing the enormous time commitment that some of these leadership challenges require. The key, however, is balance. When in command, I aspired to achieve a 10-80-10 split with my time. For every hour I spent on a disciplinary or legal issue, I was determined to spend another identifying and encouraging the top 10 percent of the organization. The challenge was less about time management than about getting out and finding the top 10 percent. In explaining the methodology behind the 10-80-10 split, I candidly admitted that the 80 percent in the middle—the center of the bell curve—would likely stay the course regardless of the proximity of myself or the sergeant major. My greatest impact, and therefore my focus, was always on the ends of the bell curve.

Picking out the bottom 10 percent is easy—they self-identify. Your job as a commander is to get out and find and mentor the future leaders of the Corps by identifying the aspiring leaders within the command. Real power and influence do not come from a position; you need to learn whom the Marines respect and why. By recognizing and empowering your "lead sled dogs," you will encourage them to pull harder. And if they are pulling harder, the whole team will be running faster! It is okay to have favorites, provided they are your top performers and the pack knows why. John Maxwell, author of *Developing the Leaders around You*, wrote: "It takes leaders to find leaders, to grow a leader, and show a leader."[1] He went on to say that the growth and development of leaders is the highest calling of leadership.

The companion to the 10-80-10 split is the truism that 20 percent of your people are doing 80 percent of the work. Here is another call to get out and learn who is doing what in your organization. Maxwell says once you identify that load-bearing 20 percent, you should give them 80 percent of your resources and time.[2] It is often our unfortunate lack of adherence to this talent-management principle that begets mediocre performance within the Marine Corps. Instead of reinforcing our superstars, we often commit our resources to propping up the weaker elements of the command. We know that in combat you should never commit the reserve to reinforce failure—only to exploit success. So why then do we send our best talent to prop up weak leaders?

In his book *The Effective Executive*, the world-renowned management consultant Peter Drucker criticized President Lincoln's selection of Union generals during most of the Civil War. Lincoln, he said, picked generals on the basis of their lack of observable faults. The Confederacy, on the other hand, Drucker argued, picked their generals for obvious strengths. It was not until March 1864 that Lincoln looked beyond Ulysses S. Grant's gruff personality and history of alcohol-related incidents and promoted him to lieutenant general. Less than a year after he placed Grant in command of all Union armies, the war was won.

Too often in the Marine Corps we manage the entire organization by focusing our policies and procedures on the bottom 2 percent. We make policies to curtail the behavior of that bottom portion, with little regard for how they will be interpreted by the rest of the command. In the civilian sector, organizations with clear values and strong cultures do not need rules and regulations. Why then does a military organization with the most revered culture and core values in the world dictate to its members how many beers can be consumed while on liberty?

DEVELOPING LEADERS

The twentieth law in John Maxwell's *The 21 Irrefutable Laws of Leadership* is "the Law of Explosive Growth." The explosive growth Maxwell refers to is the return on investment a leader begets by focusing on the leaders within the organization. Becoming a leader who develops leaders requires a special mindset, wrote Maxwell. Leaders who attract followers need to be needed. Leaders who develop leaders need to be succeeded.[3] The legacies of great leaders are the leaders they developed who carry on after their time in uniform or in office. Leaders who focus on the followers within their organization concentrate on the weak, the bottom 10 percent. Having always in mind the underperforming within their company, they are careful to treat everyone the same. Maxwell wrote that leaders who focus on the leaders within an organization are not concerned with fairness. They concentrate on the top 10 percent, and the entire organization reaps the benefits.[4]

Unfortunately, too many organizations within the Marine Corps focus on follower leadership. The truth is borne out in our retention. In the civilian sector, the people you spend the most time with will stay—and the ones you neglect, leave.[5] By spending a disproportionate amount of time developing struggling leaders, we neglect and fail to develop (and retain) our top performers. Think about it. How many times have you seen the weakest lieutenant propped up with additional talent and resources? Again, we are taught never to reinforce failure in combat, yet our poor talent-management practices do just that with personnel.

Saved Rounds—Some Thoughts and Tips

- Discipline yourself to spend an amount of time writing awards and meritorious promotion packages comparable to what you do on disciplinary cases and adverse counseling.
- Never shortchange the time and effort needed for writing proper fitness reports or evaluations; it is one of the most critical tasks a leader performs and ensures the right people are promoted—those who will strengthen the institution.
- If you delegate tasks you will develop followers; if you delegate authority you will develop great leaders.
- If you want to know who the unofficial leaders are in the organization, just ask the Marines. They will reveal who they respect most in the unit and why.

Recommended Reading

- Anything by John Maxwell. *Developing the Leaders around You: How to Help Others Reach Their Full Potential, The 21 Irrefutable Laws of Leadership: Follow Them and People Will Follow You,* and *Good Leaders Ask Great Questions: Your Foundation for Successful Leadership* are three of my favorites.
- *Grant Takes Command,* by Bruce Catton.

7

If You Treat Them like Adults, They Will Act like Adults

I call it the "Big Boy Rule"—If you treat your Marines like adults, they will act like adults. As for many of the Pygmalion effects included in this book, at the root of this self-fulfilling prophecy is trust. Trust here is achieved through reciprocity. If you want Marines to trust you, you have to trust them. Though at times I have been disappointed, I have never regretted putting my complete trust in Marines.

As the commander of the first Black Sea Rotational Force (BSRF), a Special Purpose Marine Air Ground Task Force (SPMAGTF) operating in Eastern Europe, I was often at loggerheads with the garrison commander of Joint Task Force East (JTF-E) over my liberty policies. Our command relationship did not require my adherence to the policies of our Army host, and I exercised a very liberal liberty policy during our deployment. Marines were allowed to go on liberty at the conclusion of the training day at the discretion of their small-unit leaders. They were free to "eat out" and consume alcohol outside of the eight-hour moratorium before the next training event. For accountability and security purposes, they were required to sign out and travel with a liberty buddy. My rules were simple: "You can drink, but don't get drunk. You are expected to conduct yourself as an ambassador (in other words—don't be a jackass)."

My Army counterpart approached the situation very differently. Manufacturing a threat where there wasn't one, he turned the U.S. side of the Romanian airbase into a forward operating base. The soldiers' liberty was restricted to supervised trips on the weekend, and alcohol was strictly prohibited. The Army colonel in charge, frustrated by my refusal to conform to his policies, put me on notice that I would be held accountable for any misconduct on the part of "my Marines." At the risk of coming across as flippant, I simply responded, "Yes, sir. That goes with my parking spot."

We finished that deployment with zero liberty incidents. We formed strong bonds with our host nations and secured access for an enduring Marine presence in the Black Sea region. Reflecting back, I was actually the beneficiary of JTF-E's draconian liberty policies. Without threat or coercion on my part, the Marines could see the alternative reality that awaited them should they screw up. They knew I was "hanging myself out there" on their behalf. My confidence in the NCOs to manage liberty was returned twofold. The unit policed itself.

MEANWHILE, BACK ON MAIN-SIDE . . .

If you were to ask our veteran NCOs, who have been entrusted with incredible responsibility in Iraq, Afghanistan, and the Black Sea, what their greatest frustration is, they would tell you how discouraged they are to see their authority usurped in garrison (on base). Senior leaders, aware of this problem, lament their plight but continue to pile on paternalistic policies at home station.

Take for example the issue of alcohol in the barracks. It never made any sense to me to restrict how much alcohol single corporals or sergeants living in the barracks could store in their rooms. A married private first class (second award)

living in base housing with his eighteen-year-old wife can
have as much alcohol in his house as he can afford (provided
he is twenty-one).

When a commander communicates his confidence in his
NCOs' judgment and responsibility, it creates the Pygmalion effect I mentioned above. NCOs, emboldened by their
commander's confidence, strive to validate the commander's
respect. The inverse is equally true—we demoralize our
NCOs when, in not-so-subtle ways, we communicate that we
do not believe they are responsible.

Saved Rounds—Some Thoughts and Tips

- Trust begets trust. Want Marines to act more
  responsibly? Give them responsibility!
- It's all about reciprocity—if you want to build trust
  and cohesion in your organization, you must first
  extend trust.
- John Maxwell once wrote, "Rewards are motivating.
  Rules, consequences, and punishment do not get
  people moving. They just keep them from doing their
  worst."[1]

8

Do Routine Things Routinely

When in command, I made it a point to incorporate my leadership style into my daily routine and insisted that every corporal and above do the same. The basic daily routine (BDR) for every leader in 1st Tank Battalion included four tasks that had to be accomplished before they could secure. It was their duty to:

1. Find a Marine doing a good job and thank him.
2. Find a problem and fix it.
3. Teach something.
4. Learn something.

By assigning these daily tasks to every leader in the organization, I intended to change the culture of the command. In casting my vision, I would ask, "Imagine if every leader in the battalion did these four things every day. How good would the unit be after a month, six months, or a year?" I put the leaders on notice that I would be following up. I routinely stopped sergeants and lieutenants on their way "out the hatch" at the end of the day and asked them for a read-back on whom they had thanked, what they had corrected, whom they had taught, and what they had learned. Failure to have a reply meant they were heading back in to complete their mission. Depending on the time of the day, finding a Marine doing a good job could be tough if only the Marines with extra punitive duties were left on deck. However, finding a problem to fix at that hour was never a problem.

Thank You—"We couldn't do what we do if it weren't for Marines like you." By getting out and aggressively searching for Marines doing the right thing, you accentuate the power of the positive and can change the culture of the organization. "Catching" Marines doing a good job provides you the opportunity to be purposefully grateful. Even simply trooping the lines and saying "Thank you" creates a command climate that values its members. "Thank you" and other expressions of gratitude communicate to the Marines that you value their contributions.

When you express gratitude for people when they bust their ass . . . they will continue to bust their ass. In fact, the more specific the thank-you, the greater the impact on performance (the boss noticed!). It is not rocket science. Unfortunately, most Marines assume their leaders don't know how hard they are working. Public affirmation of positive performance costs you nothing and has huge returns. This return is magnified the deeper you penetrate into the organization with your thank-yous. It is important, however, to be honest with your praise. Remember, what gets rewarded will be repeated, so don't be too loose with your gratitude. Conversely, as Andy Stanley once said, "Unexpressed gratitude is ingratitude."[1]

Leaders Find and Fix Problems. Finding and fixing problems is a leadership imperative. If you cannot see the problems in your area when trooping the lines, chances are you have been there too long and it is time to move on (refer to Maxim 21, Complacency Kills). The problems that I am referring to here are those "on the spot" corrections that keep the

standards "standard." That said, my personal focus when finding and fixing problems has shifted from correcting a private
first class on the spot to correcting the noncommissioned
officer or junior officer for leaving the correction to me.

In searching for problems to fix, I took a page out of
Kouzes and Posner's *The Leadership Challenge*. I challenged
the Marines in the command to *Eliminate The Dumb Things*
(ETDT).[2] While trooping the lines and asking questions,
I was always on the watch for the "That is the way we
have always done it" responses. If you communicate to the
Marines that you are willing to challenge the status quo to
make the unit more ready and agile, they will quickly talk
you onto target and identify stupid rules and needless tasks
for elimination.

Teach! My favorite part of leading is teaching. Probably the
quickest way a young NCO can establish credibility and have
a positive impact on the unit is by passing on the knowledge he
has acquired. Done right, the hip-pocket class develops leadership. New lieutenants are often reluctant to teach initially,
until they realize that the investment the Corps has made in
their education compensates for their lack of experience.

The best leaders never stop teaching. When I was a junior
major on the U.S. Central Command staff, the hardest general officer I ever worked for, Gen Doug Lute, took the time
to mentor and teach us. After blowing up your work, the general would turn over the placard on his desk and reintroduce
himself as "Professor Lute." He would then proceed to ask
you a series of questions until he saw your eyes light up.

Learn Something. As a new lieutenant, you build credibility
by demonstrating that you are willing to learn. As a company
commander, I had the tank leader (company gunny) clear out
"the lieutenants' office" (a room in the headquarters building
with three desks for the platoon commanders) and replace it
with a giant sand table that we used to analyze or war-game

engagements. One of the lieutenants, as bold as he was oblivious, asked where his office was now. I told him it was on the right front fender of his tank and that when he learned everything there was to know about that tank, he could move to the left fender and go over everything again. The truth is, as an officer, you have to be intentional about your professional education.

When General Mattis was the commanding general of the 1st Marine Division (MARDIV), preparing to head back to Iraq in 2004, a colleague wrote to him asking about the "importance of reading and military history for officers," many of whom he said found themselves "too busy to read." General Mattis' response has been widely republished in blogs and social media leading up to his confirmation as secretary of defense. I have heard him state on many occasions that it is our obligation as professionals to study our art. The general wrote his colleague:

> The problem with being too busy to read is that you learn by experience (or by your men's experience), i.e. the hard way. By reading, you learn through others' experiences, generally a better way to do business, especially in our line of work where the consequences of incompetence are so final for young men. . . . We have been fighting on this planet for 5,000 years and we should take advantage of their experience. "Winging it" and filling body bags as we sort out what works reminds us of the moral dictates and the cost of incompetence in our profession.[3]

General Mattis was clearly influenced by Gen Paul Van Riper when the latter ran the Marine Corps Combat and Development Command. General Van Riper would preach to young officers his concept of the "5,000-year-old mind." The general would say, "With 5,000 years of recorded military history, there is no excuse for a lack of constant study." Col B. P. McCoy took General Van Riper's message to heart. In his book *The Passion of Command* McCoy wrote, "I never wanted to look into the mirror and face the fact that I had gotten men killed due to my self-imposed limitations as a student of command."[4] Leaders like Van Riper, Mattis, and McCoy viewed professional military education as a moral imperative. Christopher Kolenda, the editor and coauthor of *Leadership: The Warrior's Art*, wrote, "The developed mind can part the shadows of chaos, disorder, and confusion to create vision and pursue it with conviction, keeping the organization on the proper azimuth to achieve its purpose."[5]

Both General Mattis and General Van Riper were (and are) what John Kotter would call "lifelong learners." John Kotter devotes the final chapter of his *Leading Change,* on implementing organizational change, to the leadership attributes required to succeed in the twenty-first century. Lifelong learning, Kotter states, is the single most reliable predictive factor concerning an executive's future potential. Lifelong learners combine their innate abilities and life experiences with competitive drive. This desire to do well leads them to seek out new information and build new skills through education and self-study. This drive, combined with growing abilities, produces a prodigious competitive capacity, one capable of dealing with today's increasingly competitive and fast-moving professional environment.[6]

Micah Zenko closes every episode of his *Power, Politics, and Preventive Action* podcast for the Council on Foreign Relations by asking his guest academics what advice they would give to a younger version of themselves. I was impressed by how many of these subject-matter experts advised future academics to be "intellectually promiscuous"—an attention-grabbing way of advising scholars to look outside of their disciplines and expand their knowledge bases. My own professional military education reading list includes books on management, economics, religion, philosophy, psychology, and even physiology. I would not consider myself "promiscuous," but I *am* curious. My curiosity goes hand in hand with humility: the more I learn, the more I discover how little I know. If smart people know when they are stupid (Maxim 23), I am a genius.

THE FIFTH STEP—HOW CAN I HELP?

When I commanded II MEF Headquarters Group, I added a fifth task to the leaders' daily duties—we were all to ask, "How can I help?" I had picked this up from the 37th Commandant when he commanded Marine Forces Central Command (MARCENT) and I was his Director of Operations (G-3). General Neller would often ask me, "How can I help?" Like most Marines, I was reluctant to dump my problems onto the general's desk. I, however, was in a unique position. As a colonel-select (aka lieutenant colonel), I was challenged every day to implement the commander's intent as a lieutenant-colonel component G-3 whose fellow G-3s were all one-star generals or very seasoned ("salty") colonels. One day, frustrated with my lack of progress with a supporting MEF on a resourcing issue, I "ghostwrote" a note for the general to send to the commanding general of that unit. When the commander asked me that afternoon if he could help, I asked him to send the e-mail. What would have taken days of cajoling with from colonel counterpart was resolved in ten minutes. Though I used those three-star-general e-mails (GEMs) sparingly, I did finally understand what General Neller was asking when he offered to help. He was not offering to do my job. He was offering to leverage the authority of his office to reduce a friction point. Think about how many man-hours are wasted by diligent staff officers struggling to gain traction that could be rectified by a thirty-second "burst transmission" by the commanding officer.

In addition to breaking down bureaucratic inertia, asking "How can I help?" can transform the culture of an organization. Can you imagine what a welcome change those four words can bring to a shop that is accustomed to being beaten down by the boss? Authenticity here is key. If you have been an Ebenezer, your epiphany had better be genuine, or you will always be Scrooge.

FRAMING FEEDBACK

Regardless of whether I was trooping the lines, inspecting a tank, or conducting an inspection, I used my daily five tasks to frame my responses in most encounters. When I would visit the tank ramp or the supply shop, I would state up front that I was not leaving until I had found a Marine doing a good job and thanked him, found a problem and fixed it, taught someone something, and learned something. Finally, before I left, I always asked how I could help. When inspecting a tank or counseling a Marine, I would normally ascertain which one of the five I would focus on, if not all of them. Is this a problem that I need to fix, or is this a Marine doing a good job? Is this a teaching moment, or am I the one who needs to learn? How can I help?

Saved Rounds—Some Thoughts and Tips

- "As the Commander, if you start the day without knowing where all of your Marines are or the location of your stuff, everything else will be suboptimal." (General Neller)
- "There is nothing new in the world except the history you do not know." (Harry Truman)
- A follow up to the question "What can I do to help?" that I found constructive is, "What can I *stop doing* that will be even more helpful?"
- Come up with your own leadership routine.

II

―――――

Toxic Leadership

9

Don't Be an Ass!

In Maxim 3 we identified the fifteenth, or missing, leadership trait as love. Here I propose for our missing leadership principle, "Don't be an ass!" No one ever wants to work for an ass. As discussed in the preface, some of these maxims have negative connotations, as they were derived from working with, or in close proximity to, toxic leaders. Unfortunately, their leadership lessons were caught more than taught. Having served with enough of these leaders, I swore never to emulate or repeat their behavior.

"Don't be an ass!"—one would think that this blindingly obvious statement is more a bromide than a leadership maxim; however, it is worth repeating. Leaders can inspire, or they can manipulate and intimidate. It has been said that fear is the lowest form of moral development—the same can be said of fear as a cornerstone for leadership. Leadership by fear and intimidation is the lowest form of leadership development.

When I was a junior officer, many of the senior leaders in the Corps of the day subscribed to autocratic and domineering leadership styles. The sea stories of general officers personally employing radar guns to enforce speed limits in base housing or scheduling inspector general visits as reprisal for leaving standing lights on were all true. One general I worked for had a policy of ceremonially firing three officers on his sixtieth day in command. He would often boast how he had relieved three officers at every level he had commanded after the second month in the seat. The morning after he relieved a battalion commander and two company commanders, he approached me on the physical training (PT) field and asked if I had heard about the firings. When I told him that I had, he asked me what I thought about it. I told him that I could not comment because I did not know the circumstances. He told me that I did not need to know the circumstances, only the consequences.

The truth is that positive leaders and negative leaders can both achieve discipline in their units; the differences are "how" and "what kind." Whether a unit is a truly disciplined unit or not can be ascertained by who enforces the discipline, not how stringently it is enforced. A well-led unit polices itself, regardless of the proximity of the commander, because its members are proud of who they are and what they have achieved.

Another adage that lends confusion for some is that it is "better to come in hard than to try and pick it up later." These folks, however, miss the point completely. They are your standards. Your standards should be introduced immediately and go higher after you have been at the helm for a while, not lower. You can be demanding without being an ass.

Unfortunately, some of the leadership styles modeled during Marine Corps entry-level training do not translate well to the operating forces. By that I am not advocating changing the role that drill instructors or even staff platoon commanders (SPCs) play on the drill field. Their authoritarian leadership style is a critical part of how we make Marines. However, as a professional, you are expected to develop and adapt your leadership style. If you are still modeling your staff platoon commander or sergeant instructor's leadership style with your

Marines in the fleet, your Marines will do exactly what you tell them to do . . . and nothing more.

Saved Rounds—Some Thoughts and Tips

- You can be tough and demanding without being an ass.
- Introduce your standards as soon as possible. Your standards should go up after you have been in command for a while; they should never go down.
- "You can shock the shit troops, but you can't shit the shock troops." (Anonymous.)

Recommended Reading—Herman Wouk's *The Caine Mutiny*. After you have read Wouk's classic, read Col Andy Milburn's dialectic piece in *War on the Rocks*, "From Captain Queeg to Winston Churchill: Lessons in Leading Up," 28 May 2020. It may change your perspective. It did mine.

10

Bad Leaders Drive Out Good Ones

An economist named Sir Thomas Gresham is credited with the three-century-old monetary principle that "bad money drives out good." The same can be said for leadership: bad leaders drive out the good ones. Said another way, good leaders don't follow bad ones . . . at least not for long.

Back in the fiscally constrained nineties, when the services underwent significant reductions in their budgets and even larger cuts to the size of their forces, an alarming number of toxic leaders ascended to senior leader positions within the Corps. They did so because these leaders got things done and were rewarded for it. The services needed better readiness rates—more readiness with smaller resources. Arbitrary metrics were ushered in with the adaptation of Total Quality Leadership (aka, Total Quality Management). Soon, however, senior leaders learned of the perils of rewarding the numbers without caring how they are made. By tying rewards (augmentation, command, and promotion) too closely to the metrics (numbers), they inadvertently encouraged manipulation, distortion, and abuse. Alarmed by the attrition rate of company-grade officers and the number of battalion commanders relieved for integrity violations, senior leadership began to take notice. Through the implementation of command-climate surveys and other feedback loops, senior leaders were able to identify and purge many toxic leaders from the ranks.

If you find yourself working for a toxic leader, there are a few constructive things you can do to accomplish the mission and still both take care of your Marines and retain your integrity. First and foremost, you should take a long-term view. Resiliency, determination, and grit all come into play here. If you are truly committed to the mission, to your Marines, and to the Marine Corps, you can weather any reign (pun intended). Loyalty, however, is a two-way street. Loyalty to your Marines requires that you provide candid feedback to your boss. Loyalty to your boss forbids you from bad-mouthing his policies or commiserating openly with the troops. In the end, if you can't reconcile your duty and loyalty with your integrity, you must resign. I worked for an extremely toxic leader as a junior major on remote duty. Fortunately, geographic separation provided a physical buffer against some of his more abusive mood swings. If I needed to speak with the boss, I called the deputy and asked how the weather was; the deputy, knowing what I was really asking, would let me know when the weather was "horrible." The lieutenant colonel, overhearing the conversation, would explode: "What are you talking about, it's beautiful out!" I knew to call back the next day. In the end, it caught up with him. He was later relieved of command, as a colonel, for command-climate issues.

The thing about toxic leaders, Lieutenant General Flynn once said, is that people are not willing to sacrifice for them. This lack of trust and commitment puts the mission at risk. Fortunately, by the time the Marine Corps went to war again after 9/11, most of the toxic senior leaders had moved on. Today Marines still suffer toxic leaders, but the institution is taking action. According to the Headquarters Marine Corps staff Manpower Management, Officer Assignments (MMOA-3) shop, twenty-one commanders were relieved from January 2014 through March 2017 for toxic leadership and command-climate issues.

As a commander, I learned that some junior leaders just don't get it and that there is a limit to what you can do to correct their bad leadership. If you encounter toxic leaders within your command, identify the leadership issues, address them with the officers, document them, and then fire them—don't delay or second-guess yourself. They are a poison! (For more on this refer to Maxim 15.)

THE BUFFER AND THE MAGNIFYING GLASS

I found an analogy useful when caring for Marines in a toxic climate: that of the buffer and the magnifying glass.

The Buffer. If you are working for a toxic or abusive commander, sometimes you have to absorb the blows in order to protect your people. A commander's ability to motivate his Marines is limited, but a caustic leader's ability to demotivate a unit knows no bounds. You can filter much of this negativity without compromising your integrity or violating your loyalty. The key is to take charge of your post and own whatever policy comes down (see Maxim 34). You can round off some of the sharp edges and repackage it to make it your own. Just do not fall into the trap of criticizing your boss to your subordinates. Marines know. They will have greater respect for you if you hold the line.

The Magnifying Glass. Sometimes the poor leadership to which we are subjected comes in the form of weakness or fecklessness. In cases where a lack of direction or focus from the higher headquarters is negatively affecting your command, it is your responsibility to turn up the magnification. In repackaging a policy or a directive to make it yours, you can always make it more stringent. Remember, as a leader you can be uncertain, just not unclear.

Saved Rounds—Some Thoughts and Tips

- Circumstances may require you to reflect back to Maxim 1 (Know Thyself) and the limits you've defined for yourself. A mentor of mine once reminded me that every officer "should know what his letter of resignation looks like."
- Take care of your Marines, and they will take care of you. Marines know. They do not need you to identify fake or toxic senior leaders. Protect your integrity and retain their respect by not bad-mouthing your boss.
- "Take heed what you say of your seniors, be your word spoken softly or plain." (Royal Navy rear admiral Ronald Arthur Hopwood's poem "The Laws of the Navy")

Recommended Reading—C. S. Forester's classic *The General* is a cautionary tale of the professional stagnation of the British officer corps that led to the carnage of World War I.

III

———

Building Cohesion

11

That Point Where Everyone Else Sucks

Above all else, cohesion is the most revealing indicator of the quality of leadership within an organization. Is the unit "tight?" Is there a sense of pride in belonging, a sense of "otherness"? Applied properly, esprit de corps is the glue that binds a unit together. Without that, it is difficult to achieve progress in any other metric of effective leadership.

In his book *Team of Teams*, GEN Stanley McChrystal, USA, recounts a conversation he had with a Navy SEAL about the optimal size of a unit. The petty officer replied, "The point where everyone else sucks."[1] Anyone who has ever been in a cohesive organization knows exactly what this special operator meant. There is a point, a critical mass, when all of the pride, loyalty, trust, commitment, motivation, and morale are fully embodied by the group.

If you can build cohesion within your organization, everything else will be relatively easy. Cohesive units are disciplined units, because their members police themselves. Cohesive units are characterized by a high degree of trust, because their members feel secure. In a cohesive unit the members are committed to the mission and have bought into how the organization intends to accomplish it. "Buy-in," though, does not come from the top—it swells up from the bottom. The members of cohesive units take great pride in their product and are fiercely loyal to the brand.

The quality of esprit de corps comes from our desire to belong. We are all herd animals. We seek to join organizations where we feel we belong, because we feel safe. When Marines know the unit has their backs, they are more confident in tackling threats or seizing opportunities.

The fact that Marines *are* Marines tells you that they want to belong to an organization with a sense of "otherness." As a company commander, I sought to tap into this allegiance by unofficially redesignating (branding) the unit "Team Bravo," as opposed to Bravo Company. Much to the battalion sergeant major's chagrin, I went so far as to reissue the company guidon with the "Team Bravo" moniker. Since Marines see through clichéd slogans, I didn't go to work on this signage until I believed we were well on our way to epitomizing the name.

In combat, unit cohesion prevents fear from becoming panic, it propels Marines forward in the face of incredible adversity, and it provides a well of resilience and the will to win. Christopher Kolenda's *Leadership* points to examples of select U.S. Army units in World War II and elements of the Israeli Defense Forces in the 1973 Yom Kippur War to demonstrate how crucial unit cohesion is to individual and unit combat effectiveness. In both conflicts, units regarded as highly cohesive had significantly fewer psychological casualties than other, similar units operating in like circumstances.[2] In World War II, the "sense of otherness" and the close affinity that paratroopers of the 82nd and 101st Airborne Divisions shared prevented widespread combat neurosis.

These units were not just more resilient, they were more lethal. *On Killing,* by Army lieutenant colonel and psychologist Dave Grossman, found that unit cohesion enabled soldiers to overcome the innate human reluctance to kill another man while providing absolution for those who did, in the unit's name. Soldiers assigned to highly cohesive units were less likely to be diagnosed with post-traumatic stress disorder and more likely to move rapidly through the postcombat stages of exhilaration, remorse, rationalization, and acceptance.[3] Finally, cohesive units are less likely to perpetrate war crimes. The same self-policing that increases discipline in cohesive units in garrison is present on the battlefield as well. Members of cohesive units will not allow anyone to bring dishonor on the unit's name.

THE "CASUAL CATS"

I discovered the power of cohesion when leading my peers in college. I am a Citadel graduate. When I attended, the Corps of Cadets was divided into sixteen companies and a regimental band. Each company had a distinctive culture, a personality that endured to a remarkable degree from class to class. The worst company in the Corps during my first three years was Charlie Company. The "Casual Cats," as they called themselves, took great pride in finishing last. Every Friday afternoon, the results of the weekly parade (which had turned into a drill competition) were announced over the PA system. The winning company, announced first, would let out a cheer that could be heard throughout the campus. When the regimental adjutant announced the last company—"and in sixteenth place, Charlie Company"—the Casual Cats' cheers would drown out the jeers.

In the institution's eye, Charlie Company took great pride in finishing last. The Commandant's office's response was to assign a student I viewed as the most autocratic martinet in the rising senior class to lead Charlie Company the following year. I took note as this hapless cadet commander flung himself against the rock that was Charlie Company, producing little or nothing to show for it. The unit's performance remained poor, the commanding officer (CO) grew frustrated, and yet the unit grew tighter. Imagine my dismay when I learned that I had been picked to lead the Casual Cats next. How did this portend for a successful senior year? More importantly, did the leadership at The Citadel see me as the rising militant autocrat of my class?

As I reflected on the challenge before me that summer, I realized that Charlie Company was in fact the most cohesive company in the Corps of Cadets. If cohesion is the most important and difficult leadership attribute to achieve, the hard work was already done. All I had to was to turn the ship around. My job was to define an alternative reality for the company, communicate the vision, and get everyone to buy in. Easy, right? Actually, I learned a lot about leadership that year. Some very talented classmates and I co-opted the senior class and produced some early wins. Building on this momentum, I doubled down on some promising initiatives. Instead of focusing on the consequences of failure, I offered rewards for victory. When the company did well, we celebrated. Our company parties (off campus) were legendary. We won the President's Cup that year: we were the honor company, a designation for the highest aggregate score in drill (parades and competition), academics, and intramural athletics in the Corps.

COMMAND CLIMATE

When you join a cohesive team, you are "all in." Marines do not just adapt to the characteristics of their surroundings, they adopt them. In units with strong cohesion, the Marines' behavior reflects the culture of the unit they joined—the good and the bad. They take on the characteristics of the group, and the norms and values of the unit quickly become their own. This command climate, the environment within the organization, can determine the unit's success as well as that of its members. When you get command climate right, there is trust and cooperation. Get it wrong, and you have a bunch of individuals out for themselves. The good news is that changing the climate of an organization is fairly easy—all you have to do is swap out one person.

Admittedly I am biased (as a proud native of Boston!), but if you are looking for a case study in effective organizational culture and command climate, take a look at the National Football League's (NFL) New England Patriots under Coach Bill Belichick. There are a lot of "haters" out there, but the effectiveness of the Patriots' culture is indisputable. In a free-agent, egocentric industry, Belichick's Patriots define organizational excellence. New players, regardless of where they fell out in the draft, fall in line and assimilate quickly into the Patriots' program. The drive to fit in is most observable among players who transfer in from other clubs with troubled pasts. Randy Moss and Chad "Ochocinco" Johnson did their jobs without the drama and self-aggrandizement that had been observed when they wore other uniforms. Even the most notorious egoists in the NFL put the team and their teammates first when wearing a Patriots uniform.

In her book *Grit: The Power of Passion and Perseverance*, Angela Duckworth discusses at length the power of conformity and the value of a "gritty culture." Duckworth concludes that there are two ways to grow resilience, or what she calls "grit." The hard way is to develop it by yourself. The easy way is to surround yourself in a culture of grit.[4] If you have a troubled Marine who could benefit from a fresh start, move him or her to your best platoon. If they are salvageable, "the way we do things around here" in their new group will become the way *they* do things too, and why.

DUNBAR'S NUMBER
In the 1990s, British anthropologist Robin Dunbar found a correlation between the size of a primate's brain and the average size of the social group. "Dunbar's number" (a term he coined) suggests there is a cognitive limit to the number of people with whom we can maintain stable social relationships. Extrapolating from the data to the average human brain size, Dunbar proposed that humans today can comfortably maintain only 150 stable relationships.

Leadership experts adopted Dunbar's work and incorporated it into organizational-design theory. My experience has borne out Dunbar's work: the biggest unit in which you can achieve an optimal level of cohesion is the company—between a hundred and 150 Marines. I knew that the battalion I commanded could never achieve the same level of cohesion I had experienced in the companies I led. As an O-6 commander, I knew my group would never be as tight as 1st Tank Battalion had been. That said, I was committed to fostering a command climate where commanders were free to cultivate cohesion within its units, provided their sense of otherness did not metastasize into suboptimization or internal rivalry.

Saved Rounds—Some Thoughts and Tips

- Cohesion requires a common purpose or a common foe. Units that lack cohesion often lack clarity with respect to their missions.
- A command's culture can be set intentionally or unintentionally—be deliberate!
- "Ritualize to actualize": in his book *Legacy*, James Kerr identifies a common technique used by elite teams and organizations. The most revered organizations use smart, sharp, recognizable phrases, mantras, and slogans to define their purpose. Remember, words start revolutions.[5]
- Branding: what symbols or artifacts are present for the Marines to identify with? An example is 2nd Tank Battalion's ubiquitous "The Ace in the Hole" moniker. I defy you to find a Marine who ever served in 2nd Battalion, 2nd Marines who does not display "Warlords" prominently, somewhere. In building cohesion with a unit, something as simple as a T-shirt is a start.
- Unit lineage and history: look for tie-ins to the unit's combat lineage and history to build cohesion and increase its resiliency for future combat.

By highlighting examples of its valor and resolve in past conflicts, you remind Marines that they must be worthy successors of the unit's name. Military units grade themselves on their accomplishments in combat. It is the stuff so eloquently evoked by Col John W. Thomason, "The Kipling of the Corps"—"Such as Regiments hand down forever."

Recommended Reading—*Legacy: What the All Blacks Can Teach Us about the Business of Life*, by James Kerr, provides many practical tips on creating a cohesive team and a culture of continuous improvement.

12

Make Winning a Habit

During the first week of my commands at the battalion and group levels, I made a spectacle of cleaning out the unit's trophy case. Borrowing a little theater from LtGen Harold "Hal" Moore's memoir, *We Were Soldiers Once . . . and Young: Ia Drang—the Battle That Changed the War in Vietnam,* I rolled a trash can up to the case and threw out all of the second- and third-place trophies in it. Some of the staff would look on in bewilderment as I chided the executive officer (XO) and sergeant major, "Holy shit, Sergeant Major, there's a third-place trophy in here!" . . . *Kaplunk* . . . into the trash. My message was not subtle—this unit would not accept anything less than excellence, and second place would never be good enough!

When I was a lieutenant, 1st Tank Battalion always took great pride in its tackle football team. Former battalion commanders like LtGen Marty Steele, MajGen Tim Donovan, and Col Bill Callahan all knew that competition was an easy and very effective way to build cohesion and unit pride. Marines are aggressive by nature, and by tapping into their competitive ethos you can rapidly forge a team. The key, however, is winning! You must dedicate the resources needed to win or do not bother.

The tank battalion's coach during those years was Master Gunnery Sergeant Graham. He would often tell the Marines to "make winning a habit." He taught us to look for the quick wins early and then repeat. When I assumed command of 1st Tank Battalion fifteen years later, I looked for an opportunity to seize an early win. The "Combat Center Challenge" presented such an opportunity. I threw the full weight of the staff behind what was little more than a field meet. We convened an operation planning team (OPT) and went through the entire Marine Corps planning process to task-organize and weight properly a winning effort. On the day of the event, we stood up an operations center to track and monitor our progress. I even had a reserve, the battalion's tug-of-war team, ready to commit if we needed some extra muscle to push an event over into the "win" column. The day indeed came down to a tug-of-war between Tanks and LAR (Light Armored Reconnaissance, our archrivals). I could not have asked for a more epic finish to seal our victory and build a bow wave of pride in the organization.

When I commanded at the II MEF Headquarters Group (MHG), I wanted to provide the battalion commanders the same opportunity that the Combat Center Challenge had given me. About three months into their command tenures, we organized the "Praetorian Challenge." (The Praetorian Guard was an elite unit of the imperial Roman army that served as the personal bodyguards and intelligence collectors for the Roman emperors. MHG's mission was to provide the intelligence, communications, supporting arms, and security for the expeditionary force. Therefore, we had selected "The Praetorians" as our call sign, logo, and crest.) Our Marine Corps Community Services coordinator secured some great sponsors. I selected only martial events for the competition. For example, volleyball was replaced with pugil-stick matches (a mock bayonet fight, with wooden sticks and football helmets). I was proud of the effort that each unit made, but more importantly, I was pleased with the culture we were cultivating. When it came time to announce the winners, I began with third place. A few thousand Marines yelled back, "Who cares?!"; I threw out the trophy without naming the recipient. The announcement of second place drew jeers of "First loser!" When I finally announced the winner, that unit erupted with jubilation while the others respectfully, if ever so briefly, clapped.

MOMENTUM

Winning builds momentum. When you have momentum, things appear to be better than they are. When you lack momentum, things can often look worse. Leadership coach Jon Gordon once said, "Winning is a great deodorant. It covers up what is wrong in an organization."[1] John Maxwell agrees. Of his *21 Irrefutable Laws of Leadership*, number sixteen is what he calls "The Big Mo." Momentum, he says, is the great exaggerator.[2] It is like a magnifying glass—it makes things look better than they are. Momentum, however, is easier to steer than to start. Creating momentum, and not just capitalizing on it, is a leadership imperative.

COOPERATION TRUMPS COMPETITION

As mentioned, competition is a great tool for building cohesion, but it must be used prudently. Left unchecked, it can become unhealthy and lead to internal rivalries that erode cohesion as opposed to creating it. The Latin root of the word "compete" means "to strive together." Striving together does not mean "everyone gets a trophy" but that—like everything else in leadership—the "why" matters more than the "what." In her book *Grit*, Angela Duckworth quotes the NFL Seattle Seahawks (and former Patriots) coach Pete Carroll: "It is your opponent that makes you great."[3] The Seahawks are known throughout the league for the intensity of their full-speed Wednesday practices. Once the season begins, most teams do full-speed practices against their practice squads. The Seahawks, however, line up their starting offense against their starting defense and go head to head. A better opponent, Carroll explained, creates challenges that help us become our best selves. "It's really the guy across from us that makes us who we are."[4]

In his book *The Generals*, Tom Ricks retells the plight of GEN Terry de la Mesa Allen, the commanding general of the "Big Red One" early in World War II. Though the 1st Infantry Division was a highly cohesive and effective fighting force, GEN Omar Bradley relieved Allen of command because of the perceived toxicity of the division for the Army as a whole. "Terrible Terry" Allen was known as a warfighter who did not care much for grooming standards or other conspicuous indicators of discipline. He *did* believe in combat readiness and aggressiveness. Allen's cocky and independent command style resonated with his men but clashed with Bradley's idea of a commander. What was worse, the division and its staff did not work well with adjacent or higher headquarters. Bradley felt "the whole division had assumed Allen's cavalier attitude."[5] GEN George S. Patton and GEN Dwight D. Eisenhower, however, respected Allen as a warfighter; he was given command of the 104th Timberwolf Division later in the war.

In researching their book *The Leadership Challenge*, Kouzes and Posner found compelling evidence refuting the conventional wisdom that competition enhances performance. Instead, they found that leaders who emphasized cooperation were far more likely to produce positive outcomes.[6] Trying to do something well and trying to beat someone are two different things. If your goal is to build cohesion while improving performance, you want your elements working together, not against each other.

When I commanded II MHG, I made the point to all my battalion commanders during my initial counseling that they were not in competition with each other. I explained that there was "room in the end zone" (top-third ranking) for all five commanders—they could all be there, provided they accomplished their missions, took care of the Marines, and worked well together. I defined my goals of cohesion and combat readiness and expounded how my leadership philosophy was predicated on trust. If our five disparate organizations with five different missions (but the same purpose) were to work effectively together in a resource-constrained environment, we needed cooperation, not competition. Cooperation requires trust, and trust requires reciprocity. I knew we were well on our way when I found warrant officers and senior staff NCOs from one battalion diligently assisting with another battalion's inspection preparation without any tasking from my staff. It worked. All five battalions passed their material readiness assessments (FSMAOs), and all five battalion commanders were selected for the war college (Top Level School). II MHG was the only command to tout clean sweeps in both metrics.

Saved Rounds—Some Thoughts and Tips

- An effective way to build momentum is to look for the "quick win" early and then repeat.
- Warning: be watchful of suboptimization within a unit. Healthy competition within a unit is an effective tool; internal rivalries can be divisive.
- Competition is effective but not as effective as cooperation. If your goal is to build cohesion while improving performance, look for opportunities for your elements to work together, not against each other.

Recommended Reading*—Win Forever: Live, Work, and Play like a Champion*, by Pete Carroll, Yogi Roth, and Kristoffer A. Garin, or *The Education of a Coach*, the bestseller by David Halberstam on the football genius of Bill Belichick, draw insightful profiles on leadership from the competitive world of professional sports.

IV

———

Instill the Will

13

True Grit

One More, One More Time

Positions are seldom lost because they have been destroyed,
but almost invariably because the leader has decided in
his own mind that the position cannot be held.
GEN A. A. VANDEGRIFT, EIGHTEENTH
COMMANDANT OF THE MARINE CORPS[1]

The warrior ethos of the Spartans is held in almost spiritual admiration within the Corps. Marine units adopt Spartan logos and slogans, and our professional reading list pays homage to Thucydides' recounting of the last stand of King Leonidas and his three hundred Spartans at the battle of Thermopylae. The Spartans, however, were not invincible: in 371 BC they were defeated by an unlikely foe. The battle of Leuctra saw the Thebans, led by Epaminondas, decisively defeat a numerically superior Spartan force. The Theban victory shattered Sparta's influence over the Greek Peninsula and was one of the most significant events in Greek history.

Much has been written on the tactics used by Epaminondas and their influence on Philip II of Macedon, who lived and studied in Thebes. Philip's son Alexander, in turn, would build upon these tactical principles to conquer the then-known world. In his book *The Warrior Ethos* author and former Marine Steven Pressfield tells how Epaminondas promised his men victory if they would give him just one more foot at the moment he commanded, by a blast of a trumpet. When the battle had been joined and the Spartan and Theban shields were interlocked, Epaminondas had a trumpet sounded, and his men found the will to push the Spartans back one more foot. That was all it took—Theban will applied at the decisive time and place. The Spartans' phalanx broke, and a rout ensued.[2]

Pressfield's story reminds me of an early mentor. In my youth I trained under a legend in the karate and mixed-martial-arts worlds, Grand Master Joe Esposito. Joe's "group classes" were renowned for their intensity. Somehow, when his students had been pushed to exhaustion, Joe always found a way to summon "one more, one more time." Those training sessions left an indelible mark on me and later influenced how I trained Marines. The best leaders can find a way to get "one more, one more time" at the decisive moment.

WILL

In defining leadership, the 1921 version of the *Marine Corps Manual* states, "The primary goal of Marine Corps leadership is to instill in all Marines the fact that we are warriors first. The only reason the United States of America needs a Marine Corps is to fight and win wars. Everything else is secondary."[3] For Marines, therefore, the one indispensable leadership trait is will. The Marine Corps includes *will* in its definition of endurance, one of its fourteen leadership traits. An objective study of military history reveals that *will* has decided every battle since antiquity. The proper application of mass and the other principles of war are necessary for victory, but at some point in every battle one side believes it has "lost"—and at that moment, it is right. The battles decided by annihilation throughout history can be counted on one's hands. They are so rare that we all know them by name—Thermopolis, the Alamo, etc. Yet Marine Corps history is replete with examples of Marine leaders who, faced with insurmountable odds, mustered the will to prevail and found a way.

INSTILL THE WILL

As the commanding general of 2nd Marine Division, MajGen John K. Love often talked about the need to incorporate *will* training into our *skill* training. As a group CO I emphasized the significance of *will* in even our most mundane tasks. Formation runs and conditioning hikes are great opportunities to accentuate the will required to succeed in combat. At the end of a long hike or run, recognize those who had the intestinal fortitude to complete it by declaring to them that they had signaled to the rest of the unit that they could be counted on when it matters. This tacit rebuke of those who had dropped out signaled to the team that those people might not be there when things got tough. I have to admit, I struggled to find empathy in these circumstances. I have been pushed to exhaustion on many occasions, but I have never been pushed to quit.

In his book *Outliers,* Malcolm Gladwell writes, "Success is a function of persistence and doggedness—it is not innate ability—it is an attitude."[4] Angela Duckworth would agree. She defines perseverance as "grit." Gritty people, she writes, those "highly accomplished paragons of persistence," are not the most talented but the most determined.[5] Gritty leaders are optimists. They believe in themselves, and they believe in the mission. Their unbridled optimism creates a self-fulfilling prophecy that fuels their resolve. Gritty leaders sustain the effort just a little longer than their opponent can. That little bit is all that matters—one more, one more time!

THE WILL TO FIND A WAY

It is the leader's job to inspire Marines to keep moving forward in the face of extraordinary adversity. Resilient leaders find the will to overcome obstacles and are not deterred by temporary setbacks or defeats. To them, initial failure is not an affirmation of a lack of capability or confidence; it is a catalyst to try harder. A favorite meme of mine is "I have never lost—I have only won or learned." To a resilient leader, defeat spurs innovation, not despair.

As a Marine officer, you are expected to be an exemplar of determination and resilience. As General Dunford once said, "It is included in the sticker price of being a Lieutenant." There is a reason why Officer Candidate School (OCS), The Basic School (TBS), and the Infantry Officer Course (IOC) are so demanding. The official motto at IOC is *Decerno Communico Exsequor* (decide, communicate, execute), but the unofficial one is borrowed from Thucydides: "He is best who is trained in the severest school." These schools' curriculums of privation—lack of food and sleep, exposure to the elements—produces a degree of misery that the protected will never know. It also immunizes future lieutenants against the stresses of combat. By overcoming tremendous adversity in training, leaders build within themselves a bulwark of fortitude that helps keep future hardships in perspective.

Today, there is in the neurobiological and psychological literatures strong evidence that justifies the rigors of entry-level training in the Marine Corps. Research has shown that extended exposure to adversity in young adulthood inoculates against hopelessness in later years. The key, however, is not enduring the suffering but overcoming it. Researchers have shown that there is "plasticity" in the circuitry of our brains. If you experience adversity—something very potent—in your youth and overcome it, you develop a different way of handling adversity in the future.[6] This is one of the reasons why Gen Charles Krulak wanted to incorporate into boot camp a "defining moment." In 1996 the Marine Corps Recruit Depots implemented an event known as "the Crucible," a rite of passage to becoming a Marine. The Crucible's fifty-four hours of physical exertion combined with food and sleep deprivation pits young men and women against a barrage of combat assault courses, team-building warrior stations, and a leadership reaction course. By imposing challenges at the peak of adversity, it instills grit while literally rewiring the brain to be more resilient.

The fortitude of any unit is equal to the sum of the grit in its members. This is one reason why the Corps puts so much stock into its recruit training. The mere fact that a Marine graduated from Parris Island or the recruit depot in San Diego tells you that this individual possesses a baseline level of grit that is significantly better than that of the average soldier. It is incumbent upon the Marine leader to strengthen the resiliency of that new Marine's unit. You grow grit one Marine at a time.

Perhaps the easiest way in which a commander can increase the resilience of his or her Marines is simply leveling with them and telling them what to expect, so they can be better mentally prepared. In combat, everything is harder than you think it will be. Your candor with your Marines will increase resiliency. It is when things seem to go bad unexpectedly, or the task appears far more difficult than anticipated, that people begin to lose their nerve.

I am a huge fan of Winston Churchill. Perhaps not since Lincoln has there been a statesman who better personified determination and grit. Upon becoming prime minister in the midst of World War II, Winston Churchill rallied the British people with his first speech to the House of Commons:

> I have nothing to offer but blood, toil, tears and sweat. We have before us an ordeal of the most grievous kind. We have before us many, many long months of struggle and of suffering. You ask, what is our policy? I will say: It is to wage war, by sea, land and air, with all our might and with all the strength that God can give us; to wage war against a monstrous tyranny, never surpassed in the dark and lamentable catalogue of human crime. That is our policy. You ask, what is our aim? I can answer in one word: Victory. Victory at all costs—Victory in

spite of all terror—Victory, however long and hard the
road may be, for without victory there is no survival.[7]

Saved Rounds—Some Thoughts and Tips

- "Success is not final, and failure is not fatal: It is the
  courage to continue that counts." (Winston Churchill)
- To prepare Marines properly for combat, you have to
  push them beyond their limits. It is only up against
  your perceived limit that you discover you have one
  more in you, one more time.
- Use historical examples, ideally from the unit's own
  past, to incorporate *will* training into *skill* training.
- In training, something as simple as declaring ahead of
  time what the pace and distance of a formation run or
  hike will be significantly reduces the number of "drops."
- "Nothing in this world can take the place of
  persistence. Talent will not; nothing is more common
  than unsuccessful men with talent. Genius will not;
  unrewarded genius is almost a proverb. Education
  will not: the world is full of educated derelicts.
  Persistence and determination alone are omnipotent."
  (Calvin Coolidge)

Recommended Reading

- Anything and everything by Steven Pressfield, a retired
  Marine lieutenant colonel and the author of *Gates of
  Fire, The Warrior Ethos,* and *The Virtues of War,* to
  name a few.
- Angela Duckworth's *Grit: The Power of Passion and
  Perseverance.*
- *The Last Lion: Winston Spencer Churchill,* vol. 3,
  Defender of the Realm, 1940–1965, by William
  Manchester and Paul Reid. Another great book on
  Churchill (and Lincoln) is *Supreme Command:
  Soldiers, Statesmen, and Leadership in Wartime,*
  by Eliot A. Cohen.

14

Embrace the Suck

Short of combat, nothing builds cohesion like tough, realistic training in the most austere environments. Marines take pride in being hard and sharing adversity. The more arduous the task and the more miserable the conditions, the greater the sense of accomplishment and the stronger affinity with the other members of the team. The quote on the cover of the manual *United States Navy Corpsman and Field Medical Service Officer*—"Tough realistic training is the best form of troop welfare"—is attributed to Field Marshal Erwin Rommel.

When in command, in the sweltering heat of the desert, or the stifling humidity on Okinawa, or the frigid cold in Norway, I would often ask Marines if they remembered that field exercise we had done in October in Camp Lejeune, when the weather was seventy degrees and sunny. After some time or thought, they would reply, "No." "Neither do I!" I would reply. "You can thank me for the story later." Ironically, they would.

"Unity is forged not forced," write Kouzes and Posner in *The Leadership Challenge.*[1] General Krulak had this in mind when he directed the revamping of recruit training and the addition of the Crucible. I had the privilege of leading a recruit training company through the "beta" test that would become the Crucible. That first Crucible was everything the Commandant envisioned—a grueling gut check. What the thirty-first Commandant did not anticipate, however, was the resistance those first "Crucible Marines" faced when they hit the fleet. In his quest to create a defining event, the Commandant had unwittingly created a seam in the fabric that united us all together. We had Crucible and non-Crucible Marines. Today, those distinctions are gone. There are very few pre-Crucible Marines left in the ranks. In September of 2016, my son Shane completed his Crucible with Platoon 3072. After hearing his Crucible sea stories, I am proud to say the system and the bonds are as strong as they were twenty years ago.

Alexander the Great understood the value of strenuous training in building his army. "Never try and please the army," he says in a historical novel about his career. "Give them hardship. Give them something that can't be done and place yourself at first hazard."[2] In giving Alexander these words, former Marine and author Steven Pressfield knew to include the most important part of the lecture—leadership by example. It was Alexander's position out in front of his men, sharing their misery, that made the difference. As the saying goes, pressure will make dust or diamonds. The difference is not the quality of the coal, it is the force of the leadership.

Never forget that wherever the friction is the greatest and the conditions are the worst is where you must position yourself. You must never underestimate the power of your attitude and example. Marines will look to see how you are doing and will mold their reactions to yours. Here you set the tone.

In his book *Primal Leadership: Unleashing the Power of Emotional Intelligence*, Dr. Daniel Goleman examines the neurology and psychology behind a leader's ability to drive such emotions within an organization. The human brain, he explains, is an open-loop system. Open-loop systems depend on external sources for management. We rely on our connections with others to regulate our feelings. Goleman describes how we can catch onto others' feelings and share moods.[3] A point that bears emphasis is the fact that a leader's personal emotions can have organizational consequences: as a commander, you must pay attention to your "emotional hygiene." Just as you would never want to bring the emotional baggage of work home, you must be careful never to bring your frustrations at home to work.

Marines are known for their morose and often dark sense of humor—situation miserable, crack a joke. As a commander I found humor a highly effective leadership tool in stressful times but one that needs to be employed wisely. Authenticity and emotional intelligence are more important than timing. It's actually the poor timing, the incongruity, of a joke in a crisis that makes it resonate with Marines. Marines like to laugh, regardless of the circumstance. Anyone who ever served with Gen Charles M. Gurganus would attest to his charisma and colorful sense of humor. When things were at their worst, you could count on the general to crack a joke to lift the staff's spirits.

Emotions are contagious. Dr. Goleman found that it is cheer that has the greatest emotional diffusion. When leaders have emotional intelligence, they are attuned to the morale of the command and to what they need to do to uplift their people. Goleman refers to this as "resonant leadership."[4] An attuned leader's message vibrates through a command. Resonant leaders communicate with more signal and less noise. When it was reported to him that the 1st Marine Division was cut off north of the Chosin Reservoir by eight Chinese divisions, Col Chesty Puller allegedly retorted, "All right, they're on our left, they're on our right, they're in front of us, they're behind us . . . they can't get away this time."[5]

Saved Rounds—Some Thoughts and Tips

- Marines want it tough and demanding and are disappointed when it is not. They will bitch about exacting training when it is under way but will tell stories about it for years after.

- If it is hard or a pain in the ass, make sure you are the first in line.
- Confident in Marines' ability to endure hardship, I never intentionally put that confidence to the test. In other words, I never planned to be miserable—it happened often enough all by itself.
- *Warning*: Draw a sharp distinction between tough, demanding training and hazing. Ensure there are no "rites of passage" for new joins.
- Check your emotional hygiene before interacting with Marines. LtGen Ronald Bailey would often preach that throughout his decades of service he never had a bad day. He had bad moments, but he knew that to be effective he had to move on quickly.
- Humor is a lubricant in good units but must be genuine to be effective. You can fake a smile, but you cannot fake a laugh. For some reason, laughing in the face of adversity resonates with Marines.
- Remember, in command your jokes are always funny . . . even when they are not.

Recommended Reading

- *Primal Leadership: Unleashing the Power of Emotional Intelligence*, by Daniel Goldman, PhD.
- *The Mask of Command*, by Sir John Keegan.

V

———

Instilling Discipline

15

There Can Be No Morale without Attrition

I n ancient Rome, when a legion was plagued with disciplinary issues the emperor would order the unit "decimated."
Decimating a unit literally meant the killing of a tenth of its
troops. The centurions would organize the legion into groups
of ten and draw straws. The soldier who drew the short straw
was dispatched by the *gladiuses*, short stabbing swords, of the
other nine. Decimation and other brutal forms of group punishment were abandoned long ago. Aside from their moral
implications, such methods could not sustain effectiveness.
Kolenda writes, "In modern armies compulsion can keep
people in the ranks but can't keep them fighting."[1] I maintain what I did in Maxim 6, that a commander will have his
greatest impact not by resorting to draconian forms of group
punishment but by focusing on the ends of the bell curve.
Specifically, failure to address properly the bottom 10 percent
can have a deleterious effect on the cohesion and morale of
the entire organization.

Xenophon of Athens, a student of Socrates, was also a
soldier and a historian whose writings on military leadership from the late fifth century BC are still referred to today.

Contrasting the leadership styles of the Spartans and the Athenians, Xenophon discovered that failing to enforce discipline can be as damaging to morale as tyranny. Clearchus, a Spartan, subscribed to a severe leadership philosophy that would have been hailed by Machiavelli: Clearchus wanted his soldiers to fear him more than they feared the enemy. In contrast, Proxenus, an Athenian and friend of Xenophon, sought to win the love of his soldiers by simply withholding praise from wrongdoers. Ironically, both commanders were despised by their soldiers. Clearchus's brutality resulted in a high rate of desertion from the Spartan ranks, and Proxenus, by failing to punish the Athenian miscreants, became an object of contempt.[2]

Today, too many Marines are disillusioned by a perceived lack of standards within the Corps. They joined the Corps because they believed it to be an elite force. However, when they find themselves surrounded by malcontents, drug users, and "fatbodies," they become disillusioned. You can prevent this problem by keeping your administrative separation process (ADSEP) pressurized. By removing Marines who are out of standards and prosecuting those who have broken our core values, we protect the Corps' elite standing and sustain its morale.

As a company commander on the drill field, I learned that properly processing your substandard Marines for administrative separation was a form of troop welfare. As the old slogan read, "If everyone could be a Marine, it wouldn't be the Marines." Drill instructors (DIs) are taught that it is their job to train Marines, not to screen them. When drill instructors feel undue pressure to retain substandard recruits, however, the lesser among them may be tempted to take matters into their own hands. Having investigated and reviewed too many hazing incidents, I find that this phenomenon—hopeless cases kept on board too long—is often the common denominator. I am in no way excusing or condoning maltreatment; I am pointing out an unintended consequence of arbitrary retention goals. A retention policy that applies undue pressure on leaders to reduce attrition can place substandard Marines, their leadership, and the entire organization at risk.

As a commander, it is crucial that you apply even more scrutiny to the organization's poorly performing leaders than you do to poorly performing Marines. Nothing will destroy the morale of a unit faster than saddling it with leaders who are incompetent or have compromised their integrity. Lieutenants are supposed to make mistakes. Provided they learn from them and continue to grow, this actually strengthens the organization. However, when a commander appears to sanction incompetence through inaction, the commander's credibility is called into question.

My single greatest regret as a battalion commander was not firing a company commander whom I believed to be toxic. Most toxic leaders survive, even flourish, because their seniors, oblivious to their means, appreciate their results. My reluctance to relieve this particular officer, however, was a product not of my ignorance but of my arrogance. I thought I could "fix him." Concerned by his callous demeanor and his lack of trust and respect for the senior enlisteds in his company, I would take him for walks in the desert. The problem was that I kept bringing him back. The situation finally came to a head less than a week before the unit was scheduled to deploy. Coming out of the field to inspect the battalion I could see a rare desert downpour over its area. Knowing the unit was scheduled to lay out all of their kit on the tank ramp, I turned and commented to the sergeant major that surely they must have moved the inspection into the maintenance bays. The sergeant major, having heard the SNCOs' gripes, did not share my optimism. When we pulled onto the ramp, there were the Marines standing at attention in the pouring rain while the gear they were about to deploy with was washed away. I was incensed—not at this gross lack of leadership and judgment but at my own failure for letting things get this far.

With this leadership failure ingrained in my mind, I made certain not to make that mistake again. When I had group command, a particular subordinate commander's caustic attitude and unconcern for troop welfare was brought to my attention several times during my orientation. I made it a point to meet with the officer right away. The meeting didn't go well. I decided it was in the command's best interest that this officer be reassigned to a billet that didn't expose a large number of Marines to his toxicity. When he challenged how I could make such a call after being on deck only for a couple of weeks, I told him I knew how the episode would end.

A decade ago, the management philosophy of General Electric's Jack Welch heralded the benefits of ranking your organization and continuously removing the bottom 10 percent. This "rank-and-yank" philosophy, however, has an insidious and corrupting effect. Taken to its logical conclusion, this modern-day form of decimation will destroy unit cohesion and erode integrity. In an article for *New Yorker*, "The Talent Myth," Malcolm Gladwell pointed to the collapse of Enron to highlight the perils of "rank and yank." Enron, he wrote, had epitomized the "talent mindset" philosophy.[3] Here, internal competition encouraged employees to prove they were smarter than their peers. The result was a narcissistic culture that rewarded deception and discouraged integrity. By the time of its demise, the leaders of Enron were all the smartest guys—and the most smug and insecure show-offs—in the room.

Saved Rounds—Some Thoughts and Tips
- Marines should not have to suffer fools or toxic leaders. Some junior leaders just don't get it, and there is a limit to what you can do to correct poor leadership.
- Identify, address, and document toxic leadership and then dismiss the leader—do not delay or second-guess yourself.
- One of the few mantras adopted by the New Zealand All Blacks professional rugby team is "No Dickheads."

The philosophy of the All Blacks' coach (until 2019), Sir Stephen Hansen, was that no one is bigger than the team. Hansen shocked the small island nation on several occasions, "passing" on very talented Kiwis because, in his assessment, the players lacked character.

Recommended Reading

- "Coaching the Toxic Leader," by Manfred F. R. Kets de Vries, *Harvard Business Review* (April 2014).
- "From Captain Queeg to Winston Churchill: Lessons in Leading Up," by Andrew Milburn, *War on the Rocks*, May 28, 2020.

16

Praise, Correct, Praise (PCP)

The Nobel Laureate economist Daniel Kahneman once wrote, "Rewards for improved performance work better than punishment for mistakes."[1] This proposition is supported by volumes of critical research involving everything from mice to fighter pilots. Unfortunately, the "carrot and stick" methodology, though incessantly ingrained in military leadership dogma, is inconsistently applied. Immature leaders fail to extend the carrot for worthy performance that they dismiss as "just doing one's job" and are far too eager to swing a big stick to assert their authority when a Marine screws up.

Marines screw up—and some mistakes are bigger than others. They will at times disappoint you. When a Marine fails to perform as expected, I try to assume good intent (refer to Maxim 5). Effective counseling—the ability to correct Marines' behavior without crushing their spirit—is the hallmark of a mature and caring leader. I have been blessed to serve under some remarkable leaders who employed a "grandfather"-like approach to discipline. The most devastating thing Col Walt Davis, LtGen John Sattler, LtGen Keith Stalder, or MajGen Lee Miller could ever say to you was, "You really disappointed me today." A counseling like that from any of these leaders would leave you wishing they had chewed your butt instead and desperate to make it up to them.

Take it from General Neller: "Marines don't join the Marine Corps because they want to screw up."

I learned, when correcting Marines, to separate the individual from the wrong action and to identify what was right before I addressed what was wrong. In making a correction, I try to follow the acronym PCP—Praise, Correct, Praise. It goes something like this: "Tom, I have really been impressed with what you are doing with 1st Platoon. But this morning's performance was not what I expected. I trust you understand what needs to be done, and I'm confident the platoon will look like 1st Platoon again tomorrow." Though never afraid to make a correction, I always tried to remember that no one was more aware of or remorseful about an error than the person who made it. Piling on is rarely helpful or constructive.

Counseling does not come easily to a lot of leaders, and counseling hard-driving, type A subordinates can be a particular challenge. In his book *Developing the Leaders around You*, John Maxwell writes that you have to "care enough to confront" your top performers when they could benefit from some constructive criticism.[2] When I called in a subordinate for counseling, I found it critical to relieve their fear and apprehension up front. This allowed them to be more focused on and receptive to what I had to say. I would assuage their concerns with "You're not in trouble," or "I think you are doing a good job," before I focused on how they could improve. The key at that point is to make them see the WIIFM—"What's in it for me." You do this by walking them through how changing their behavior or approach will benefit them.

IS IT WORTH IT?

Remember, no one likes to be critiqued. Strong, driven, type A leaders often disdain criticism directed at them. Though candor is a leadership attribute, its application may not be as constructive as a leader may intend. Judgmental comments, "nitpicking," and other noncontributive remarks are rarely received positively. Before critiquing a junior leader's product or performance, I have learned to ask myself, "Is it worth it to do that?" Sometimes it is not a matter of whether or not the comment is true or warranted. Are the benefits of my correction likely to outweigh the damage it may cause to a rising leader's drive? Frequent, inconsequential critiques are destructive to leadership development, morale, and the command climate.

SOME PEOPLE JUST DON'T GET IT

When I was at The Citadel, on the cover of the cadet regulations, the *Blue Book,* was the Greek definition of the word "discipline," which is "to teach." Unfortunately, some subordinates are slow learners. When counseling a Marine over and over about a repeated behavior, at some point the conversation has to go from "what good things will happen if" to "what bad things will happen if not." At this point you need to leave a mark. Clarity here is paramount. When counseling chronically underperforming subordinates, you must ensure they understand:

- What they did wrong.
- What right looks like, and what you expect.
- What the consequences look like if the behavior continues.

If the counseling is verbal, I would ask the challenged Marine to reiterate what we had just discussed, in their own words. With Marines today, you need to make it their responsibility to understand what leadership thinks about their performance. Depending on how they grew up, this may be the first time they ever heard it. If you harbor some doubt about this, remember the first few weeks of the original *American Idol* seasons? Those kids really believe they could sing, because no one ever told them the truth. Recall the confused and devastated looks on their faces when judge Simon Cowell would say "Absolutely dreadful." Then picture the look on their parents' faces in the lobby after the fact. That is what real failure looks like.

Saved Rounds—Some Thoughts and Tips
- Assume good intent. Remember "Hanlon's Razor": "Never assume malice when stupidity will suffice."
- "Marines do not join the Marine Corps to screw up." When a mistake has been made, no one is more aware of or remorseful about the error than the Marine who made it.
- Care enough to confront your top performers.
- Remember when correcting, "to be unclear is to be unkind."

Recommended Reading—*Ender's Game*, by Orson Scott Card.
Card's novel is more than a science fiction classic: its central theme is leadership development.

17

Enforce All the Standards All the Time

In his influential book *Common Sense Training*, LTG Arthur S. Collins Jr., U.S. Army (Ret.), writes, "The CO who directs a lot of special effort because a general is coming had better look at his own standards."[1] Commanders confident in their units do not jump through their "third point of contact" for VIP visits. When informing the staff of an upcoming VIP visit, I used the opportunity to communicate my confidence in the unit's leadership. I would remind them that our standards were higher than those of anyone who was coming to visit. It always resonated well and called on the staff members' pride to make sure things were as tight and right as I indicated.

NEVER WALK PAST A PROBLEM

In response to a recent scandal, General Neller reminded all Marines that the Corps is built on discipline. "It's a rock; it's the foundation of our house," said the thirty-seventh Commandant. "Every time you walk by something you know that is wrong, it's the equivalent of taking a hammer and hitting that rock and putting a chip in it. If enough people walk by, pretty soon that thing is going to crack."[2]

Here is a challenge I often faced: on my way to a promotion or awards ceremony, without a minute to spare, I would pass a group of Marines performing an unauthorized maintenance procedure or doing something else they were not supposed to be doing. Though careful not to make eye contact, they knew I was there, and they knew they had just been caught cutting an unauthorized corner. I was conflicted: I didn't want to be late to an important event but knew allowing whatever transgression had occurred to go unchecked was equally damning. What do you do?

Though I still have not figured out how to leave enough margin in my schedule to account for transit time, I have learned to never walk by a problem. When you walk by an infraction without taking corrective action, your inaction has just made whatever was wrong okay.

As commissioned officers, we don't get to pick and choose what orders and regulations we are going to enforce and which ones we will ignore. Again, people are watching. The "sea lawyers" and the disgruntled smell hypocrisy and will use such sins of omission to discredit your leadership. Further, when junior leaders observe you disregarding an order or a regulation, you communicate to them that it is acceptable to disregard orders they don't like.

I am not advocating mindless adherence to regulations. The special trust and confidence bestowed upon you implies a degree of latitude to exercise good military judgment. The institution trusts you to deviate where appropriate. Provided any deviations you make are required to accomplish the mission and are consistent with your moral and legal obligation to care for those in your charge, *do the right thing and fear no man.* As in most situations, the "why" is far more important than the "what."

I DON'T CORRECT LANCE CORPORALS ANYMORE

At the risk of sounding arrogant, when I corrected an NCO or junior officer for not enforcing discipline after hours or on weekends, I would begin, "At this point in my career, I don't correct lance corporals anymore." The scenario would go something like this. My wife would ask me to go to the convenience store on base to pick up milk on Sunday morning. Before departing, I would shave and put on appropriate civilian attire (I won't define "appropriate civilian attire here," but know I still wear web or braided belts). Inevitably, standing in front of me in line will be the "senior lance corporal," unshaven, in shower shoes, the sleeves cut off his inappropriate T-shirt, and, well, let's throw in a baseball cap . . . on backward . . . indoors. Since "I don't correct lance corporals anymore," I scan the area quickly and make eye contact with the first staff noncommissioned officer I see. They are pretty easy to spot, and I won't belabor the stereotype. Let us just say they know I am a colonel and I know they are SNCOs without the need for rank insignia or other conspicuous symbols of authority. I call the SNCO over with one hand while pointing at the lance corporal to my front with the other. "I got him, sir," the Gunny, say, will reply. "No, actually you don't. That is why we are having this conversation," I would chide, outside the earshot of the offending Marine. At this point in my career, the corrections I need to make are on those who are derelict in enforcing the standards out of apathy or, worse, fear.

THE ROAD TO PERDITION

As we will discuss later in the "broken windows" theory of leadership (in Maxim 44), there are bigger issues at play when discipline breaks down in such ways than inappropriate civilian attire or shaves on the weekend. When you do the forensics on the recent atrocities at the hands of U.S. service personnel in Iraq and Afghanistan, they look remarkably similar to those committed in Vietnam and the European and Pacific theaters during World War II. The common denominator is a breakdown in discipline at the small-unit level, exacerbated by a lack of leadership at the company-grade level.

I recommend reading Jim Frederick's *Black Hearts: One Platoon's Descent into Madness in Iraq's Triangle of Death*. The book is about a small group of soldiers from the 101st Airborne's 502nd Infantry, part of a combat team known as "the Black Heart Brigade." Deployed to Iraq's Sunni Triangle in 2005, the leadership of 1st Platoon, Bravo Company broke down. Under continuous pressure from the insurgents, the platoon descended into a death spin of indiscipline, substance abuse, and brutality. By the end of their tour four soldiers from the platoon had raped a fourteen-year-old Iraqi girl and then executed her and her family.[3] The *Black Hearts* story reads like the investigation into the 800th Military Police Brigade's abuses inside Abu Ghraib prison. The fragility of character in combat is nothing new, but it is entirely preventable. Some of our worst atrocities can be traced back to a breakdown in small-unit discipline.

Much like our fights today, our future conflicts will be information wars. Think General Krulak's "three-block war" on a global scale.[4] In his book *Scales on War: The Future of America's Military at Risk*, MG Bob Scales, USA (Ret.), reminds us that one bad soldier acting badly can do damage that a thousand good soldiers can't undo.[5] So how then do we mitigate this strategic vulnerability? How do you control the uncontrollable? The solution lies in the consistent application of discipline. In building a disciplined unit, the first things you must eradicate are the inconsistencies in your own standards. If you allow a "field-versus-garrison" mindset to arise at home station, it will inevitably carry over to when you deploy. This will then lead to a combat-versus-stateside mentality. When you allow Marines to act differently in the field than they do in garrison, then it will be alright for them to act differently somehow in combat. I assure you these different standards are rarely better and even less likely to be constructive.

Saved Rounds—Some Thoughts and Tips

- How does the unit look on the weekends? Hit the barracks on a Sunday morning and observe shaves, civilian attire, etc.

- Never walk past a problem. As an officer, make "on the spot" corrections that focus on those not enforcing discipline rather than on those lacking discipline.

- When you conspicuously ignore or fail to enforce an order or a regulation, you signal to your subordinates that it is acceptable to selectively ignore your own orders too.

Recommended Reading

- *Four Hours in My Lai*, by Michael Bilton and Kevin Sim.

- *Black Hearts: One Platoon's Descent into Madness in Iraq's Triangle of Death*, by Jim Frederick.

VI

Increasing Proficiency

18

People Do What People See

The sign in front of the Marine Corps Officer Candidate School reads *"Ductus Exemplo!"* For a leader in the Marine Corps, "leading by example" is not the main thing, it is the only thing. We are taught from the start that it is "Follow me!," not "You go ahead and I'll catch up!" As a leader, it is imperative that you be out front setting the example. Whether it is the PFT, gunnery qualifications, or professional military education, Marines will gauge their performance by yours. You can have the greatest impact on the unit simply by modeling the way it is supposed to be. Nothing increases a unit's performance faster than the proficient example of its leader.

Alexander the Great's favorite formation in battle was the diamond. At the forward point of the diamond was the commander—the king himself. Alexander selected this formation for his cavalry charges because it gave his men the best view of their leader's heroism. Seeing the valor of their comrades out front would "light a fire in the men's hearts."[1] Alexander knew that a man witnessing the selflessness of another would be compelled by the nobility in his nature to emulate that virtue and join the fight.

Leadership is a "performing art," write Kouzes and Posner.[2] Leaders do not act, they enact the purpose of the organization with every decision they make. Marines will obey the orders of the "officers appointed over me," but they will follow with their eyes and ears. Do the words match the actions, and does the action match the words—is there congruence? Your authenticity and integrity as a leader will determine whether you are one worth following.

When I was in command, the worst job to have in 1st Tank Battalion was the CO's "Humvee" (HMMWV) driver. I never complained about the long hours in command, in fact I enjoyed them—well, almost all of them! I was always busy and did my best to break "laptop defilade" (sitting behind the computer) regularly and get out and see the Marines. Aside from the months of March and October, the weather in the Mojave Desert was intense. The heat in the summer was stifling, and the cold winds in the winter were sharp. January and February brought short but torrential rains that often resulted in flash floods. Whenever the weather was truly miserable or the conditions were at their worst, I made a point to get out and check on the Marines. A wise commander once said that wherever the friction is greatest, there is no substitute for your presence. Nothing increases your capital as commander more than arriving unannounced in a storm, in the dark, and helping to secure camouflage netting or filling sandbags. When the Marines would discover that their commander was beside them in the mud, they would ask, "Sir, what are you doing here?" My response was always the same: "Embracing the suck!"

THE LAW OF THE LED

In his book *Start with Why*, Simon Sinek writes that there are two ways to influence behavior—you can manipulate it, or you can inspire it.[3] The essence of leadership by example is inspiration. The extent to which leaders can motivate their subordinates is limited. A leader who inspires through his own example, however, leaves an enduring benchmark that the members of the organization will strive to achieve.

When I was a company commander on Parris Island, I worked on my master's degree in the evenings. I studied management and wrote on leadership. A theory I worked on was "The Law of the Led." The notion held that an organization's performance is limited by the proficiency of its leader. In order to test the theory, I tracked the average run times for my unit over a series of cohorts ("cycles" on the Depot). During morning physical training (PT), the first sergeant and I would alternate our paces on individual effort runs, running some events at the front of the pack and in others policing up the run drops in the rear. The next cycle on the same training day, I would alternate and run with the other end and then record the results. My sample size was too small for the result to be statistically significant, but there was a measurable increase in the company's average run time when the first sergeant and I were pushing ourselves out front. Why? I believe the recruits gauged their performance by the first sergeant and me. If they were behind us, they would try and catch up. If they were in front of us, they might not be inclined to push as hard. Even though they were not giving it their best effort, they thought, they were at least beating the CO.

As the 1st Tank Battalion commander, I put my professional reputation on the line twice a year when my crew and I ran our tank through the gunnery qualification tables. Gunnery was one of my three focus areas, and I had put the company commanders on notice that their evaluations would rest in part on how well their units performed at gunnery. Tank table VIII is the final test of an individual crew's ability to employ its weapons systems against a complicated array of target scenarios. Preparing a tank crew to qualify in tank table VIII takes time, time that many battalion commanders elect to apply elsewhere. When I was a lieutenant, my battalion commander, then-LtCol Mike O'Neil, was the first battalion commander to qualify on the M1A1 main battle tank. He not only qualified but was the battalion "Hot Shot" (top scorer). When I was a tank company commander, the battalion commander, LtCol "Wild Bill" Callahan, qualified his crew with my company. He and I actually had a heated exchange as to who would have the honor of going downrange first. Unfortunately for the tank community, the commitment of and example set by these two commanders was rare. As a battalion commander, I was determined to live up to the expectation of my mentors and set a proper example. The workups were not always pretty, but the crew of "Mufasa" tied as the Battalion Hot Shot in 2009. We were the first crew downrange, and all of the battalion's master gunners evaluated the run.

Admittedly, as a colonel (O-6) commander, I found that ensuring my headquarters led by example was a struggle. The focus within II MEF during that time was readiness. As a tanker, I knew what "right" looked like when it came to material readiness, and I knew we had quite a way to go before we got there. I directed the staff to track and display the detailed material readiness statistics for the command element and each of the five battalions every week during the staff meeting. When the results posted, I did not say anything to the battalion commanders. There was no need to. By simply measuring it comparatively in a public forum, I knew their material readiness would improve. My challenge was that, I knew, they were gauging their performance against the command element's numbers, and, quite frankly, my stats were not that great. In order to fix the problem, I had to swallow a little humble pie: I reached down into the battalions and pulled up a couple of subject-matter experts (warrant officers) to help me fix the headquarters' readiness issues. I knew I needed to fix my own house before I could expect to see the improvements I was looking for in the battalions.

YOU'RE A BETTER MAN, SIR, THAN I AM

When BG John C. "Doc" Bahnsen commanded the U.S. Army's 1st Aviation Brigade back in the 1980s, he awarded a "Gunga Din" certificate to any soldier who bested him. Gunga Din was the central character in a Rudyard Kipling poem (and a film by the same name released in the 1930s). In his poem Kipling, writing from the perspective of a British soldier in colonial India, tells the story of an Indian water bearer who repeatedly exposes himself to enemy fire to deliver water and ammunition to ungrateful British soldiers. Gunga Din is eventually shot and killed. In the final three lines of the poem, the soldier, ashamed of how he had abused Din, finally realizes what Din had really been:

> Tho' I've belted you and flayed you,
> By the livin' Gawd that made you,
> You're a better man than I am, Gunga Din![4]

Receiving a Gunga Din certificate from Brigadier General Bahnsen was a big deal to the soldiers of the brigade. He was one of the most decorated leaders of his day, having received eighteen awards for valor in Vietnam, including the Distinguished Service Cross and five Silver Stars. Before commanding the brigade Bahnsen had successfully commanded an air cavalry squadron and a tank battalion in combat. If you beat this "Old Man," you had accomplished something.

Though not worthy to carry Bahnsen's helmet bag, I drew inspiration from his example. When I commanded II MHG, I had poker chips made with "Praetorian Six" on one side and crossed gladiuses on the back. The inscription read, "For Excellence." Whether running a Combat Fitness Test (CFT), qualifying with the pistol, or "rolling" in the martial arts (MCMAP) pit, I always had a pocketful of chips to give out to any Marine who beat me . . . though I never gave one out without a fight.

CAN YOU SEE MY ASS?

The caustic U.S. Army general in charge of the China-Burma-India Theater during World War II, "Vinegar Joe" Stilwell, is credited with the axiom, "The higher a monkey climbs, the more you see of his behind."

Life in command is analogous to living in a fishbowl. You are under constant observation, and not all of your onlookers wish you well. Never forget that there will be those rooting against you. My advice is to "Starve them of ammunition!" Admittedly, as a junior officer I did not always set the best example off duty. Had there been the now-ubiquitous camera phones and social media when I was a lieutenant, I might not have kept my security clearance, let alone reached colonel-level command!

What you do on your own time matters. Remember, the "whole you" is on display every day. Have a drink too many at the club and drive home, and people notice. Hit the gym unshaven on a Saturday morning, people notice. Post pictures of yourself on social media being an idiot, people notice. Unfortunately, there is no expiration date on stupidity posted online. It may not seem like a big deal now, but you may have to adjudicate the misbehavior of a Marine someday that you yourself displayed online.

A quick way to show your ass is by losing your temper. Again, this was a personal shortfall of mine. Over time, I learned not to allow my "Irish" to come out (without a purpose). Outbursts of profanity, throwing or slamming objects, and theatrics like that do two things: first, they demonstrate a lack of maturity and control on the part of the leader; second, they signal to the junior leaders that such behavior is acceptable. Do not get me wrong, showing emotion can serve a purpose—but it should be done sparingly as you move up the chain of command. Controlled releases of anger can get people moving with purpose or can quickly rout any resistance to change. However, keeping your cool when everyone else is losing theirs is the epitome of leadership by example.

Saved Rounds—Some Thoughts and Tips

- "When deeds speak, words are nothing." (Anonymous)
- There is no substitute for your presence—position yourself where the conditions are the worst or the friction is the greatest.
- By being visible and allocating your time and energy in accordance with your declared priorities, you build credibility and model behavior Marines will replicate.
- You do not have to run the farthest or the fastest, but whatever you do—*never quit!* Marines will admire a leader who gives it all but on occasion comes up short. But if they ever see you quit, you are dead to them.
- "Example isn't the main thing that influences others, it's the only thing." (Albert Schweitzer)
- If your lieutenants don't want to be you someday, you did it wrong.

Recommended Reading

- BG John C. "Doc" Bahnsen's essay "Charisma," in *Leadership: The Warrior's Art*, edited by Christopher Kolenda.
- *Credibility: How Leaders Gain and Lose It, Why People Demand It*, by James M. Kouzes and Barry Z. Posner.

19

Balanced Excellence

When I commanded 1st Tank Battalion, our annual training plan focused on three lines of effort: gunnery, tactics, and maintenance. The analogy I used was that of a three-legged stool. If any leg was not as long or as strong as the others, the stool would not withstand the weight of our mission. Regardless of the unit type, an effective training plan must properly balance the technical and tactical with maintenance.

I have discovered a balanced training regime is more about managing tension than resolving conflict. It is important for a commander to distinguish between healthy tension and a problem that you need to solve. For example, there will always be dynamic tension between the company first sergeant and the tank leader or battery Gunny. The tank leader will always push to have the Marines down on the ramp, pulling maintenance on the tanks or working on their crew drills. The first sergeant, on the other hand, will be focused on basic Marine skills, professional military education (PME), and other measures of standards and discipline. As a company commander, I saw the benefit of allowing this tension to exist. When two men pull on a net, the holes close up as it grows taut. When the holes close up, things do not fall through.

At the battalion level, there should be a similar tension between the operations and logistics sections. You want an aggressive operations officer who will seek out every opportunity to get the unit more "reps" (training). On the other hand, the S-4, the staff logistics officer, having heard from the maintenance management officer, will insist that every field training exercise be followed with the requisite period of postoperation maintenance. Since they are both right, I only weighed in when I had to to avoid the scales being inadvertently tipped.

As a colonel in command at the major subordinate command (MSC) level, I watched and learned from the commanding general of the 2nd Marine Division, MajGen Brian Beaudreault. Despite a command climate that appeared singularly focused on material readiness, he was careful not to overcorrect and to retain a balanced approach to readiness. General Beaudreault's training philosophy espoused "balanced excellence," and he withstood tremendous pressure to increase his material-readiness numbers. Acknowledging his own commander's intent, he stayed true to his philosophy and did not allow the regiments or the separate battalions to lose focus on their predeployment training requirements.

The pillars of the best training philosophies I have seen are the following:

- *Mental*: When he was the commanding general of 2nd Marine Division as a major general, P. K. Van Riper declared that Marine officers must possess "five-thousand-year-old minds." The general was referring to the five millennia of written history that undergirds our professional art. *History is a religion to Marines.* Like the Roman god Janus, one head facing forward and the other backward, we often look to our past to find our future. As a company commander I would gather the platoon commanders around a sand table, where we could fashion a terrain model, every Thursday afternoon, while the Marines conducted field day (cleaned the barracks). The lieutenants and I would dissect a particular historical battle and then replay how we would fight it today. One of my favorite sources for these tactical vignettes was *The Defense of Hill 781,* by James R. McDonough. This book, written in the spirit of E. D. Swinton's 1904 *The Defence of Duffer's Drift* (a widely reprinted and translated classic that works through ways in which a small-scale tactical problem might be handled) is replete with great examples of high-intensity combat you can replicate on a map of the Army's National Training Center (NTC) in California.[1]

- *Physical*: In his *The Passion of Command*, B. P. McCoy quotes Napoleon's linkage of fatigue with cowardice. The truth is that severe physical fatigue can make Marines vulnerable to a wide range of afflictions.[2] An effective PT regime focused on combat conditioning and functional fitness can prepare your Marines for the rigors of combat and inoculate them against some of its stressors. Done effectively, a good PT program develops junior NCOs, builds cohesion, and increases stamina and resiliency. Overdone and unchecked, it can devolve into hazing and needlessly injure Marines. I am a huge fan of the Marine Corps Martial Arts Program. MCMAP builds confidence, stamina, and relevant skills. The NCOs I sent to the martial arts instructor MAI course returned infused with more small-unit-leadership and instructor skills than any professional military education in our curriculum.

- *Spiritual*: You can incorporate spiritual fitness and build resilience within the command without prosely-tizing. Tactical decision-making exercises can include ethical decision-making problems. As discussed earlier, ethical dilemmas always present themselves as "pop quizzes." By thinking through ethical problems with your leaders beforehand, you can ensure they have a better appreciation of the second and third effects of their decisions and where you, as the commander, sit on particular issues.

- *Technical*: Tankers are in the business of putting "steel on target." All of these Marines' "mass" and tactical genius means little if they cannot hit what they are shooting at. The key is preparation and conditioning. As a company commander, my mantra was "boresight, boresight, boresight." As a battalion commander, I would assess the degree of technical proficiency of a given unit by the presence or absence of a boresight panel in its assembly areas. For Marines not on a tank crew I emphasized combat marksmanship. Known-distance marksmanship training is great for entry-level training and cutting scores, but its relation to combat proficiency is limited. To be effective, marksmanship training should be conducted in combat conditions and in "full kit." Be it on a tank or behind a sandbag, all marksmanship training must include fire discipline and control as well as immediate feedback. In combat, it is not enough simply to hit a target. I expected our crews and machine gun teams to hit the *right* target, *when directed*.

- *Tactical*: Battle drills reduce fear by increasing confidence and proficiency through repetition, by instilling reflexive responses to likely threats. Drills, repeated until they become instinctive, enable tactical teams to reduce dramatically the cycle time between identifying and defeating a target. The best tank crews, for instance, can deliver steel on a target within a few short seconds of identifying it, as all its members instinctively doing their parts. At the platoon and company levels, units with effective standard operating procedures can rapidly respond to contact and seize the initiative with decisive maneuver. "Action right!" or "Hammerhead left!" are all the CO of a disciplined unit needs to say to unleash the violence of collective action. To be effective, though, battle-drill rehearsal should incorporate the expected friction. Mechanical or communication failures may require degraded modes or alternative signals. When rehearsing battles, leaders should require the unit to execute alternative signal plans and without various elements or capabilities.

Saved Rounds—Some Thoughts and Tips

- A unit that performs highly across all measures is better than one outstanding in some areas but critically deficient in others.
- Ensure you incorporate *will* training into skill training during martial-arts or conditioning runs/hikes (see Maxim 13, "True Grit: One More, One More Time").
- When drafting standard operating procedures, I have found the process more valuable than the product. By tasking the NCOs and platoon commanders to develop their own load plans, immediate-action and contact drills, etc., you create ownership. The key, though, is enforcement. A unit SOP that sits on the shelf and is not exercised can be more dangerous than a nonexistent one. "Jumping vehicles" in contact (moving to another tank) is not the time to discover that one of your elements has been on its own program.

Recommended Reading

- *Common Sense Training: A Working Philosophy for Leaders*, by LTG Arthur S. Collins Jr., is timeless, as relevant today as it was three decades ago.
- *Scales on War: The Future of America's Military at Risk*, by MG Bob Scales, is a thought-provoking look at how we need to prepare for the most likely and dangerous threats of tomorrow's battlefield.

20

Brilliance in the Basics

LtGen John Sattler and MajGen Lee Miller had the same mantra as commanding generals—"brilliance in the basics." I have found this maxim as relevant to discipline as it is to proficiency. You can normally assess what type of unit you are working with after only a few minutes observing it in the field. The fluidity of battle drills, the establishment of local security, and the adherence to vehicle load plans and personal protective equipment (PPE) are all great indicators of the state of training discipline, and, in turn, the quality of the leadership. Well-led units are excellent in the ordinary.

First published in 1978, Lieutenant General Collins' *Common Sense Training* is a must-read for commanders aspiring to create combat-ready, disciplined units. According to General Collins, too many military leaders have misconceptions about what real training is and think they must focus on large tactical exercises. Collins lays out a program for implementing "best practices" for improving tactical proficiency necessary not just to "move, shoot, and communicate" but also to master all those sustaining functions required to succeed. General Collins passed away in 1984. I fear that if he observed an Army brigade mission rehearsal exercise (MRX) at one of the joint training centers or a Marine Mojave Viper training exercise in Twenty-Nine Palms today, he would roll over in his grave. We have replaced a focus on the sustaining actions required to keep a unit in the fight with discrete, situational training exercises and have outsourced to contractors many of our sustainment requirements.

HABIT OF ACTION

At the most basic level, we conflate military proficiency and discipline, much as the Spartans or the Roman legions did. The intent of our individual skills training is to create what General Mattis refers to as "habit of actions." The repetition associated with individual skill training creates primal, implicit learning. We literally rewire a Marine's brain. B. P. McCoy wrote, "Discipline is reinforced habit designed to produce a specific character, or personal behavior that is strong enough to override creature comforts, personal wants, and lapses in fortitude."[1]

On War, the 1832 treatise by Carl Von Clausewitz that is an archetype of Marine Corps maneuver warfare, includes several chapters on the necessity of achieving reflexive habits ingrained through the repetition of drill. Clausewitz wrote, "Habit hardens the body for great exertions, strengthens the heart in great peril, and fortifies the judgment against first impressions. Habit breeds that priceless quality, calm, which passing from Hussar [light cavalryman] and rifleman up to the general himself will lighten the commander's task."[2]

Modern military training techniques can be traced to the research of the psychologist B. F. Skinner. In 1938, Skinner coined the term "operant conditioning" for how behavior is changed by reinforcement of desired responses. Skinner believed the best way to understand human behavior was to look at the causes and consequences of an action. Skinner discovered that behavior that is reinforced (somehow rewarded) tends to be repeated (or strengthen) and that behavior not reinforced tends to die out (or weaken). Responses to behavior, or *operants*, are broken down into reinforcing and punishing reactions. "Reinforcing responses" increase the probability of a behavior being repeated. Reinforcement can be either positive or negative; negative reinforcement strengthens behavior by stopping or removing something unpleasant. "Punishing" responses decrease the likelihood of a behavior being repeated or weaken the behavior.[3] Marine Corps basic training is rooted in operant conditioning. Marksmanship and combative training today are all forms of operant conditioning. In his *On Killing*, Lieutenant Colonel Grossman holds that the risk of death or serious injury in combat is still a very effective operant (negative reinforcement) underlying our tactical training today.[4]

Those who have never served in the military associate military leadership and discipline with punishment and coercion. Negative stereotypes are reinforced by movies about basic training and extrapolated from stories of hazing or abuse. When I speak with Ivy League students or executives in New York City on leadership, I am alarmed by the number of members of the "learned elite" who associate military leadership with sanctions and the autocratic leadership style of a drill instructor. Having served as a company commander on the drill field, I use such opportunities to pivot and explain that the methodology used early at boot camp to instill discipline gives way to a more sophisticated approach aimed at developing self-disciplined but audacious risk takers in the fleet. During entry-level training, DIs first instill discipline through an operant (carrot and stick) approach that relies on the proximity of the supervisor. It is a minimalist approach that builds a necessary foundation but doesn't take us much further. I witnessed a lot of desirable qualities in the recruits on Parris Island, but initiative was not one of them. Our maneuver-warfare philosophy, though, rests on the initiative of subordinate leaders, enabled to exercise it by decentralized decision-making authority. Disciplined legionnaires, pressed by centurions, conquered the known world two thousand years ago, but their model is of limited utility on today's battlefields.

Lord Moran believed discipline must first be imposed externally before it can be replaced by more intrinsic motivations. In his *The Anatomy of Courage* he wrote, "If discipline is relaxed when it has not been replaced by high morale you get a mob who will obey their own primitive instincts."[5] By morale, Lord Moran meant esprit de corps. As discussed, units with a high level of cohesion maintain high degrees of discipline. These units police themselves, whether the leader is on hand or not. This collective self-discipline establishes the underpinning for what Christopher Kolenda describes as an "initiative-based organization." Kolenda argues that discipline builds cohesion, cohesion builds self-discipline, and the combination of cohesion and self-discipline creates the trust that makes decentralized operations possible.[6]

THE 10,000-HOUR RULE

In his third book, *Outliers,* Malcolm Gladwell defines success as a function of persistence and doggedness. It is not an innate ability—it is an attitude.[7] Gladwell, Angela Duckworth, and other leadership authors often cite psychologist Anders Ericsson's "10,000-hour rule" when defining mastery. Ericsson studied Olympic athletes, world-class musicians, chess masters, and the best doctors in the world to identify the determinative factors in their success. The learning curve for skill development, Ericsson discovered, was not surprising but the time scale was. Duckworth asserts that Ericsson's work went viral because of the visceral sense of scale his treatise suggests.[8] Mastery requires a degree of intentionality the layman cannot comprehend. Experts practice differently, declares Duckworth: they practice deliberately. Training to achieve "brilliance in the basics," therefore, does not in Duckworth's view require more time on task but *better* time on task. According to her, to be effective training to achieve excellence requires full concentration and effort and immediate feedback, followed by repetition, reflection, and refinement.[9]

In other words, just going through the motions will not achieve the habits of action or the brilliance in the basics needed to fight effectively. To be effective, time spent on immediate actions and battle drills should push Marines to the brink of exhaustion but not beyond their attention span. Leaders can hold their attention through supervision and immediate feedback. "Hot washes" after a run should dissect what the unit did right and where improvements are needed. Then repeat . . . ten thousand times.

Saved Rounds—Some Thoughts and Tips
- The best do ordinary things better than everyone else.
- Routines are helpful . . . especially when things are hard.
- Never miss an opportunity to train. As a tank company commander I forbade "admin" moves—just traveling in the most expedient way. If the company was leaving the ramp to stage for a training evolution, we turned the trip into a "movement to contact," complete with five-paragraph order, terrain model, and back-brief. Once while moving the unit across the New River to complete gunnery qualifications at Camp Lejeune's Greater Sandy Run range complex, I turned the event into a tactical river-crossing exercise, complete with rotary-wing close air support and rafting operations from 8th Engineer Support Battalion.
- By focusing on immediate and continuing action, providing immediate feedback, and repeating drills after refinements are applied, you will create a combat-ready, disciplined unit.

Recommended Reading—*The Passion of Command: The Moral Imperative of Leadership*, by Col B. P. McCoy, is a short read that pulls together works of S. L. A. Marshall, Clause-witz, and other paragons of combat leadership into a useful training plan.

21

Complacency Kills

The Marine Corps Intelligence Activity (MC IA) 2016 report on the future operating environment begins with a quote from the thirty-second Commandant of the Marine Corps, Gen Charles Krulak. General Krulak frequently used the Roman legions' experiences in Gaul to highlight the dangers of complacency in the face of emerging threats. The Roman legions decisively defeated the Germanic tribes on the northern edge of the empire, only to be soundly defeated by the same tribes years later. Quoting a Roman proconsul, General Krulak's selected quotation reads, *Ne cras, ne cras* (not like yesterday). An adaptive enemy had learned from its earlier defeat, explained the general, whereas the Romans had learned little from their success.[1]

I wake up every morning acutely aware that someone somewhere in the world is training to kill me. Like the Roman proconsul, military leaders must never forget that what worked on the battlefield last time is unlikely to work again. History is replete with military organizations that, resting on their laurels, surrendered the initiative to rising adversaries. Stagnation and complacency are not only strategic vulnerabilities: they ruin strong battalions and companies every day.

When you first take over a command, you can see all of the warts. They are everywhere. However, after a year or so at the helm, problems are not as apparent.

WHEN EVERYTHING SEEMS TO BE GOING VERY WELL, BE CONCERNED

The truth is that for most organizations complacency is the default mode. People readily believe that "what got us here will keep us here" and naturally push back when a leader attempts to change the status quo. The irony is that this phenomenon is most prevalent within successful organizations. Someone wiser than I once said the greatest threat to future success is current success. The best leaders know that success is temporary. Just as mutual funds warn, "Past performance is not a guarantee of future returns." Change, on the other hand, is inevitable. We change either when we want to, or when we have to.

The antidote to complacency is change—change not for its own sake but constant/continuous improvement that leads to professional growth or competitive advantage. Strong leaders know they have a moral imperative to change. They understand that organizations, especially bureaucracies, are resistant to change and that it is up to the leader to break through the inertia to keep the organization growing. In his book *Good Leaders Ask Great Questions,* John Maxwell chides the reader, "Never complain about what you allow."[2] He dares leaders to change what needs to be changed, not what is easy to change.

Motivational author Jules Ellinger is credited with the saying, "There has never been a statue erected to the memory of someone who let well enough alone."[3] In his leadership podcast Craig Groeschel says, "Comfort is the enemy of progress. Growth and comfort can never coexist."[4] Successful leaders have the courage and the will to get the staff out of its comfort zone and effect real change.

The best book that I have found on implementing change within large complex organizations is *Leading Change,* by

John Kotter. The author begins by listing the eight most common errors organizations succumb to while trying to implement change:

1. Failing to instill urgency. (Leaders too often overestimate their ability to implement change in large organizations or underestimate resistance. Ironically, failing to instill urgency can actually reinforce the status quo.)
2. Failing to create a powerful guiding coalition.
3. Underestimating the power of vision.
4. Undercommunicating vision.
5. Permitting obstacles to block the new vision.
6. Failing to secure early/quick wins.
7. Declaring victory too soon.
8. Neglecting to anchor change in corporate culture.[5]

As a leader, you can effectively implement change within the organization by flipping Kotter's eight errors on their head, by:

1. Establishing a sense of urgency.
2. Creating a guiding coalition.
3. Developing a vision and strategy.
4. Communicating the change vision.
5. Empowering broad-based action.
6. Generating short-term wins.
7. Consolidating gains and producing more change.
8. Anchoring new approaches in culture.

Through Kotter's prism, change should be easier to implement in the Marine Corps than in civilian organizations. In fact, Gen Victor H. Krulak's *First to Fight* ("Brute" Krulak was Gen Charles Krulak's father) is replete with examples of the Corps' adaptive corporate culture. It is far easier for Marines than for our civilian counterparts to establish and sustain a sense of urgency. Our outside opposition is easily recognizable and is known to be seeking to do us existential harm. The thirty-seventh Commandant, General Neller, was a disruptive thinker. On his "road shows" he reminded us all that if we did not continue to adapt, innovate, and change, we risked being defeated in our next battle. General Neller continuously challenged the status quo. Everywhere he went he asked:

- Are we doing the right things and in the right way?
- What do we need to do differently?

Nevertheless, over the past eighteen years the Corps has become myopically focused on counterinsurgency operations, while peer and near-peer competitors have watched us, learned, and markedly improved. The *Marine Operating Concept* warns that at the tactical edge, our overmatch has significantly narrowed—and in some cases been reversed. In future conflicts, we will be contested in every domain. Our superiority in the land, sea, air, space, and cyberspace domains can no longer be assumed.[6] We are going to need to reinvigorate and leverage our adaptive culture if we are to confront and overcome the numerous challenges that define the future operating environment. To take advantage of emerging technology, we will need leaders with change-oriented personalities. Fortunately, most young Marine officers today have a "bias for action." To be successful on tomorrow's battlefield, we will need officers who epitomize the leadership General Mattis espoused when he addressed the 1st Marine Division before taking it back into Iraq in 2003: "We must think like men of action and act like men of thought."

I DON'T WANT TO LOSE TO LEARN
During my first week on the job as the Commandant's military secretary, I had the opportunity to sit in on a meeting with General Neller and Steve Hansen, then coach of the New Zealand All Blacks. The All Blacks were (and are) the most successful professional rugby club in the world. If the

All Blacks were the New England Patriots (of the Tom Brady years) of rugby, then Steve Hansen was the Bill Belichick of the game. The Commandant, aside from being a big rugby fan, had just put on the Commandant's reading list the book *Legacy: What the All Blacks Can Teach Us*, recounting Hansen's leadership secrets.

During the meeting, Coach Hansen said something profound: "I don't want to have to lose to learn." But, he added, success "is a lousy teacher." To combat complacency, Hansen then routinely shook up the organization when it was on top. In an attempt to outflank the inevitable declines predicted by the sigmoid growth curve, Hansen's coaching philosophy called for continuous change. Adaptations to the All Blacks' game plans were never in reaction to an opponent or other external influencers, but were parts of a systematic series of deliberate actions. Hansen wanted a degree of discomfort in his locker room; he believed the irritation brought on by continuous change creates both opportunities and a desire to improve.

Saved Rounds—Some Thoughts and Tips

- If you are not getting better, you are getting worse.
- Andy Stanley once said, "Time in [an organization] erodes awareness of . . ."
- The thought that "what got us here will keep us here" is as naïve as it is dangerous.
- The antidote to complacency is change.
- "Comfort the agitated and agitate the comfortable." (Col Dennis "Dolf" Sampson)
- People are for change until they are personally required to change. You will face resistance whenever people are pushed out of their comfort zones.
- Never complain about what you allow. Do not ever say "Marines will never go for that," or words to that effect. Marines will go where they are led.
- The most successful leaders are continually dissatisfied. Though proud of what has been

accomplished, they are constantly frustrated that they
are not further along. General Gurganus would often
close staff meetings by saying he was "happy but never
satisfied."

Recommended Reading

- *Leading Change*, by John P. Kotter.
- *Hope Is Not a Method: What Business Leaders Can Learn from America's Army*, by Gordon R. Sullivan and Michael V. Harper. Sullivan, the former Army Chief of Staff, lists eleven leadership tenets, of which seven focus on change and making organizations more competitive.

VII

Personal Development

22

Find Your Blind Spots

Anyone who has ever commanded can attest to the fact that when you first take over an organization, you can see all of its warts. Problems jump out at you, and you dutifully knock them down as quickly as they pop up. After nine to twelve months in command, however, you no longer notice so many blemishes. We would all like to believe that this is because, after some time at the helm, we have righted the ship and that the organization is now policing itself. Ideally, this is true. Yet, our relief will have no problem finding a whole new set of warts nine to twelve months later. The truth is that we all have blind spots. Understanding how and why blind spots form can help you locate and mitigate them. Remember, success is an intoxicant that can blind you to your weaknesses. There are psychological, physiological, and spiritual, even theological, aspects to this axiom.

THE DELUSION OF SUCCESS

In his illuminating self-help book *What Got You Here Won't Get You There,* executive coach Marshall Goldsmith exposes what he calls the "success delusion." Successful people believe they are successful because of their behavior. Goldsmith argues that though this may be true, there are often personality flaws that hold good leaders back from being great. Here, some successful people may be confusing causation with correlation. Where they believe they are successful because they behave a certain way, Goldsmith offers an alternative hypothesis—perhaps a person is successful in spite of their behavior. Successful people already know what they need to do to be prosperous. Goldsmith argues that to be a better leader, successful people need to learn what they need to *stop* doing.[1] Many successful people maintain a level of self-confidence that borders on the delusional. This self-confidence, reaffirmed by personal success, creates a cognitive dissonance that stunts future growth.

Goldsmith's coaching is based on the work of Joseph Luft and Harrington Ingham, two American psychologists best known for their "Johari Window" theory. The Johari Window was originally proposed in 1955 to help people better understand their relationship with themselves and how they were perceived by others. The window's four quadrants represent what we know about ourselves and what people know about us—think Donald Rumsfeld's "known unknowns."

Goldsmith proposes that when leaders discover their blind spots, the parts of their personalities known to others but not to themselves, a "Road to Damascus" moment

THE JOHARI WINDOW

1 Open	2 Blind
Known to self and to others	Not known to self but known to others
3 Hidden	4 Unknown
Known to self but not to others	Not known to self or others

occurs (a sudden revelation that changes everything). It is only through greater knowledge of themselves that good leaders become great.[2]

WE ARE BLIND TO OUR BLINDNESS

The first time I saw the "invisible gorilla" video was at the Commanders' Course back in 2008. If you have never seen it, I will not give it away, but I highly recommend you watch it.[3] I admit I missed the gorilla, but I didn't miss the message. Absorbed in the moment, we can be blind to the obvious. Worse, we are blind to our blindness. As mentioned above, I highly recommend you read Daniel Kahneman's *Thinking, Fast and Slow.* Once you begin to understand how your brain works, you can better understand how you make decisions. A "cognitive reflection" test can tell you whether you are an intuitive or analytic decision maker. Intuitive decisions (Kahneman's "System 1") are quick, because they appear self-evident. Analytical decisions ("System 2") can better account for complex situations or ambiguity.[4] Military leadership often requires "heuristic" decision making (using rules of thumb to simplify things for the moment). but such decisions are heavily influenced by our emotions and subconscious biases. Operational experience enhances the recognition required to make intuitive decisions, but it also exposes such decisions to predictable biases. By understanding how bias forms ("halo effect," "anchoring," etc.), you can better account for them.

In his book *Smarter, Faster, Better* Charles Duhigg introduces a condition he calls "cognitive tunneling," to alert us to the fact that when our brains become overwhelmed with stimuli they focus on the most obvious and often least appropriate factors. For example, when you suddenly realize you're speeding past a highway patrol car, you automatically hit your brakes. Though Duhigg was not writing for combat leaders, some of his research and recommended techniques can apply. To mitigate the adverse effects of mental tunneling, Duhigg advocates "mental modeling." Mental modeling involves telling yourself beforehand a story about what you think things should look like, so you detect and focus on what is wrong or different in execution. The most productive people, he says, know what to focus on and what they can ignore.[5]

In Maxim 35 ("Command and Feedback"), I will introduce Dr. Daniel Goleman's work on emotional intelligence. In his book *Primal Leadership: Unleashing the Power of Emotional Intelligence,* Goleman suggests that the first "domain" of emotional intelligence is self-awareness. Self-aware leaders are deliberate in their self-assessment.[6] They are honest with themselves about themselves. This self-reflection produces self-confidence and greater empathy and understanding for the people they work with. Unfortunately, these self-aware leaders are rare. Instead, too many senior leaders become alarmingly less introspective the higher they rise.

The remedy for our blindness, Goleman suggests, is obvious, a matter of common sense, yet it is not common practice: actively soliciting *negative* feedback. By polling those who know us best, we can discover the discontinuity between our actual self (how we are perceived) and our ideal self. "Three-hundred-sixty-degree" evaluations have become very popular. The Marine Corps War College and other top schools have incorporated "360 evaluations" into their curriculums. They are also popular in the business world, because of the different perspectives they offer. Goleman points to research that finds the "subordinates' views" in a 360 evaluation far more accurate predictors of executive potential than seniors' assessments alone.[7] If a leader is genuine, the feedback received from a 360 evaluation or other form of constructive criticism can serve as a wakeup call. Constructive criticism should be a catalyst for change. It is only when leaders know where they need improvement that professional growth can occur.

At the direction of the thirty-seventh Commandant, General Neller, the Marine Corps began incorporating 360 evaluations at the Commanders' Course and the War College in 2018 to provide feedback to leaders before and after their command tours. When this program began I had already completed my colonel command, so I reached out to the Naval War College, in Newport, Rhode Island, to see if I could still participate. They were kind enough to connect me with (and pay for) the Leadership Practice Inventory (LPI) referenced extensively in James Kouzes' and Barry Posner's works. In preparation for the evaluation, I provided contact information for all of my former subordinate commanders and other "direct reports" who I knew would provide candid, anonymized assessments. I deliberately included associates I knew were not "fans." The assessment illuminated some blind spots, and I am glad I did it. I expected negative feedback from some, got it, and it was clear where it came from. What was most insightful, though, was how I was perceived by staff members, especially in the beginning of my tour. They say everyone sees an open door in the mirror, but the truth is that others rarely see the same thing. Many respondents, attempting to be positive, tried to be indirect in their criticism. Admittedly, I did not pick up on their subtlety initially. My wife, however, had no problem reading what they were trying to tell me. Her direct approach was what I needed to hear.

WE ARE ALL BIASED

In his most popular book, *Blink*, Malcolm Gladwell introduces the reader to the "Implicit Association Test" (IAT) as a means to measure the influence our unconscious bias has on our decisions. The test involves a series of words listed under two columns. At the beginning of the test readers are asked to decide whether a word is masculine or feminine and to time how long it takes them to make connections. For example, the word "John" quickly goes in the male column, "Karen" under the female heading. But words such as "career" and "kitchen" may cause the reader to pause for a second before deciding the "right" column.

When I took the test, I started to feel uncomfortable in the next series of questions. Instead of male/female questions,

Gladwell asked you to associate words under either "European or Good" or "African American or Bad." Then the headings were changed—"European or Bad" and "African American or Good." According to Gladwell, 80 percent of people who took the test had demonstrable pro-white associations.[8] Even of the fifty thousand African Americans who took the test, 50 percent had a pro-white bias, including Gladwell himself.[9] In other words, it took measurably longer for them to complete answers when in effect matching "black" with "good" and "European" and "white" as "bad." The IAT and Gladwell's research illuminate the fact that when making decisions, our conscious attitudes reflect what we choose to believe. We need to be aware that our immediate, automatic associations may be subconsciously biased.

WE ARE ALL PRIDEFUL

There are two types of pride—affinity and arrogance. There is nothing wrong with being dedicated to your work or in prizing the affinity and kinship we find when we belong to an elite organization. This pride is the essence of what it means to be a Marine and is the source of our greatest strength as a service. A debilitating side effect of this pride, however, can manifest itself as arrogance, conceit, or egotistical blindness. Such hubris has befallen great leaders since Alexander and the ancient Greeks. It is when our pride becomes self-righteousness that we become blind.

The irony is that the same pride that pushes us to be the best can actually keep us from being the best. All of the major religions in the world today agree on one thing—that pride is the most insidious of the mortal sins, because pride separates us from God. It is our pride that convinces us that we don't need any help and that we "can do it" alone. I strongly recommend C. S. Lewis' seminal *Mere Christianity*, or, if you prefer a more contemporary interpretation, Jon Gordon's *Training Camp*. (For me, though it wasn't a pleasant journey, my own walk of faith led me to realize I couldn't do it alone. It was only at the breaking point that I discovered that some things you just need to give up to God.)

Micah Zenko's *Red Team* is packed full of practical techniques and procedures for finding blind spots in your organization or plan. This book is a must-read for your S-2 staff intelligence officer, tactical safety specialist, or whoever manages your operational risk program. My takeaway from this book, however, had more to do with leadership and self-awareness than risk mitigation. In his chapter on military "Red teaming," Zenko explains how our greatest source of strength as Marines—our pride—can be our most insidious weakness. In researching his book, Zenko spent considerable time in Quantico and with the MEFs talking directly to the officers assigned to the Corps' few standing Red teams, specialized in modeling the actions of an adversary. In a double dose of irony, he recalls how when Gen James Amos, then Commandant, institutionalized Red-teaming in the operating forces, the pushback came from senior officers who believed they were already receptive to dissenting opinions.[10]

Ironically, most leaders believe they welcome dissenting opinions and challenging viewpoints. If this is true, then why doesn't it occur? Zenko cites years of War College surveys of lieutenant colonels and colonels showing that the most successful officers in the U.S. Army (new brigadier generals) score much lower than the general American population on openness to new ideas. In other words, the group selected for their strategic- and critical-thinking abilities are the most closed-minded officers in the military.[11]

Saved Rounds—Some Thoughts and Tips
- "For by the grace given me I say to every one of you: Do not think of yourself more highly than you ought, but rather think of yourself with sober judgment, in accordance with the faith God has distributed to each of you." (Romans 12:3, NIV)

- Submit to a 360 evaluation and share the results with your spouse. They will tell you what is written between the lines.
- Finding your blind spots has a lot to do with self-awareness (see Maxim 1). Self-awareness can be measured. John Maxwell includes a useful test in his book *The 21 Irrefutable Laws of Leadership*. He recommends you ask yourself the following questions, then ask them to three people who know you well and compare their answers with yours:
  o What is my single greatest strength/asset?
  o What is my greatest weakness/deficit?
  o How well do I communicate/relate with others?[12]
- Finding the blind spots within your organization is most important during the second half of your tenure in command. A robust internal inspection process is a necessity, but *you can't grade your own homework*. Bring in external inspectors or don't bother.

Recommended Reading

- For more on effective decision making, see Maxim 47.
- As part of my personal professional military education regime, I spend a lot of time reading about "metacognition," thinking about thinking. "Metacognition" comes from the root words *meta* (Greek, beyond) and *cognition* (from the Latin, how we think). By learning how you think and learn, you can better develop strategies for professional education and problem solving. I read up on neurology and psychology in order to learn how the brain works, in hopes of improving my decision-making abilities. The Commandant's reading list is replete with the works that help you do just that. In *Start with Why: How Great Leaders Inspire Everyone to Take Action*, Simon Sinek does a great job of explaining the physiologic

aspects of leadership and how our responses to leadership are governed by chemicals in our brain. *Thinking, Fast and Slow*, by Daniel Kahneman, explores the psychology behind our intuition (and our biases). Many authors borrow from Kahneman's System 1 and 2 and apply them to their own work on decision making. *The (Honest) Truth about Dishonesty: How We Lie to Everyone—Especially Ourselves*, by Dan Ariely, focuses on the ethical aspects of our decisions but also provides some moral bulwarks to keep our "honor clean." Lastly, *Blink: The Power of Thinking without Thinking*, by Malcolm Gladwell, illuminated many biases I did not realize I had.

- If you want to learn more about how physiology and psychology affect your brain's ability to make timely, accurate, and just decisions, I recommend:
  - o Dan Ariely's *The (Honest) Truth about Dishonesty: How We Lie to Everyone—Especially Ourselves*.
  - o Daniel Goleman's *Primal Leadership: Unleashing the Power of Emotional Intelligence*.
  - o Richard Restak's *Mozart's Brain and the Fighter Pilot: Unleashing Your Brain's Potential*.

- If you want to explore the theological aspects to our blind spots, C. S. Lewis does a great job of explaining how pride and hubris destroyed many of the most learned and noble men the world has known. Lewis holds that pride is the most insidious of all the mortal sins, because it blinds us to the existence of all of our other vices.[13] A short read of *Mere Christianity: The Case for Christianity, Christian Behaviour, and Beyond Personality* or *The Screwtape Letters* can illuminate the greater forces at work around us.

23

A Smart Man Knows
When He Is Stupid

He who knows the most, knows how little he knows.
THOMAS JEFFERSON[1]

My grandfather's only advice when I told him I was pursuing a commission in the U.S. Marine Corps was that "a smart man knows when he is stupid." A World War II veteran and Silver Star recipient from the battle of Anzio, he had some strong feelings about "know it all" officers. Despite my grandfather's sage advice, I entered the service severely lacking in the virtue Stephen Covey calls "the mother of all values"—humility. Covey holds humility in such high regard because, he believes, it begets all the other leadership traits.[2] Today, experience has taught me what my grandfather failed to impress upon me in my youth—I do not need to know everything, and the worst thing I can do as a leader is to pretend that I do.

Lieutenants are often tempted to pretend to know something they do not. Doing so, however, not only stunts their professional growth but quickly erodes their Marines' confidence. Worse, it exposes a lack of character. Trust me when I say—they know that you do not know. I remember completing a precombat inspection (PCI) as a company commander before departing the tank range at Camp Lejeune. To guide their precombat checks, I told the platoon commanders that I would be inspecting the tanks for brass and ammunition, stowage of sensitive items in accordance with the load plans, and proper installation of the eye-safe laser filter (ELF) device prior to departing the range. (The ELF is a lens that the mechanics placed over the laser range finder when not in use to prevent possible permanent eye damage from an errant firing of the laser.) Not satisfied with the results of the inspection, I questioned one of the lieutenants about whether he had checked his tanks' ELF devices, after I found a .50-caliber round on the turret floor of his own tank. He told me he had. "How?" I asked. "How did you check?" Caught in a lie, he dug himself in deeper: he told me that he had verified that "the wires had been connected." The ELF device, however, has no wires. It is a simple filter, distinguishable when properly installed by a bright yellow tag beside the laser range finder. The truth was the lieutenant did not know what an ELF device was and lacked the courage to admit it. Not knowing what an ELF device was as a second lieutenant was forgivable; lying was not.

PREDICTIVE HUBRIS

I will never forget how woefully ignorant I felt after sitting through a PME session with Gen Paul Van Riper on quantum physics and nonlinear thinking in 1995. If a smart man knows when he is stupid, I was truly a genius that day. Today, I am no more conversant than I was then in Lorenz's butterfly effect or chaos theory, but I am a staunch believer in its byproduct— "predictive hubris." Predictive hubris is the fallacy of believing that something is going to happen just because it happened that way before. Fifteen years of operational experience in the Central Command (CENTCOM) area of responsibility (AOR) taught me that, just as in forecasting the markets or the weather, small things in complex environments can have a small impact, a huge impact, or no impact at all—and that it is impossible to know which.

The former Joint Special Operations Command (JSOC) commander, GEN Stanley McChrystal, recognized the dangers of predictive hubris and the inevitability of surprise in his book *Team of Teams*. General McChrystal argues that scientific management and reductionist managerial models were designed for the industrial age and are incompatible with the much greater complexity and unpredictability of today's information-infused global environment. Instead, he ascribes to what David Salt calls "resilience thinking."[3] Salt's model embraces humility by recognizing that true knowledge is knowing that we do not know.

THE LEARNED ELITE

Andrew Carnegie allegedly wanted his epitaph to be, "He was smart enough to surround himself with people smarter than himself." Carnegie knew that it was a sign of poor leadership to aspire to be the smartest guy in the room. As a Citadel graduate who twice served as a fellow in academe, once at the Massachusetts Institute of Technology (MIT) and later with the Council on Foreign Relations, this was never a problem for me. Those experiences, however, did expose me to the "learned elite," the highbrows who are very comfortable letting you know what they know and you don't.

I encountered this intellectual and professional intimidation most often at Harvard's Kennedy School of Government. Having taken courses at both MIT and the Kennedy School, I can attest that there is a clear "culture divide" between these two learned institutions. At the Kennedy School there was pretentiousness in the air in every class I took. Students would respond to questions and share their opinions with little cross talk or "peer review." Each believed he or she was the smartest in the room but did not want to provoke a contentious debate that might expose the limits of their knowledge. The atmosphere at the "tech college downriver," however, was quite different. While not as socially refined, the MIT students regularly engaged in cantankerous debates. Should students let fly with what they (wrongly) considered informed opinions, their peers would (without animosity or pretense) brutally critique their positions. The opportunity to take classes at both institutions was incredible. Equally valuable was the exposure to how differently elites learn.

I DON'T KNOW

Humility is conspicuously absent from the Marine Corps' list of leadership traits. Over the years, I have benefited greatly from some great leaders who modeled humility so well. Anyone who ever had the pleasure of working for Major General Gurganus appreciated his self-deprecating sense of humor. General Gurganus taught me that saying "I don't know" was a sign of leadership. Though you would be a fool to underestimate his intellect, his candor about what he did not know built trust and energized the staff to find solutions. In 2012, the general was charged with drawing down the Marine Expeditionary Force Forward in Afghanistan from 19,301 Marines to a force of less than seven thousand with no reduction in their specified tasks or an appreciable decline in the threat. As his lead planner, on loan from Marine Forces Central Command (MARCENT), I found the general frank about his uncertainty but always clear about his intent and desired end state. The polar opposite of egoism and an elite mindset, General Gurganus' style was the best way to solicit good ideas and avoid big mistakes.

THE VALUE-ADDED FALLACY

I once worked for a chief of staff who always had to add his "two cents" to the discussion. He was a brilliant, experienced officer, but he was bound to ensure everyone on the staff knew how smart he was. Whenever an officer or a section would come up with an initiative to improve the efficiency or effectiveness of the command, the chief always felt obliged to improve upon the idea. These inconsequential "improvements" demoralized the staff. I don't know how the commanding general perceived the chief's suggestions, but I saw them kill the staff's initiative and ownership of ideas. By always insisting on improving proposals on the margins, the chief of staff unknowingly stripped the staff members of their desire to implement them.

THE FOUR LEVELS OF LEADERSHIP

It has been said that a leader goes from "unconscious incompetence" to "conscious incompetence" to "conscious competence" to "unconscious competence." These are the four levels of leadership taught in the Naval Reserve Officers Training Corps' Leadership and Management Course to freshmen in NROTC programs across the country. The levels go from not knowing what you don't know ("unconscious incompetence") to knowing what you don't know ("conscious incompetence") to understanding with reflection ("conscious competence") to implicit learning—now having the "muscle memory" to do it right ("unconscious competence").

Saved Rounds—Some Thoughts and Tips
- If you are in command, ideally you are not the smartest guy on the staff.
- "Doubt is an uncomfortable condition but certainty is a ridiculous one." (Voltaire)
- You can be uncertain, just not unclear.

Recommended Reading—If you really want to feel stupid, read *The Black Swan: The Impact of the Highly Improbable,* by Nassim Nicholas Taleb. This book focuses on the impact of rare and unpredictable events and our predilection to finding simplistic explanations for them afterward. A "black swan" is an unpredictable event (an outlier), the consequence of which has a large or extreme impact. These events are later explained away by theories concocted after the fact. Taleb's black-swan logic holds that what we do not know is far more relevant than what we do know. More than just a statistician's and philosopher's rebuke of economics and the social sciences, his work blows up conventional thinking and with irrefutable logic. Taleb's examples demonstrate the fragility of our knowledge and our blindness to the risk of random events. His work is particularly germane to the military decision-making process. Our war-gaming and operational risk-management processes now focus on probability. Taleb argues we should emphasize instead the consequences, not the probabilities. We can never know the risks, only their effects. By focusing on the effects, we can better mitigate the consequences. A thousand days in command cannot prove you right, Taleb might say, but just one day can prove you wrong.[4]

24

Don't Allow the Urgent to Displace the Important

An organization's most precious resource is its people. As a leader, your most precious resource is your time. It is the one thing that you can't make more of, and you can never get back what you squander. The best commanders and executives know this and "don't allow the urgent to displace the important."

The difficulty in distinguishing the urgent from the important is nothing new. Dwight D. Eisenhower is credited with saying, "What is important is seldom urgent and what is urgent is seldom important."[1] Stephen Covey built on this idea in *Seven Habits of Highly Effective People.* Covey's time-management matrix is divided into four quadrants. I've applied them to Marine Corps life:

- *Urgent and important.* This is crisis management.
- *Not urgent but important.* Here is where commanders should be dedicating their time.
- *Urgent but not important.* Here is where commanders end up spending too much time.
- *Neither urgent nor important.* Time-sinks for the distractible.[2]

The best commanders I know are deliberate with their schedules; they realize that where they spend their time signals to the rest of the organization what is important. Great leaders schedule their values. Your staff can ascertain the degree to which readiness is important to you by the amount of time you dedicate to readiness reporting briefs or inspections. Conversely, the same could be said about training, intelligence, leadership development, or personnel management. As a commander, you are responsible for all of the functional areas, but how things are scheduled will, intentionally or unintentionally, signal your priorities. So when planning your day, don't major in the minors!

FILLING AN AMMO CAN

A time-management metaphor I like to share involves filling an ammunition can with rocks, gravel, and sand. The amount you can pack into a can is determined by what you put in first. If you start with the big rocks, then the gravel, and then the sand, you can quantifiably increase the weight of the load. The takeaway for operations officers is, if you put the big rocks—the nonnegotiables—in first, you can find time around them for all of those grating little tasks. The reverse, however, is not true. If you become distracted by the ankle biters, you won't have time for your core competencies. You keep "the main thing the main thing" by doing "first things first." That may be splicing two clichés together into a corny jingle, but research has demonstrated people's relative propensity to recall the first and last items in a series. In what is known as the "serial position" or "primacy" effect, the first thing said is the most remembered.

THE BEST THINGS HAPPEN IN THE MARGINS

Now that I have discussed how you can fill every waking moment of a commander's day, let me change course. One of my most arduous billets was as then–Lieutenant General Neller's director of operations (G-3) at MARCENT. The hours were long, and the travel schedule was demanding. Though the time spent flying to and from the AOR often took me away from the headquarters "battle rhythm" at inopportune times, I learned to relish the opportunity to think critically in the back of a plane. I found that my best thoughts and ideas came when I had the opportunity to "unplug," even if for only a few hours. How this relates to "margins" came to me while listening to a sermon by Andy Stanley. Andy was preaching on the concept of margins and how the best things happen when you create space for yourself. Be it in personal finance or time management, when we allow the margins in our life to collapse, our stress level goes up, and we become less effective. If you are barely covering your obligations financially or have not a minute left in the day, you become trapped in your current situation. By deliberately building in margins, you create opportunities for growth. Margins create opportunities to seize opportunities. The biggest barrier to both a successful command and a meaningful life is overcommitment.

If you do not have enough time to accomplish the tasks you have now, find the space to create margins by creating a "do-not-do list." When Col Gary Johnston, the chief of staff of II MEF, managed the transition for a new commanding general, he tasked the staff to come back to him with a "do-not-do list," so he could find "white space" in the battle rhythm in which the new commanding general could process information and think critically. Colonel Johnston looked for meetings or products that sucked away time without supporting decisions. Gary understood that the primary purpose of the staff was to assist the general in making timely and accurate decisions. He also understood that his role as the chief was to clear the calendar of nonessential tasks that distracted the commander from doing what only he could do.

Several of John Maxwell's books on leadership focus on this very subject. Maxwell argues that leaders should spend most of their time where they are most valuable to their organizations. CEOs' time should be spent doing what only they can do. Everything else should be delegated. Delegation, Maxwell writes, is about trust, value, and time. If someone else in the organization can do something 80 percent as well as you can, let them. Researching the calendars of hundreds of CEOs, Maxwell found that 20 percent of their time equated to 80 percent of their impact. In other words, these CEOs could, by properly delegating, buy back 80 percent of their time and reallocate it for more strategic endeavors.[3]

PROFESSIONAL DEVELOPMENT

Kevin Eastman, formerly assistant coach of the Boston Celtics under Doc Rivers, now dedicates his time to coaching coaches. In a podcast he once said, "You don't find time for professional development, you make it."[4] It is the obligation of every officer to seek and find time for professional development. Research has shown that implicit learning goes on in the background of your brain, if reading and other forms of professional development have been made habitual. Once you have incorporated professional reading into your basic daily routine, take it to the next steps—think, and apply. Find time for critical thinking. During this quiet time, reflect on how you can incorporate what you have learned into the organization. See what fits and how you can apply it. Make it yours.

Saved Rounds—Some Thoughts and Tips
- Determine what you value most that you are not doing.
- "If the devil can't make you bad, he'll make you busy." (Anonymous)
- Share your schedule with the staff and subordinate commanders. They need to see how you are allocating your time.
- Be draconian about your schedule and hold your executive officer accountable for keeping you on time. Nothing says you don't respect subordinate commanders' or staffs' time more than keeping them waiting.

- When faced with a bunch of meetings, schedule them back to back, as a forcing function to keep the staff from running over.
- When meeting with stakeholders outside of the organization, do it in their spaces. If the meeting runs over, you can always get up and leave. There is nothing worse than being trapped in your own office with a long-winded individual.
- Schedule time for PT, professional reading, and critical thinking and stick to the schedule. First, you need it; second, by doing so you are modeling constructive behavior. Remember the three "musts" for maintaining balance and peak performance—proper sleep, regular PT, and eating right.
- The twenty-ninth Commandant of the Marine Corps, Gen Al Gray, espoused "education through defecation"—take a book to the head with you!

Recommended Reading

- Google this: "Important vs. Urgent," by COL Mark Blum, USA, Commander, 212th Artillery Brigade.
- *The Leader's Bookshelf*, by ADM James Stavridis, USN (Ret.), and R. Manning Ancell, lists and assesses fifty books every leader should read. Retired four-star generals and flag officers contributed reviews. Stavridis, the former Supreme Allied Commander, argues that by replicating the reading patterns of senior military leaders, future leaders can gain unique insights. Most Marines are familiar with the Commandant's reading list. I would also recommend reviewing the Army Chief of Staff's and General Mattis' reading lists.

The Eight-Year Rule

I am at the point in my Marine Corps career where I spend a lot of time at friends' and classmates' retirement ceremonies. At these events I have discovered a common theme of things unsaid. I have yet to attend a retirement ceremony in which the retiree expressed regret for not spending enough time in the office, in the field, or deployed. Instead, with tears welling up in their eyes, they would look to their families in the front row and thank them for their sacrifices and ask for their forgiveness.

This maxim, when presented in the form of a question, provides practical advice. In eight years, will you be proud of how you balanced your obligations as an officer of Marines with your responsibilities as a husband or wife, or as a mother or father? As a leader, are you demonstrating to your Marines the proper balance between the demands of command and obligations to family? No success in the Corps will ever take the place of failure at home. Whether you serve four years or thirty-four years, your time as a Marine will be a seminal period of your life. It will also be a relatively short period. In eight years you will be entering a different phase of your life or career. If you find eight years arbitrary, select your own interval. The point is to identify a reflection point, at which to atone and ensure your priorities are properly set before continuing on.

Demonstrating the proper balance between family and duty is essential to leading by example. Your work ethic is not just about dedication, determination, and drive. It is also about balance. Your Marines will not take leave, take time off for children's sporting events, etc., if you don't. Every battalion and squadron in the Marine Corps is replete with lieutenants and captains on the fence. They have a spouse and a young child (or two) at home and are trying to decide whether to take orders next summer or get out. Informing their decision are the personal battle rhythms of their battalion operations officer and executive officer. They ask themselves, is that who they want to be in eight years? What, judging by the executive officer, do they have to look forward to?

Once when running along River Road in Camp Lejeune as a captain, I bumped into Lieutenant General Sattler, then a colonel commanding 2nd Marines. The colonel had backed his car up against the tree line and was doing paperwork in the front seat. Without prompting, he answered the question I would never have asked but that he knew I was wondering about—"What are you doing back here, sir?" He told me he had a rule: in garrison he never went into the office before 7:00 a.m. Doing so, he explained, would force the executive officer and the staff to be in well before he was.

By any measure, LtCol Jon Bradley was a superior battalion commander. Second Radio Battalion (RadBn) under his watch was the most deployed and engaged unit in the MEF, was the first to pass the new material and readiness assessment (FSMAO), had the fewest disciplinary issues of the five battalions I was responsible for, and maintained a uniquely tight and cohesive command climate. The "Quiet Professionals" of RadBn were truly superior. But the quality I admired most about Jon Bradley was his ability to balance properly his responsibilities as a father and husband with the demands of command. If Jon faced some challenges doing that, you would never know it. Despite an exhausting operational tempo, Jon found time to coach his sons' athletic teams and attend his daughter's athletic and school events. Never losing sight of the big picture, Jon knew where he needed to be. Selected for Top Level School (TLS) and a shoo-in for colonel, Jon elected to turn down school and retire, to be with his children. I know this decision was not easy for him, but he truly lived the eight-year rule.

The reality is that the demands of the current operational tempo tilt the scales toward the Marine Corps more often than not. I missed the first four out of my youngest daughter's five birthdays. But that doesn't mean I'll miss the next five. In applying the eight-year rule, ask yourself, "In eight years, will I or someone I love remember my attendance (or absence) from this event?" The fact is, I love going into the field, traveling on temporary additional duty, and spending time with Marines. This is never a sacrifice for me, but it is a sacrifice I transfer onto my family.

Saved Rounds—Some Thoughts and Tips
- Take leave. Leave work early to catch your kid's recital, track meet, or lacrosse game.
- Don Shula kept his priorities in order. They were God, family, team, and coaching. If he lost a game, he never lost his perspective.
- Everyone has to decide for themselves when the burdens of "taking the king's shilling and doing the king's bidding" during their military careers are too much. That said, do not think the civilian world will expect anything less.

Recommended Reading—GEN Stan McChrystal's article "How I Keep Up with an Unrelenting Work Pace," published on *LinkedIn,* 1 February 2016.

26

Keep Little People Little

Every organization will have a few malcontents. Be careful how you acknowledge them, or you may inadvertently empower them or legitimize their malfeasance. Remember, the loudest voices of discontent do not necessarily represent the majority. I refused to focus the energies of the command on the bottom 2 percent.

I expected platoon commanders, as lieutenants, to know their Marines and to tackle personnel issues head on. As a commander, however, I always maintained a degree (or two) of separation from my discipline cases until it was time to adjudicate them. There is a strong legal imperative here (see Maxim 38, "The Best Legal Advice I Ever Received Was to Get Good Legal Advice"). Your quasi-judicial role prescribed in the Uniform Code of Military Justice for COs means that you must maintain your objectivity and the perception of impartiality. For a new commander it is easy to get too close to a problem. It is natural to take discipline problems personally. You must fight the urge, however, to reach personally into your leadership toolbox and address the issue directly if there is a chance the matter will eventually be referred to a legal or administrative proceeding.

"Little people," or those without the character to accept responsibility for their poor performance or misconduct, will often attempt to redirect culpability for their transgressions onto the chain of command. Their reflexive response is either to lie, deny, or counter-accuse. The target of their counter-accusations is most often an individual they perceive to be biased against them or to be applying the most pressure on them to straighten up. When the chain of command receives a counter-allegation, it is obligated to investigate it. The degree to which you have allowed your separation from the problem to collapse will determine whether it will be you who investigates the matter or be you who is investigated.

Every Marine and sailor has a right to "request mast" (at which to file a grievance) before the first general officer in their chain of command or to communicate, without fear of retribution, with their elected officials. Most senior officers, by the time they are commanding generals or inspector generals (IGs), have heard dozens of request masts and similar grievances. More often than not, the disgruntled member just wants to be heard. In the case of congressional inquiries (CONGRINTs) you receive, remember, the inquiry has been drafted by a staffer. Just answer the question. Qualifying your responses or attempting to impugn the motives of the member involved will delegitimize you more than the most disgruntled Marine could.

Ironically, more officers have gotten themselves into serious trouble attempting to shape or deter request masts or IG complaints than anything that may have ever come out of the allegation itself. (Remember Maxim 4, "Do Right and Fear No Man"). If you or those within the organization have not done anything wrong, there is no sense fretting over grievance proceedings. Conversely, you reap what you sow. If there is an issue, the sooner you own it, the better your chances of getting in front of it. It is acceptable to ask Marines or sailors if you can resolve their grievances yourself, but if they say no, the conversation is over. Send them on up the chain of command.

Your boss will not think you are passing on your problems. Request masts coming in at 16:30 on a Friday go with the parking spot!

Saved Rounds—Some Thoughts and Tips

- Remember: The lion doesn't turn when the small dog barks. (African proverb)
- "The loudest boos come from the cheapest seats." (Babe Ruth)
- These maxims only work with Marines who want to follow and be productive members of the unit. An individual's adverse response to your leadership does not necessarily make you a bad leader. Bad leadership is tolerating it.
- Maintain a degree, or two, of separation from your disciplinary cases until it is time for you to adjudicate them. That familiar warning "Everything you say can be used against you" cuts both ways.
- One of "Vinegar Joe" Stilwell's best maxims: *Illigentimi non carborundum,* "Don't let the bastards wear you down!"

VIII

Professional Development

27

If You Have to Tell People You're in Charge, You're Not

When I first heard those words directed at one of my fellow second-lieutenant platoon commanders by our company first sergeant, First Sergeant Martinez, I thought they should be engraved in stone in front of O'Bannon Hall, the old bachelor officer quarters at TBS in Quantico. Margaret Thatcher made a similar observation: "Being in power is a lot like being a lady. If you have to tell people you are, you are not."

When I joined the Corps, the senior leaders of the day were Vietnam veterans. In combat in Southeast Asia, they had learned to lose their shiny rank insignia or else fall quickly to a sniper's bullet. More importantly, they had learned they did not need them. In combat or in a crisis, leaders should be distinguishable by their activity and presence, not by insignia alone. In a crisis, people will look to the person they trust, not the person with the shiny rank devices.

The fact remains, however, that no one can lead without authority. Your commission as an officer establishes your authority to lead in the armed services, and the Uniform Code of Military Justice (UCMJ) defines its limits. In the military, deference is paid to rank, we honor the office—but respect is always earned. The power to influence—to inspire—does not come from an appointment or assignment; it comes from your character.

In his book *Leading the Charge*, General Zinni tells how he expected his junior officers to develop their power to lead beyond that of their rank or commission. Power, he said, cannot be assumed—it must be earned and used wisely. After his retirement, as a college professor, he would caution his students to know the limits of their power, along with its possibilities. "A leader who does not understand his power will lose it," wrote the general.[1]

Exceeding your authority as a senior officer is a mistake from which you are unlikely to recover. Such overreach, if known by your men, will result in a loss of credibility; if discovered by your seniors, it is grounds for relief. In preparing a decision brief for (then) MajGen William Beydler at II MEF, I knew the general would pay significant attention to the references. He knew from his experience as the director of plans (J-5) for CENTCOM that any authority he may have was derived from higher up the chain. Before the commanding general would authorize anything, he wanted to be sure that it was his decision to make and that any position he staked out was on a solid footing.

MORAL AUTHORITY

John Maxwell once wrote, "True leadership cannot be awarded, appointed, or assigned. It comes from influence."[2] In a later work, *Developing the Leaders around You*, Maxwell lists the five levels of leadership as position, permission, production, personal development, and personhood. Position is the lowest level: "A person who stands on his position will never have influence beyond his job description."[3] His statement is more significant today to leaders of the new generation than it was to leaders of Maxwell's generation or mine. Today's generation is skeptical about positional power; for millennials, power is more about personal authority. Today, more than ever before, moral authority trumps positional authority.

Lou Holtz, a college football coaching legend, said, "Titles come from above, leaders come from below." "Great leaders," Andy Stanley says, "rarely leverage their position, they leverage their moral authority." He went to explain how moral authority is derived. In his book *The Next Generation Leader*, Stanley listed three sources:

1. Their character—character is the will to do what is right regardless of the cost.
2. Their sacrifices—an inspirational vision will always require more resources than are readily available. Great leaders build moral authority by demonstrating the will to sacrifice their own resources.
3. Their time—developing and building one's moral authority takes a long time. Will Rogers is credited with saying, "It takes a lifetime to build a good reputation, but you can lose it in a minute."[4]

A unique aspect of moral authority as it pertains to military leadership is the extent to which it derives from sharing the same hazards as your people. The commander of 3rd Battalion, 4th Marines ("Darkside") during the "march up" to Baghdad in 2003 was Col Bryan McCoy. Taking a page out of the memoirs of GEN Matthew B. Ridgway, McCoy led from what Ridgway referred to as the "zone of aimed fire."[5] Aside from the tactical advantage of positioning oneself at the point of friction, McCoy wrote, nothing builds the bonds of trust and affinity faster than shared danger and hardship.[6]

Saved Rounds—Some Thoughts and Tips
- Develop and expand your power beyond your position—but know your limits.
- Identify and co-opt the unofficial leaders in your organization.

- James Stockdale—retired admiral, Medal of Honor recipient, and onetime president of The Citadel—once said, "Great leaders gain authority by giving it away."

Recommended Reading—Anything from General Zinni. His *Leading the Charge: Leadership Lessons from the Battlefield to the Boardroom* is referenced above. Additionally, I routinely reread the last chapter of Tom Clancy's nonfiction account of General Zinni's career, *Battle Ready*, in which General Zinni shares the advice he gave his son on graduating from the Marine Corps Officer Candidate School.

28

With Great Power Comes Great Responsibility

Regardless of whether you believe this maxim is derived from Peter Parker's grandfather or the Gospel according to Luke, it forms the foundation of "servant" leadership. Servant leadership is defined as prizing service over self or station. As Marine officers, we are taught from Day One that command is a privilege. The chief justice of the Supreme Court in 1913, Oliver Wendell Holmes, once said, "The prize of the General is not a bigger tent, but command." In the Marine Corps, the privilege of command is not having a bigger tent or a car and driver but the honor and privilege of leading the best this nation has to offer. With this privilege, however, comes the heavy burden of responsibility. The mothers and fathers of this country have given their sons and daughters to us because they trust we will care for them as our own. They expect us to protect their kids as if they were in fact our own—because they are.

Quoting the *Marine Corps Manual* (1921 edition), the plaque above the entrance to the Center House (the old officer quarters) at the Marine Barracks, Washington, D.C. (known as "8th & I") reads: "The special trust and confidence which is expressly reposed in each Officer by his commission is the distinguishing privilege of the Officer Corps. It is the policy of the Marine Corps that this privilege be tangible and real. It is the corresponding obligation of the Officer Corps that it be wholly deserved."[1]

NOT SO WITH YOU

In the Gospel of Matthew, Jesus rebukes his disciples for quarreling among themselves about who should have the position of authority next to Him in His coming kingdom. The world's people may think that way, He told them—"Not so with you. Instead, whoever wants to become great among you must be your servant."[2] Despite his earlier parables on servant leadership and how the "first shall be last and the last first," Jesus' disciples were still missing the point. His teaching on leadership here was a radical departure from the practices of the day, the pursuit of positions of authority for wealth and gain. The concept of a leader serving his subjects was completely foreign, but here was Jesus, "the Son of Man," who "came not to be served but to serve."

In one of my favorite leadership podcasts, Simon Sinek is asked what it means to be a leader. He responds that being a leader is not about being in charge but about taking care of those in your charge: "We call you leader because you had the courage to go first."[3] When I interview prospective officer and warrant-officer candidates, I am always skeptical of people who want "to be" something. In screening the future leaders of the Corps, I look for people who want *to do* something. The narcissist seeks positions of power for personal affirmation or fulfillment of aspirations. A leader seeks a position of responsibility in order to have a greater impact. Positions and titles define success to the narcissist. Their success is about *them.* Servant leaders do not pursue success, they pursue significance. Significance is personified in leaders who desire to see others succeed.

POWER

In physics, power is the transference of energy. "The more amps you push through an incandescent bulb, the brighter the light," says Sinek. The same is true with leadership: the more power you push down, empowering those subordinate to you, the greater the effect. In *The Leadership Challenge,* Kouzes and Posner write, "We become more powerful when we give our power away." By allowing subordinates to assume more responsibility, a leader is able to expand her influence in other areas.[4]

It has been said that when you properly delegate a task, you develop good followers but that when you delegate authority, you develop great leaders. John Maxwell has written that in order to empower subordinates properly, leaders must be given both the authority and responsibility for the task. They have to own that task. In the Marine Corps, we are taught that you can delegate authority but that you can never delegate responsibility. This is because the accountability of command is absolute, a situation without comparison in the civilian sector.

LEADING ALPHAS

The truest test of leadership occurs when you are placed in charge of people who do not consider themselves compelled to do what you say. This phenomenon is seen at the Commanders' Course twice a year, in Quantico. Some hapless major on the Marine Corps University staff is assigned as the action officer for the Cornerstone Course (aka the Commanders' Course, a two-week preparation program for lieutenant colonels and colonels recently selected for command). Charged with herding the largest group of "AAA type" officers in Corps, this unfortunate officer has to cajole the class to stay on schedule. Whenever you assemble this many Alphas together, they naturally size each other up, spending the first two days trying to figure out who has the most testosterone— who has the most game. By refusing to break contact with their smartphones fifteen minutes into the ten-minute break, answering e-mails, and otherwise no doubt performing what would seem to onlookers vitally important tasks, many are posturing to show they are more important than the rest.

Turning a group of Alphas into a team is the pinnacle of leadership. As the director of operations (G-3) for the Marine Forces Central Command, I learned to lead Alphas managing the planners assigned to the Future Operations Division. Whether in Tampa or forward in Afghanistan, I observed a phenomenon with these high-performing officers: whenever I put two "rock stars" against the same problem, there was tremendous competition. Each was always trying to outdo the other. However, when we added a third planner, they began to cooperate. Perhaps this is why we do not read much about dynamic duos but everyone knows all-star teams.

In *The 21 Irrefutable Laws of Leadership*, John Maxwell writes that there is only one way to lead leaders: to become a better leader than they are. People naturally follow leaders stronger than themselves. In the Marine Corps, I have seen this strength best demonstrated through humility. As a group commander, I had to learn to keep my ego in check when commanding five remarkably talented battalion commanders, all at the pinnacles of their occupational specialties. I learned often to defer to the battalion commander best positioned to run a particular event. If you always have to be directing the show, your top leaders will grow frustrated and disillusioned.

Saved Rounds—Some Thoughts and Tips
- Do not aspire to be someone; aspire to do something.
- People will submit to a position but will follow a leader.
- If you always have to be the Alpha, other top dogs will not work for you.

Recommended Reading
- If searching for a book on how to turn a group of headstrong "Alphas" into a cohesive team, try

Lee's Lieutenants: A Study in Command, by Douglas
Southall Freeman.

- I would also recommend *Ridgway's Paratroopers:
The American Airborne in World War II,* by Clay Blair.
General Ridgway was hard on his subordinates but
even harder on himself. His performance both in
World War II and Korea bears that out.

29

Watch Your Pronouns

Col Bill Callahan, the CO of 2nd Tank Battalion while I was a company commander, would often say, "Watch your pronouns, because your Marines will." He was right. Over the years, I have found this maxim to be a remarkably good indicator of leadership. It does not take long to spot the "I" guys within the organization. They are quick to use the first-person singular when pointing out the unit's achievements and equally adroit at deflecting responsibility for any short-comings or failures on to the hapless "they" or "them."

Marines are remarkably quick at identifying the self-serving leaders in their midst. Most revealing is their body language when one of these so-called leaders takes credit for something they themselves had done. Conversely, most good NCOs have difficulty hiding their disdain when a weak lieutenant tries to evade responsibility for a shortfall. You can see it in their eyes.

When I had tank-company command, I failed to account for an expensive and radioactive component on one of my tanks. Prior to deploying to Twenty-Nine Palms for a double combined-arms exercise (CAX), our maintenance chief had (without my knowledge) directed that the muzzle reference systems (MRSs) be removed from the tanks we were leaving in Camp Lejeune. The MRS is a small device on the end of the gun tube used by the ballistic computer to maintain the alignment between the gun and the sight. In the humidity of Camp Lejeune, in North Carolina, these devices can fog over if condensation forms inside. To prevent this, the Gunny had stored them inside the climate-controlled maintenance bay. When we returned from the desert, one of the MRSs was missing. This is not something you just lose. After an exhaustive search, I went to see the battalion commander to report the incident. I told him I had taken the MRSs off and lost accountability of one. My unqualified use of the first-person singular left no question in the battalion CO's mind that I "owned" the issue. When pressed for an explanation, I offered no excuse and accepted complete responsibility for the incident. I fully expected to be held financially responsible for the loss and would not have been surprised if the event negatively affected my next performance evaluation. Instead, my stock went up. I later learned from the battalion XO (after he chewed my ass about this) that my loyalty to my maintenance chief and sense of responsibility had impressed the boss.

Unfortunately, I failed to instill that same degree of personal accountability in one of my company commanders. After his company failed one of my pre-inspections in preparation for a material readiness inspection, I put the commander on notice that I would return in a week to re-inspect. When I returned to find that some of the original discrepancies had not been corrected, the company CO blamed his executive officer for not following through. Loyal in the face of total disloyalty, the XO admitted the CO had instructed him to make the corrections and took responsibility for the discrepancy. I was incensed and would later regret not firing the company CO on the spot.

In his book *Good to Great* Jim Collins has a great analogy for responsibility and accountability. Great leaders, he writes, look upon an organization's success as if looking through a window, constantly searching for who should be given credit.

For failure, on the other hand, they need only look in the
mirror.

Saved Rounds—Some Thoughts and Tips
- Perform a self-assessment—Are you the guy who takes
  responsibility or who takes credit?
- Leaders never assess blame, they take responsibility.
- Remember, it is:
  - "*I* screwed up, *I* missed it, or *I* failed to . . ."
  - "Yes, *they* did great, or *they* deserve the credit . . ."
  - "*We* got this."
- "The only thing I own in this job is failure.
  Where there was success, it belongs to the Marines."
  (General Neller)
- Pronouns cut both ways. Gen Joe Dunford always
  took notice when Marines referred to a lieutenant
  as "my Lieutenant." He would say, "That is what
  winning looks like."

Recommended Reading—*Good to Great: Why Some Companies Make the Leap . . . and Others Don't,* by Jim Collins, is the
best case study that I have read on effective servant leadership.

IX

Taking Command

30

The Two Most Screwed-Up People in the Marine Corps

Who are the two most screwed-up people in the Marine Corps? Everyone knows. They are the guy you replaced and the guy who replaced you. Whenever this conversation came up, General Neller was always quick to retort that he "never met a guy who took over a good unit or turned over a bad one."

If you are trying to build trust and credibility as a new commanding officer, do not get caught in the trap of criticizing your predecessor. Regardless of the perceived level of popularity of the person you replaced, you are more likely to lose credibility with your Marines and your boss by blaming the organization's present shortfalls on the last CO. Like the college football coach who continues to blame his predecessor for losing season after losing season, there is a finite period of time in which you can blame the last guy without abdicating your role as the commander. As a battalion commander, you have about sixty days. For a company commander it is about half that time. Therefore, it is incumbent on every new CO to ensure that the initial inventories and inspections are thorough, because anything you find after your "discovery period" has your name on it.

When a new CO would drop in my lap a problem he attributed to his predecessor, I would often ask if he knew who Boris Yeltsin was and if he had ever heard the parable about his transition from Mikhail Gorbachev. Now, I cannot attest to the veracity of the story, but my message was clear. The story went something like this:

Supposedly, when Yeltsin was taking over what was left of the USSR to become the first president of the new Russian Federation, he met with his predecessor, Gorbachev. Originally a supporter of Gorbachev, Yeltsin had by now emerged as one of his most powerful political opponents. It was not a surprise, then, when Yeltsin rebuffed Gorbachev's offer to help. Still a proud Russian, Gorbachev, the story goes, left behind two numbered envelopes for Yeltsin to open in order should the weight of the office become too great. Sure enough, Yeltsin's initial popularity was short-lived. Russia suffered terrible inflation and enormous political corruption. It wasn't long before the soup lines grew long and many of Yeltsin's initial supporters were starting to question his leadership. With the prospect of economic collapse of his empire before him and a tall glass of vodka in his hand, he decided to open the first envelope. In it he found an index card with a handwritten note: "Blame me." So he did. Yeltsin held a series of press conferences to blame Russia's economic calamities on years of poor governance under Gorbachev. It seemed to work— at least for a short time. But a year later, economic collapse appeared imminent. So with another tall glass of vodka, he decided to open the second envelope. In it he found another index card. This one simply read, "Make out two envelopes."

THE NEW SHERIFF

In his book *A Passion for Leadership*, former Secretary of Defense Robert Gates issued a stark warning to leaders whose turnovers display open disdain for their predecessors, sometimes without saying a word. Even before they arrive, these "conquering heroes" assume they have the solutions to the organization's problems. Once in command, they are quick to show everyone that there is a "new sheriff in town," issuing directives, striking down standing policies, or both, on their first day. The result is often resentment among the people to be led. By maligning previous commanders for their errors, you condemn their hard work and effort as well. You come across as an arrogant know-it-all. Gates advocates embarking on a "listening tour" before issuing a single directive. By listening, a leader will gain insights into the health of the organization and an appreciation of who will be candid about its problems.[1] By taking the time to listen first, a new commander demonstrates confidence in and respect for the Marines assigned to the command.

SUCCESSORSHIP

A great way to distinguish between servant leaders and self-serving leaders is how they approach relief. American writer and political commentator Walter Lippmann is credited with saying, "The final test of a leader is that he leaves behind in others the conviction and will to carry on."[2] Our days in command are always numbered. Just when you feel you have caught your stride, Headquarters Marine Corps will announce the name of your relief. Every commander knows that melancholy feeling when this list comes out. The good ones turn their attention toward successorship.

For his best-selling thesis on corporate culture *Good to Great*, Jim Collins assembled a team of researchers to study what distinguishes truly great companies. From the thousands of firms that had appeared on the Fortune 500 from 1965 to 1995, Collins' team chose eleven that met his criteria. Studying these companies, the team members were astounded by what they discovered, the type of leadership required to make a good company great. Collins defines this pinnacle of the leadership hierarchy as the "level V executive." He wrote, "Level V leaders build enduring greatness through a paradoxical blend of personal humility and professional will."[3] Another factor that distinguished level IV leaders from level V was successorship. Level V CEOs were far more concerned with the companies' success than their own personal reputations and ambitions. In comparison, three-quarters of the other CEOs either set their successors up for failure or picked weak successors to begin with.[4]

In his *The 21 Irrefutable Laws of Leadership*, John Maxwell lays down a "Law of the Legacy"—that "a leader's lasting value is measured by succession."[5] In their book *Transition Plan*, Bob Russell and Bryan Bucher liken the process to the passing of a baton during a relay race. The guy receiving the baton must be up to speed before he gets the stick, while the guy passing it needs to ensure that the issues are solidly handed off.[6]

Saved Rounds—Some Thoughts and Tips
- Avoid blaming your predecessor. You have a finite period in which to determine the material readiness and accountable-property status of your new command—use it wisely.
- Upon taking command, avoid implementing significant policy changes until you have had an opportunity to listen to the staff and senior enlisted.
- Courtesy-copy your relief in the unit's biweekly update (SITREP). This is an easy way for him to build situational awareness.

Recommended Reading—A Passion for Leadership: Lessons on Change and Reform from Fifty Years of Public Service, by Robert M. Gates, is a frank and honest discussion about the challenges he encountered taking over and leading the CIA, Texas A&M, and the Department of Defense.

31

Marines Who Know Where They Are Going Are Easy to Lead

When Major General Beydler was the commanding general, 1st Marine Aircraft Wing (MAW) in Japan and the director of plans (J-5), U.S. Central Command in Tampa, he routinely met with lieutenant colonels (O-5) and colonels (O-6) newly selected to be commanders to provide leadership primers before they took over. I was the beneficiary of one of his mentoring sessions, and this maxim is a direct lift from him. The general's advice, as elegant as it was simple, encouraged us to take time to define our goals before taking command. He recommended we select only two or three areas to focus on. Too many goals will dilute your message, he said, and will prevent the focus required to achieve your ends.

As the commanding general of II MEF a year later, by-then Lieutenant General Beydler encouraged the battalion and squadron commanders to "point the bat and then knock it out of the park!" This Babe Ruth metaphor was a compelling vision of what could be and should be. Before a unit underwent an FSMAO assessment or commanding general's readiness inspection (CGRI), he wanted to review the commander's published goals. I believe his purpose was twofold:

first, he wanted to ensure the commander had a solid under-standing as to where the unit stood, but second, and more importantly, he wanted to ensure the commander's goals were worthy of the effort required to achieve excellence.

I do not know if General Beydler was a follower of Stephen Covey, but his message nests well with Covey's legendary *Seven Habits of Highly Effective People.* Covey's second habit is to "begin with the end state in mind."[1] This familiar adage is often applied to the military planning process, but it is something that can be overlooked by leaders mapping out their command tenures. What does success look like? Where do you see the command in eighteen months? In two years? These are critical questions the commander must ask of his staff and subordinate commanders up front.

In defining your leadership goals and mapping out a strategy to get there, I would be very careful not to publish anything without first making an opportunity to listen to the staff and senior enlisted leaders. It is fine to have some goals in mind, but I would strongly recommend spending the first few weeks listening before grabbing the rudder. You do not want to come across as a blank sheet of paper vacillating in the wind, but you also do not want to be perceived as arrogant. After spending time listening to the senior enlisted and the warrant officers, you will undoubtedly adjust your plans. You will have a better appreciation of what changes you need to make right away and which can be deferred. As a new com-mander, you have a limited amount of capital you can expend right away. If you try to accomplish too much too quickly, antibodies will start to form.

In *Built to Last,* the sequel to his seminal *Good to Great,* Jim Collins advocates defining "big hairy audacious goals" (BHAGs), in order to inspire the organization. Collins believed the clearer the vision, the greater the motivation.[2] If your goal as commander is to maintain the status quo, the command-selection board got your case terribly wrong. As a leader of Marines, you can set goals as grand as you can imagine, provided you can convince the unit they are achievable. I encouraged commanders to, when selecting their goals for command, select a few measurable goals that fit within mine and my boss' intent.

Bold and aggressive goals will often be met at first with resistance from within. Rarely an open rebellion (a "mutiny," in the naval services), this resistance will often manifest itself as an "insurgent slow roll." The larger the organization, the slower the roll will be. We do not like to think of the Marine Corps this way, but it is a bureaucracy, and all bureaucratic organizations are resistant to change. It is natural to want the staff and the senior enlisted to buy in, but be wary of what is presented to you as consensus. When it comes to implementing changes within large organizations, Secretary Gates recommends that you look closely at any recommendation for action characterized as the consensus of a group.[3] The consensus course of action to fulfill your vision is often aimed at a watered-down version of your vision. Before acquiescing, ask yourself, "Will it achieve the end state? Is it as bold as it needs to be?" Goals must be achievable, but do not be too quick to walk back your vision.

In defining and implementing your goals, leadership coach and author Jon Gordon used the metaphor of a telescope and microscope to describe the challenges of working with struggling professional athletic teams. To be successful, a leader must possess bold goals and communicate them "with a telescope and a microscope." The "telescope" is the vision, the organization's goals—that is, they should be far enough away to require a telescope to see them. The "microscope" is needed to define all of the minute details required to make that vision a reality. Goals alone do not get you where you need to be, he concludes. It is the commitment to goals as defined in painstaking details that distinguishes championship teams.[4]

PLAN OF ACTION AND MILESTONES

Once you have published your goals, turn your staff loose on developing a plan of action and milestones (POA&M) to accomplish them. Reverse-planning from your desired end state, the staff owes you quantifiable milestones by which you can assess progress. If your goals are bold, you will need some immediate and assessable milestones to develop momentum.

In implementing his change initiatives at Texas A&M University and later at the Department of Defense, Robert Gates found value in milestones with short deadlines. Short deadlines, he says, signal the importance of the initiative and reduce the opportunity for opposition to form. Most importantly, short deadlines generate energy and create momentum.[5]

In his world-renowned work on leading change, John Kotter lists securing "short-term wins" as the sixth of eight steps in a transformational process. These short-term wins must be unambiguous and related to change efforts. Focusing on some early milestones builds momentum, Kotter emphasizes; quick wins can turn fence sitters into active participants while undermining those resisting the change. They provide evidence that the effort and sacrifices are worth it and help keep the boss or your higher headquarters on board. Finally, they offer you and the staff an opportunity to fine-tune the message and test the vision against concrete evidence.[6]

THE MARINE CORPS IS A SPRINGBOARD

When I first wrote this maxim I was focused on defining organizational goals. After further reflection, however, I thought it appropriate to add some thoughts on developing personal goals for your Marines. More than half of the Marine Corps turns over every two and a half years. That is over 100,000 Marines returning to society every thirty months. We have a moral obligation to ensure they are set up for success.

When counseling Marines on their futures during reenlistment or exit interviews, I used the metaphor of a springboard to illustrate how their service could propel them into a successful future. For those with ambitions to climb the ladder, their service in the Corps should provide the bounce to land them where they wanted to go. Unfortunately, too many have no idea where that is. John Kotter once said, "Some people don't lead their lives, they accept their lives."[7] They wake up and ask themselves, "What is going to happen to me today?" I believe that it is the obligation of every leader to know, and to help set, the personal goals of his or her subordinates. If they cannot qualify their goals, encourage them to draft a personal mission statement and define where they see themselves in five years.

In *Grit*, Angela Duckworth retells the story of a mentorship session between Warren Buffett and his personal pilot. In a cross-country flight, the billionaire tycoon pressed the pilot to define his own personal goals. The pilot was unsure but did not see himself flying corporate jets the rest of his life. Buffett encouraged him to list twenty-five career goals, prioritize them, and then circle the top five. Buffett counseled the pilot to stay away from the other twenty as distractors that would pull him off course.

Saved Rounds—Some Thoughts and Tips

- Even the greatest American presidents are remembered for accomplishing only a few things.
- You cannot hold people accountable for your unspoken or unrealistic goals.
- Short deadlines signal the importance of the initiative, reduce the opportunity for opposition to form, and generate energy and momentum.
- Write down your own personal goals. Doing so will create personal accountability.

Recommended Reading—Stephen R. Covey's most popular book, *The 7 Habits of Highly Effective People: Powerful Lessons in Personal Change*, is full of simple, practical, and principled life lessons.

32

Know and Meet Standards

"What is the standard?" That was often Lieutenant General Beydler's refrain when reviewing training readiness throughout II MEF. Unfortunately, his question often went unanswered, because the Marines genuinely did not know. As an aviator, the general was accustomed to defining readiness with clear, quantifiable standards. Every function within the Marine aircraft wing can be measured against the appropriate training and readiness (T&R) standard. In the wing, these standards drive resources. Everything from flight hours to maintenance can be traced back to a published standard. If you want to learn how standards can drive readiness, talk to a pilot.

This is a service that distinguishes itself by its high standards; I was disappointed to discover that Marines often failed to meet a given standard because their leaders failed to define the standard properly. After more than a dozen years of continuous combat rotations, the Corps' material readiness became abysmal. Successive generations of officers had no idea what "right" looked like when it came to material readiness. Our automated systems were not providing accurate reports of our readiness, because our accountability was so poor. Principal end-items were erroneously entered into the systems of record, skewing the numbers. It was "garbage in, garbage out," as the saying goes. When the material readiness assessment results came back, the results were ugly.

Paraphrasing the father of modern management, Peter Drucker, "What gets tracked, gets done . . . and what gets measured improves." There is a culture of disdain for management within the Marine Corps. The Corps heralds its combat leaders, not its managers. But to be a successful commander, you need a solid understanding of management. Planning, controls, and supervision are all managerial functions. While it is true that we lead Marines and manage things, it is equally important to remember that you cannot manage what you cannot measure.

As the commander of 1st Tank Battalion, I had numerous advantages over my infantry brethren during my first round of material readiness inspections. For one, I had "scar tissue" from previous FSMAO inspections as a lieutenant and then as a company commander in the tank community. Back then, a single formal finding (a significant discrepancy) was grounds for relief. Secondly, both of the executive officers during my tenure, Maj Dave Bardorf and Maj Ron Storer, were prior enlisted Marines who appreciated the level of detail that was required to be successful.

Increasing proficiency and enhancing readiness within a command starts with clear expectations from the commander. The commander sets the standards, teaches the standards, models the standards, and leads others to exceed the standards. John Maxwell writes, "Not knowing what is expected is confusing and demotivating."[1] It is the leader's job to define what success looks like. In my group-command tour, when the material readiness bar had been raised and the three-star general was holding commanders accountable, I pulled in additional subject-matter experts to help increase our material readiness standards. First, I got an unvarnished look at our current status from experts whom I trusted outside of the command. Fortunately for me (and the Marine Corps), Logistics Command (LOGCOM) had hired CWO5 Dusty Cooper (Ret.) and MGySgt Curtis Jefferson (Ret.) as liaisons. Dusty and Curtis identified some serious discontinuity in our records. More importantly, they taught me what questions I needed to ask. Once I had a better understanding of our shortfalls, I solicited the help of some remarkable chief warrant officers to create a plan of action and milestones for each unit. We defined the end zone and the yardage markers along the way. We incorporated quantifiable metrics and measures of effectiveness and held some very talented battalion commanders accountable for meeting them. Readiness improved, and a generation of leaders were taught what "right" looks like.

MEASURE WHAT YOU VALUE AND VALUE WHAT YOU MEASURE

The "expectancy theory," first proposed by Victor Vroom of the Yale School of Management, proposes that "motivation is always in direct proportion to the level of expectation."[2] My standards changed after my first company command experience, at Marine Corps Recruit Depot Parris Island (MCRD PI). Leading over forty drill instructors as they made over three thousand Marines, I saw firsthand what an NCO and SNCO could do when empowered to enforce clear and challenging standards. When I returned to the operating forces, I expected the same degree of professionalism and dedication from the SNCOs and NCOs in the tank company as had been modeled on Parris Island. They did not disappoint me.

In his book *A Passion for Leadership*, former secretary of defense Robert Gates says, "used properly, metrics can be invaluable in tracking and evaluating performance in a myriad of categories. However, in my experience, the danger is that people get so focused on successful statistical outcomes they fail to see how reliance on numbers can distort reality and lead to unintended consequences."[3] During my colonel command, I saw what happens when meeting the metric becomes the end in itself. In order to meet unreasonable measures of effectiveness, certain units in the division "heavy barreled" their preventive-maintenance records. The units did not become more ready; instead, the erroneous records exacerbated their maintenance issues and were exposed during the unit's FSMAO inspection. The result was mission failure and sullied reputations of all involved.

Saved Rounds—Some Thoughts and Tips

- You cannot manage what you cannot measure.
- Be careful not to declare arbitrary and unreasonable standards—you just may get what you ask for (or at least, you will be told so).
- Metrics should be used as a tool to evaluate, not prop up, your programs. Secretary Gates once quoted a Scottish poet, Andrew Lang, to rebuke a staff officer: "He uses statistics as a drunken man uses lamp posts—for support rather than illumination."
- If you are not an expert, find an expert who can help you and your unit meet the standard.
- "Readiness problems are not like fine wine—they don't get better with age!" Identify your command's issues early and make deliberate plans to fix them.

Recommended Reading—For Marines, read the training and readiness standards for your specific military occupational specialty (MOS) published in the Marine Corps Order (MCO) 3500 series. The Marine Corps Training and Readiness manuals have long been used to great effect in the Marine aircraft wings. The first T&R manual for the ground combat element (GCE) was introduced, for the tank occupational field back, in the mid-nineties. Since then, the GCE has been slow to adopt a standardized training approach to developing and measuring unit combat readiness. Before you can build an effective training program, you have to know the standard.

33

Can Do Easy

The second maxim that I lifted directly from Major General Beydler when he was the commanding general of 1st Marine Aircraft Wing was his definition of "superior unit" for his aspiring squadron commanders:

- Works hard, but not so hard as to crush itself.
- Produces superior results that are widely acclaimed outside the organization.
- Has fun in the process, making the hard work seem nearly effortless (can do easy).

Anyone who has ever worked in close proximity with the British Royal Marines can attest that they personify the "can do easy" mindset. Cheerfulness and a positive attitude in the face of adversity are the essence of the Royal Marine commando culture. Admittedly, I overuse the "embrace the suck" adage, but it resonates well with Marines. Marines do not want it easy, and they welcome a challenge. Provided there is a purpose to their misery, Marines welcome hardship they share together.

In terms of superior results, the "widely acclaimed outside the organization" criterion is critical. Too many commanders are receptive only to the information and feedback that fits their own narratives. Within the Marine Corps, a unit's reputation is normally a good indicator of its proficiency. Marines want the unit to their left or right or in their support to be competent. Units that "have game" are held in high regard. Those that do not are mocked. There is a strong reinforcing effect here. Superior units tend to remain good, while troubled commands have difficulty breaking out of the doldrums.

Having fun while appearing to produce at high levels effortlessly takes a lot of work up front. Marines take pride in accomplishing difficult tasks or achieving high standards. This pride builds esprit de corps and morale. Unit pride and cohesion create a recursive effect—success breeds success. As I've stated, momentum is hard to start but easy to build.

Most Marines have an " 'I love me' wall." Blessed with an understanding wife, I have an " 'I love me' *room*." My favorite memento is an old ship's engine-order telegraph welded to "all ahead full." On the base is an inscription: "Face it, Sir, you only have one speed." The token came from the lieutenants of my battalion, originally as their retort to one of my favorite phrases before a long weekend. When delivering the requisite "safety brief," I would proclaim that I had only two speeds— "I'm either wide open or off! This weekend we're off, and I want you to enjoy some well-earned time with your friends and families." Admittedly, I looked for every opportunity to push the unit to its limits during the workday, but whenever there was "white space," I never had a problem securing the unit early or cutting out for a long weekend.

BE THE ORGANIZATION THAT SAYS "YES"

I don't know when it became okay to say "no" in the Marine Corps, but it is not okay. When in command, the staff knew that I was the only person authorized to say "no" to a tasking or a request from a subordinate or adjacent command (matters of morality or ethics aside). They also knew I did not know how to spell it. When the Marine Corps was short of route-clearance companies for mission in Iraq, I, as the commanding officer of 1st Tanks, I said "yes" to "remissioning" tank companies for this critical task. When the component command in charge of Marine Forces in MARCENT needed a security force company to guard Camp Leatherneck in Afghanistan, we remissioned another tank company. The remainder of the battalion was offered up as the core of a proposed armored motorized task force to meet a shortage of light armored reconnaissance battalions for the expanding mission in Afghanistan. When the "Task Force Iron Wolf" course of action (the plan to use a tank battalion to replace an LAR battalion) died at the service headquarters, we were promptly remissioned instead as the first Black Sea Rotational Force Special Purpose Marine Air Ground Task Force (SPMAGTF). Any Marine who had the opportunity to deploy to Eastern Europe, though disappointed not to be in Afghanistan instead, will have stories to tell about that deployment for the next thirty years—and of course, the stories will get better every time he tells them! The point is that you gain credibility with your higher headquarters when you find a way to say "yes." Remissioning may over the short term degrade core competencies, but that is a risk we are willing to take to find a way to accomplish the mission. Furthermore, by establishing a default "yes" reputation, when you say, "There is too much risk here," your reclama will not be questioned. When you say something can't be done, your professional judgment will be accepted.

Saved Rounds—Some Thoughts and Tips

- A unit's reputation is normally a good indicator of its proficiency. Guard yours like your career depends on it . . . because it does.
- Don't be afraid to secure the unit early or to ask the boss for a well-deserved long weekend.

34

When in Charge, Take Charge

Here is the deal: never tell your subordinates that you are doing something because "the captain wants" or the "colonel said." I realize that a junior lieutenant or corporal may not grasp how disloyal they are being when they do so or realize that they are abdicating their authority. Assuming good intent, I believe that they are simply trying to put an exclamation point on their directive. Immature leaders mistakenly believe that an order from the "commander" is more important than if it came from them. The fact is, however, that by directly attributing their orders or directives to the commander they are effectively removing themselves from the chain of command. Instead of leading, they are simply messengers. Worse, this otherwise innocuous statement may put the junior officer or noncommissioned officer in the untenable position of having to defend the order. Marines bitch—that is a fact of life. If they are griping among themselves about the little stuff, this is normal. However, when leaders separate themselves from orders, they avail themselves to complaints. They, in turn, place themselves in an untenable position in which they must either defend the CO or completely forgo any loyalty they have to the chain of command and join the gripe session.

Commanders can help junior leaders avoid falling into this trap by focusing on the "why" behind their orders and directives. This is not just good leadership. Mission orders are fundamental to our warfighting philosophy; Marine Corps Doctrinal Publication 1, *Warfighting*, states, "There are two parts to any mission: the task to be accomplished and the reason or intent behind it. The intent is thus a part of every mission. The task describes the action to be taken while the intent describes the purpose of the action. The task denotes what is to be done, and sometimes when and where; the intent explains why. Of the two, the intent is predominant."[1]

Therefore, the most important part of any order is everything that follows the "in order to." The tenets of maneuver warfare—speed, focus, shock, and surprise—are achieved through decentralized operations. Decentralized operations require rapid and audacious action, and that in turn requires a high degree of trust, shared understanding of the intent, and delegated decision-making authority. The future operating environment will be characterized, much as is the battlefield today, by ambiguity and a lack of attribution—"Where'd *that* come from?" Commanders must be prepared for rapid change, even chaos. Subordinate commanders, closer to the problem, will often have better understandings of the situation. Armed with the commander's intent, subordinates are expected to adhere to the scheme of maneuver until the plan no longer makes sense or a better option presents itself. Mission-type orders and decentralized decision making enable subordinate commanders to seize the initiative and take advantage of fleeting opportunities.

The Marine Corps isn't looking for automatons or messengers. If it is to be successful in battle, the Marine Corps requires bold and decisive subordinate leaders, people who will take charge. This relationship is defined in, again, MCDP-1: "Relations among all leaders—from corporal to general—should be based on honesty and frankness regardless of disparity between grades. Until a commander has reached and stated a decision, subordinates should consider it their duty to provide honest, professional opinions even though these may be in disagreement with the senior's opinions. However, once the decision has been reached, juniors then must support it as if it were their own."[2]

COMMAND RELATIONSHIPS

As the director of operations (Assistant Chief of Staff for Operations, G-3) for MARCENT, if I had only sixty minutes to frame a problem or brief General Neller on a course of action, I would spend fifty of them on the command relationships. Unity of command, the first principle of warfare, remains as paramount today as it was in Napoleon's day. Complex, combined, and joint operations require absolute clarity as to who is in charge, who is supported, and who is supporting. The authority to conduct contingency operations is derived from the highest level of government and is deliberately delegated down. It is crucial that the agency responsible for the execution of a critical task have the authority necessary to accomplish it.

In preparing numerous orders and directives as the G-3 at the Marine expeditionary brigade, Marine expeditionary force, and Marine Corps component levels, I found a useful technique that involved the "find and replace function" in Microsoft Word. When reviewing an order, if I found that the words "responsibility" and "authority" could be used interchangeably, then the command relationships were aligned. In other words, if you were to replace the word "responsible" with "authority" and the resulting document read the same (allowing for the conjugation of the verb "to be—" and replacing "is responsible for" to "has authority for"), then the policy is sound. However, if you discover that someone has authority but is not responsible or is responsible but doesn't have authority, then the policy or plan violates the first principle.

INSPECTOR-INSTRUCTOR DUTY

If command is the most rewarding billet in the Marine Corps, then inspector-instructor (I&I) duty is the most challenging. The inspector-instructor staff is a cadre of active-duty Marines that serve as the full-time counterpart to a reserve component (the Army and Air Force equivalent is the AGRC). Here the Marine Corps violates the first principle (unity of command) by design: it decouples responsibility and authority. The commander of the reserve unit, by all legal (Title X) authority, is in charge. But the I&I is the "responsible" officer, fiduciarily liable for the organization's property and material readiness. The reserve CO has the authority to promote and punish, but the I&I retains the authority to give effect to said promotions (or reductions) on the unit diary. In such connections, instead of adhering to the more parochial command-relation policy described above, I recommend a more nuanced position.

When Gen Thomas Waldhauser was the MARCENT commander, he took a distinctly nuanced stance on command relationships. The general would often say, "Command relationships are not as important as relationships between commanders. If everyone is working well together, command relationships do not matter. But if the commanders are not working well together, then command relations do matter." Fortunately, when I was an I&I, I got along great with the unit's commander. Many of my peers were not as blessed. The truth is, the Marine Corps expects you to work it out. Disagreements elevated outside the unit will end up at the general-officer level before there is a common boss to serve as the arbiter. This does not do anyone any favors. Inspector-instructors must have the experience and the maturity to guide their reserve commanders properly. Commanders must have the self-awareness and humility to understand that they ignore the I&I's advice at their own peril.

Saved Rounds—Some Thoughts and Tips

- When giving an order to your unit, own it. Never push an unpopular or demanding task off on your boss.
- Always include the "why" behind what you are doing. Informed by the commander's intent two levels up, empowered subordinates will often find a better way.
- When reviewing an order or policy, ensure the commander who is responsible for something has the commensurate authority. Conversely, a situation wherein a commander who has authority to task but is not accountable for the outcome is misaligned.

Recommended Reading—Nathaniel Fick's autobiography, *One Bullet Away: The Making of a Marine Officer*.

35

Command and Feedback

The "capstone" doctrinal publication for the U.S. armed forces defines *command and control* as a commander's ability to exercise authority, responsibility, and direction over assigned and attached forces to accomplish the mission. "Command at all levels is the art of motivating and directing people and organizations into action to accomplish missions," it reads. "*Control* is inherent in command. To *control* is to manage and direct forces and functions consistent with a commander's command authority."[1]

As the CENTCOM commander, General Mattis took umbrage at the conventional concept of command and control, subscribing instead to a leadership philosophy of "command and feedback." He knew that control over large, complex organizations could be an illusion. He chose instead to exercise "mission command" with his component commanders, expecting them to operate from his intent. As combatant commander (COCOM), the general replaced the long and laborious commander's update brief (CUB) by his staff with a daily dialogue (in person or by video teleconference) with his commanders. General Mattis knew that feedback can be filtered by staff. He wanted the commanders to hear his tone when passing them guidance, and in turn he wanted to read their body language when he pressed them for concerns. The result was clarity and unity of effort within a geographic combatant command that was fighting simultaneous campaigns in Iraq and Afghanistan while concurrently deterring Iran.

I know of no other general officer who would penetrate more deeply into the organization in search of feedback than General Neller did when he commanded Marine Forces Central Command. His "battlefield circulation" schedule was exhausting and his requests for information (RFIs) insatiable. General Neller was renowned at MARCENT for a carryover from when he had commanded 6th Marine Regiment and the 3rd Marine Division, reaching deep into an organization to locate and engage the "truth tellers" so as to learn what was "really going on." He may not have always agreed with them, but he always appreciated the discussions.

EVERY DAVID NEEDS A NATHAN

Most Americans, regardless of their religion, are familiar with the story of David and Goliath, when a young shepherd boy defeated a giant warrior with a sling and a stone. What many do not know is that David, a most unlikely heir, rose to be the king of Israel. As a king, David lost his way. The Bible reads, "At the time when kings go off to war, . . . David remained in Jerusalem."[2] As Marine officers we are immediately troubled by that verse, but it gets far worse. The passage introduces one of the most notorious acts of treachery in the Old Testament. While his army was off fighting on his behalf, King David had an adulterous affair with the wife of his top lieutenant, Uriah, whom he then had murdered. His mistress was Bathsheba. If you have never heard of the "Bathsheba syndrome," it is worth reading up on.

Much has recently been written on ethical failures of successful leaders since the fall of GEN David Petraeus (among others), but Nathan has been omitted from the contemporary discussions. Nathan was a prophet with the courage to call

David out. In a well-crafted parable Nathan relates to the king a story about a treacherous rich man who stole a sheep from a poor man. Incensed by the injustice, David demanded to know the identity of the thief. "You are the man!" replied Nathan.[3]

Command is intoxicating. Your jokes are always funny, and everyone around you genuinely tries to please you. It is easy to see how successful people can believe their own press and succumb to hubris. Going into command, I knew that I would be the last to know of my shortcomings. Over thirty years in uniform, I had observed that the higher one rose in an organization, the less likely people were to tell them the truth. In my favorite novel, *Once an Eagle*, the character Sam Damon states it bluntly: "Your people will lie to you. They will try and please you by telling you what you want to hear."[4] The best leaders know that truth trumps flattery. As a commander, I did not tolerate sycophants. Instead, I made it my mission to identify, cultivate, and protect the "truth tellers." I found the best way to protect them and the feedback I needed was to give public credit to those in the command who showed me they had the guts to speak up. I would recognize them in formation or other public settings. While the subjects of our conversations were confidential, the fact that we had them was not.

In his *Primal Leadership*, Dr. Goleman dedicates an entire chapter to a phenomenon he calls the "CEO disease"—the vacuum of information that surrounds many top CEOs. This vacuum occurs when subordinates withhold information from the boss because of the human reluctance to be the bearer of bad news. This syndrome produces and is compounded by an acute lack of feedback. Subordinates suppress negative facts and withhold information because of a natural desire to feed the boss good news. This problem is magnified in cases of CEOs with overdeveloped self-importance and ego. The higher these CEOs rise, the more evident is their lack of self-assessment.[5]

Secretary Gates once wrote, "Creating a climate of candor is cheap job insurance for the person in charge."[6] He then quoted

George Washington: "I can bear to hear of imputed or real errors. The man who wishes to stand well in the opinion of others must do this, because he is thereby enabled to correct his faults, or remove prejudices which are imbibed against him."[7]

Author and leadership coach Ken Blanchard once wrote that you can distinguish true servant leaders by how they receive constructive criticism. Instead of growing defensive, servant leaders welcome any feedback that that will make them better leaders.[8] If you truly desire honest and candid feedback, you need to go out and actively seek it. People will be reluctant to provide it until you establish trust. Before people will tell you what you need to hear, they need to know that you will listen and to trust that you will not hold their candor against them.

A good indicator of how receptive a commander is to constructive feedback is the degree to which he tolerates humor in the workplace. Moreover, I have found humor normally a good indicator of the overall health of the command climate. Often, subordinates will artfully use humor to soften implied criticism when presenting feedback. Likewise, commanders who adopt self-deprecating humor appear more willing to receive critical feedback. In General MacArthur's famous "Duty, Honor, Country" speech to the cadets at West Point, he told them "to be serious, but don't take yourself too seriously."[9] The best commanders know they can take their responsibilities seriously without taking themselves too seriously. Lieutenant General Sattler, Major General Gurganus, and MajGen Charles Chiarotti were all masters of self-deprecating humor.

John Wooden, the famous coach of the basketball team at the University of California at Los Angeles, once said, "People are more likely to listen to people who listen to them."[10] John Maxwell, who claims Wooden as a mentor, credits him with the adage "Listen, learn, and then lead." Maxwell goes on, "One of the best ways to persuade others is with your ears."[11] The corollary to this point comes from Andy Stanley:

"Leaders who do not listen will eventually be surrounded by people with nothing to say."[12]

When in command, I aspired to replicate the synergy General Mattis achieved with his commanders while balancing the need for constructive feedback from the ranks. I found "open door" policies trite, having witnessed how they often eroded the authority of the chain of command. Instead, I purposefully created multiple unfettered feedback loops across the command. The following is a list of my most effective feedback channels and the ways in which I tried to cultivate them.

Senior Enlisted Advisor

It has been said that leadership is a relationship founded on trust. As a commander, no relationship is more important than the trust you must have in your sergeant major—you will find no more valuable source for feedback than your senior enlisted advisor. I was blessed with some truly superior sergeants major. Each balanced me while providing excellent counsel. SgtMaj Conrad Potts would often tell me after a staff meeting or an address to the battalion, *"I know what you said, but let me tell you what they heard."* I would often bristle at first, arguing back, "That is not what I said!" Conrad, the quintessential Southern gentleman, would calmly repeat, "I know what you said, but let me tell you what they heard." His candid advice was instrumental to me, a hot-headed Irishman, in my development as a commander.

Commander's Breakfast

Every Tuesday, SgtMaj Rene Salinas and I would have breakfast with a different group of Marines. The first Tuesday of the month was always reserved for commanders, but for the rest of the month we ate with different groups of SNCOs, NCOs, and junior Marines. Stealing a page from General Neller's playbook when he was the commanding general of 3rd Marine Division, we had breakfast with a group of Marines being separated for misconduct or poor performance. The feedback and insight we received from them was always genuine and insightful. We drank coffee and listened. Using a trick acquired from the counterintelligence Marines, I never filled the awkward silences that occasionally occurred. Instead, I sat back and remained silent, knowing the best insights were yet to come. After a few moments a junior Marine would work up the courage and fill the void with something he really wanted to get off his chest. When I did ask questions, I normally focused on:

- Who in the unit is busting their ass that no one knows about?
- If you were in my seat, what would you do differently?
- What will you tell me that no one else will?

The purpose of these commander's breakfasts was twofold. More than just great forums for feedback, the meetings themselves were a calculated display of respect. I wanted the Marines, NCOs, and SNCOs we were dining with to know I respected them and valued their opinions. Whenever sitting down to eat or talk with Marines, I treated them as colleagues. As I said in Maxim 27, if you have to remind Marines that you are in charge, chances are you are not.

Staff Meetings

Probably the best-established feedback resource for the commander is the weekly command and staff meeting. Done properly, the event can be a great opportunity to synchronize the subordinate units and the staff, expose all to the "bigger picture," cross-level ideas and concerns, and issue guidance and direction in a clear and concise way. Done poorly, it devolves into the doldrums of PowerPoint slides interrupted with bursts of self-promotion and infighting. Rick Warren once tweeted that "meetings are more effective when you approach them as a servant who leads rather than a leader who serves."[13] If, as the commander, you are doing the majority of the talking, you have either the wrong staff or some serious control issues. In presiding over the weekly staff meeting, I ascribed to the philosophy of "Listen first, speak last." Andy Stanley once said, "You can't learn while you are talking."[14]

Executive officers ordinarily organize and run these meetings. Here are a few things you might suggest they consider:

- Start on time, end on time, and limit it to one hour. Nothing says you do not respect the commanders or the staff like being late or running over.

- Change the meeting location one week a month. When BGen "Wheels" Weidley was a group commander, he had the squadrons take turns hosting the weekly meeting. Bringing the staff to the squadron enhanced group-staff/squadron-staff coordination and gave commanders the opportunity to walk the spaces of sister units. The good ones rapidly noticed best practices that could be brought back and incorporated into their own units.

- When General McChrystal commanded the Joint Special Operations Command (JSOC), he ran operations and intelligence briefings differently than his predecessors. Instead of focusing on what had happened, he framed the discussion as "What, so what, and therefore"—this is what happened, this is why it matters, and what action it means we should take. He used this refrain to drive home the fact that the "why" matters more than the "what."[15]

- As a commander, if you start a staff meeting with "I think," everyone else will stop thinking.

Surveys

As a commander, you are required to complete command-climate and equal-opportunity surveys within your first ninety days and repeat them annually. The results of the surveys are reported to your commander. Since the first command-climate survey is far more about the previous guy than how your initial policies are received, I tried to order the survey for my successor and have it done, ready for my relief as part of our turnover. That way, they knew up front where the problem areas were. Second, ambiguity over who owned the issues was eliminated. Further, it allowed the new guy's policies and procedures to germinate before being subjected to anonymous review.

As a group commander, I received the battalions' surveys but never dwelled on them. This was the commander's business. Surveys are a feedback loop and nothing more. They are not popularity contests, and you are not running for reelection. When you conduct a survey, provide feedback to the command and include a plan of action and milestones to rectify any issues you believe are legitimate. Major General Beydler put the entire command element in the base theater for a three-hour, public marathon session in which he addressed directly every issue (gripe and concern) that had been raised. I too chose to assemble the unit to discuss the results of the survey, but I filtered the chaff and focused on the constructive suggestions (see Maxim 26—"Keep Little People Little").

The most adroit use of command-climate surveys I witnessed was that of 8th Communications Battalion under LtCol Derek Lane. Derek combed through the surveys looking for quick wins that he could take on and so deliver not just feedback to the Marines but some results as well. The projects and policies that came out of those first surveys had the double benefit of both improving efficiency and morale while providing instant credibility to the new commander. In one of my favorite leadership podcasts, Craig Groeschel says, "If you don't care what your people think, you either have the wrong people or you are the wrong leader."[16]

Uncle Chief

Perhaps the most constructive feedback I have benefited from was received from senior mentors. I have been the recipient of great counsel from various mentors throughout my career.

Finding a mentor is an informal, haphazard process. You have to seek out mentors, but the best mentors will seek you out. One such leader, one who still retains great influence over me, is Col John Holden. Colonel Holden, a thirty-year colonel, was scheduled to retire when he agreed to continue to serve ("retire retain") as the chief of staff for General Gurganus when he commanded the Marine Corps Air Ground Combat Center in Twenty-Nine Palms, California. The Holdens were our neighbors; the "Chief's House" anchored the commanders' houses on Lejeune Circle. Colonel Holden's wife, Lisa, was every bit the mentor to battalion commanders' wives that John was to the COs.

As the base chief of staff Colonel Holden was not in my chain of command, so when something would catch his eye that led him to call me, he would introduce himself as "Uncle Chief." At the time, I was responsible not only for the Marines and sailors of 1st Tank Battalion but also for the newly reformed 3rd Combat Engineer Battalion, which the division commanding general had placed under my command until their slated commander arrived later that summer. Additionally, because of force-management level ("force cap") considerations, two line companies from 3rd LAR were attached to 1st Tanks while their battalion was deployed to Iraq. Commanding over two thousand Marines as a lieutenant colonel was an incredible opportunity but it came with a lot of "threat space." Far from thinking of them as intrusions, I learned quickly to value Uncle Chief's questions. Inevitably, the questions he asked were the same questions the division CG, Gen Thomas Waldhauser, would soon ask. Having already researched the facts for Colonel Holden, I had ready, cogent responses for the division CG when he or "my own" chief of staff called.

OBSTACLES TO CONSTRUCTIVE FEEDBACK
Not all feedback loops are constructive. Here are few I recommend you avoid.

The Suggestion Box. Whenever I see a suggestion box in a unit, I immediately question the command climate. Often its presence points to a climate in which people are only comfortable expressing their opinions anonymously. On one of my staff assignments, my counterpart in the plans section (G-5) had a very serious command-climate issue within his directorate. I had known him for a long time and had seen the problems coming. The situation reached a tipping point when the general directed the inspector general to investigate the command climate within the "-5." The results were brutal. When confronted with them, the colonel made a genuine effort to be more receptive to his planners' ideas by placing a suggestion box in the office. The irony was he would often get incensed by the suggestions he received there and lash out at his Marines. When the planners in the operations directorate (G-3) heard of the trials and tribulations of their peers, they joined the fight, filling the box with sophomoric satire. I have to admit I was amused when someone covered the shredder in the "-3" with a large cardboard box, labeled "Suggestion Box," with an opening that fed directly into the chute. The G-5 "actual" did not share my amusement when he saw it outside my office.

FITREPs. Our performance evaluation system is horribly inflated. When fitness reports are inflated, a single bad report or even temperate wording can be damning. This atmosphere encourages timidity and produces subordinates unwilling to challenge their seniors. Conversely, when you do have a poorly performing subordinate, previous inflated reports can make it difficult to hold them accountable.

Saved Rounds—Some Thoughts and Tips
- Writing about the advent of the telegraph, Field Marshal Helmuth von Moltke the Elder (lived 1800–1891), chief of German General Staff, said of command and control, "The advantage which a

commander believes to achieve through continuous
personal intervention is mostly an apparent one[;] . . .
he denigrates [his commanders'] abilities and increases
his own duties to such a degree that he can no longer
fulfill them completely."[17]

- Identify the truth tellers in your organization—and
  protect them.
- Be careful not to take yourself too seriously. In a few
  months, someone else's name will be on the sign out
  front of the headquarters.
- Create feedback loops that keep you close to critical
  events within your organization.
- Aggressively seek out constructive criticism. If the
  answers do not sting, you are asking the wrong
  questions.
- If you fight honest feedback, no one will give it
  to you.
- Chances are, the more you push back against criticism
  on a subject, the more you need it!
- By carefully listening to your Marines' concerns, you
  demonstrate that you care. Your Marines, however,
  will not see you as a leader until you are doing
  something about them.
- You can tailor the command-climate, equal-
  opportunity (Defense Equal Opportunity Management
  Institute, or DEOMI), and safety surveys to assess areas
  of concern within your command.
- Do not "chase" survey results—you will never please
  everyone.

Recommended Reading (and Watching and Listening)
- For more on effective feedback, see Maxim 22.
- Watch the Craig Groeschel Leadership Podcast 27,
  "Giving and Receiving Feedback, Part 1," at https://
  www.youtube.com/watch?v=FMrKPGlpiMA.

36

Spartan Spouses

In Steven Pressfield's best-selling work of historical fiction *The Gates of Fire*, King Leonidas selects the three hundred Spartans with whom he will make his heroic final stand against the Persians at Thermopylae. He picks them not because of their warrior prowess but because of the stoic resolve of their wives.[1] Leonidas knew that he and his men would not return and that it would be up to the women left behind to rally the city-state of Sparta to war. My takeaway from that book was to find those "Spartan Spouses" within the command, recognize them, and empower them.

As the commanding general of II MEF, Major General Miller always emphasized that those we leave behind when we deploy have the tougher job. During our predeployment briefs to the families, I would dovetail onto General Miller's remarks the necessity of locating and cultivating these Spartan Spouses. These spouses would serve as exemplars to emulate during challenging and difficult times. When a Marine unit deploys, rumors often spread before the embarkation process even begins. Social media has only exacerbated this phenomenon. As the commander, I needed to find spouses who would limit the chatter and provide calm, reassuring presences for the families.

Since 9/11 our families have endured the disruption and heartache of a continuous cycle of predeployment training, deployment to combat, and reunion and reintegration. The ratio of operations to dwell-time for some units has fallen below 1:1; in other words, Marines have spent less time at home than in combat. Though this operational tempo was difficult on the family, it was predictable for them. For the most part, a family knew when its Marine would deploy and return. This was a far different family-readiness problem than what I faced earlier in my career (or will likely face in the future). Marines are charged with being the most ready when the nation is least ready. This must apply to our families as well. Back in the 1990s, when I was a lieutenant and captain, we were required to keep our bags packed, always ready to go. Families knew what that seabag in the garage meant. Marines who deployed to the first Gulf War, Somalia, and Kosovo had hours—at most a few short days—to prepare their units and their families to deploy in response to contingencies, duration unknown. It is incumbent on the commander, therefore, to ensure the unit's families are as ready as the Marines. This requires deliberate engagement and rehearsal.

Before we hired civilian family readiness officers (FROs) (deployment readiness coordinators, today), commanders were required to recruit volunteers—"key wives"—to do the family-readiness heavy lifting. The success or failure of this volunteer force could make or break a unit on deployment. Results overall, then, were mixed: When the key-wives program was bad, things could get really bad; in contrast, a solid family-readiness program was the hallmark of truly cohesive units.

As mentioned throughout, I aspired as a commander to create the most cohesive, combat-ready units possible. I knew we could never achieve the required level of cohesion without the support from the families. I learned the best way to achieve their buy-in was from the inside out, rather than from the outside in. I looked for spouses within the command who had solid reputations (particularly as not being gossipers) and personal influence (but didn't "wear their spouses' ranks") and were willing to serve. In recruiting volunteers, I found spouses and parents of Marines who wanted to have an impact and were willing to donate their time and energy to help other families and support unit events. I discovered that what these volunteers most desired in return was something they would never admit to—recognition. We started by printing T-shirts with the unit crest printed on the front and "SPARTAN SPOUSE" boldly across the back. Spouses would wear these shirts at unit events to identify themselves to the families having questions or needing assistance. The shirts became status symbols. Ladies would wear them to the gym and to the commissary. Others would ask where they had gotten them and were referred to the Family Readiness Officer, my wife Candace, or me. We in turn would use the T-shirt as a recruiting tool. During our "meet the CO" nights, we established "T-shirt covenants" with family members willing to serve.

MUGGINGS

A great way to make a positive first impression and reach out to new families is to form a welcoming team to deliver a coffee mug with the unit crest, along with some key contacts and information on upcoming events. We called the events "muggings," and the responses were overwhelmingly favorable. The spouses we recruited to deliver the mugs were often greeted at first with shock: "No one has ever done something like this for us!" Regardless of their affinity toward the Marine Corps or the unit, no family assigned to II MHG could ever say that "No one ever reached out" or "No one cared."

Families are vital parts of the organization and must be included in your team-building measures. The most important things to Marines are their families. As a former Assistant Commandant of the Marine Corps (ACMC), Gen Jay Paxton, once said, "We enlist Marines, we reenlist families." How a family is first received when joining a command sets an important tone. First impressions are hard to undo. If you have relegated your sponsorship program to an overworked admin chief, you are making a colossal mistake.

In my career, I saw no one build a command team better than Derek and Jill Lane did at 8th Communications Battalion. The battalion was huge, with over 1,200 Marines initially when Derek inherited it, but it was scheduled to lose 20 percent of its structure and then be manned at only 80 percent of its new table of organization, with no corresponding reduction in operational tasking. Additionally, the previous commander had implemented termination proceedings on the battalion's FRO. The FRO in turn was appealing and had filed her own grievances against the command. I did not need to see the initial command-climate survey to know Derek was going to have his hands full. Derek and Jill's approach in addressing this family-readiness challenge was the perfect combination of self-deprecating humor and bold vision of what could and should be. Jill—a younger commander's wife than many, with an engaging personality—was able to bring together a team of officers' and SNCOs' spouses and junior Marines. They recruited an impressive network of volunteers who enabled the battalion to do all of the little things that separate a good unit from a great one. Derek energized the battalion's intramural athletic teams, while Jill ensured that all of the sporting events were well attended by the families. There she recruited the wives to form their own teams and enter various kickball and other sports leagues in the area. The result was the most cohesive battalion in the Headquarters Group, and, I would contend, the MEF.

Saved Rounds—Some Thoughts and Tips

- Locate, identify, and empower the "Spartan Spouses" within your unit.
- At the colonel level, I was careful not to encroach upon the battalion commanders' space when scheduling family-readiness events. My job was to set the conditions for their success and resource their

events to the greatest extent possible. Where we could do something more effectively at the group level, we did so, provided it enhanced the cohesion within the battalions.

- *Muggings*—recruit a welcoming committee and ensure they personally welcome new families to the command within thirty days of their joining the unit.

Recommended Reading—*We Were Soldiers Once . . . and Young: Ia Drang—the Battle That Changed the War in Vietnam*, by LtGen Harold G. Moore and Joseph L. Galloway. The book is best known for its heroic portrayal of General Moore (which is the focus of the blockbuster 2002 film), but it also includes a stalwart example of a military spouse. During ninety-six hours of intense combat in the Ia Drang Valley in Vietnam, the soldiers of the 1st Squadron, 7th Cavalry Regiment (Air Mobile) killed more than a thousand Vietcong and North Vietnamese regulars while losing more than 250 of their own. Holding things together on the home front—before there was a key-volunteer network or family readiness officers—was the consummate and caring Mrs. Julie Moore.

37

Pin It Where You Win It

Our awards process is too slow!

If you want to maximize the effect when recognizing a Marine for going above and beyond, ensure the acknowledgment takes place in front of his peers, as soon as possible, and, ideally, at the completion of an event. In recent years, the popularity of challenge coins has grown, and they are a great tool with which to recognize and thank a hardworking Marine or sailor for a job well done. I liked the challenge coins and even purchased poker chips (at my own expense) that I could give away without the drudgery of accounting for the coins. But there is no substitute for that colored piece of cloth—and remember, what gets rewarded gets done.

As a battalion and group commander, I charged my sergeant major to have a Navy Marine Corps Achievement Medal always in his pocket. To the chagrin of our professional administrators I would on occasion award a deserving Marine with one on the spot—before the citation or the summary of action had even been drafted, let alone approved. I was not in compliance with the procedures set forth in the Marine Corps awards order—I even made a point of "putting the cart before the horse"—but then, I was also the awarding authority: I was confident that we would follow through with the appropriate documentation. The impact, meanwhile, was unmistakably raw and powerful. Imagine the Marine, still hot and filthy from the action, standing in an impromptu formation, completely oblivious to what's going on, when his commander pins a medal on their chest. During the spontaneous ceremony I always challenged the Marine's immediate leaders to have the write-up to me within twenty-four hours. Then "drop the mic" and walk off. The Marines will tell the story for you.

Now, I am not recommending circumventing the Marine Corps award process on a regular basis. In fact, I am advocating that you pressurize the system to make sure it works for the Marines in your command. If a Marine nominated for a personal award leaves the command before the award is presented, someone should be explaining why to the commander.

Service awards are another opportunity to recognize excellence. Unfortunately, too many of these nominations go unanswered. There are literally dozens of opportunities to recognize excellence across a diverse cross section of the unit every year. I took care to submit a deserving nominee for every philanthropic, equal-opportunity, veterans' organization, or community-service award obtainable.

A unit award is a great way to recognize the team for sustained excellence. The 1st Tank Battalion received a Meritorious Unit Citation (MUC) for the period I was in command. Unlike personal awards, your higher headquarters rarely initiates unit awards. Documenting the superior actions of your unit and nominating the unit for a commendation is an easy process, but plan on starting it yourself. Paraphrasing Napoleon, Marines will do a lot for a little piece of ribbon cloth—so when they deserve it, give it to them.

MANAGEMENT 101

People repeat behavior that is rewarded. Management-science research attests that rewards are most effective when highly specific and given in close proximity to the behavior.[1] Our "pin it where you win" program is also an accepted practice in the business world. Read Kouzes and Posner's *The Leadership Challenge* or Peter Drucker's *The Effective Executive* to discover similar practices in great organizations. Such programs are ubiquitous, because they work. For example, Tom Watson, the former CEO of IBM, would often walk the office spaces and factory floor of Big Blue with his checkbook, issuing monetary rewards on the spot for superior performance.[2]

The Marine Corps award process is very different from the monetary awards programs of corporate America, but it is no less effective. Kouzes and Posner write, "It is not what gets rewards that gets done. It is what is rewarding."[3] They found that the value of extrinsic motivators (things you are given) is limited and can even block an organization's potential. Transactional leadership is a math problem, bounded by dollars and cents. But intrinsic motivation (fulfillment) is limited only by the leader. Perhaps in the Marine Corps it's not "What gets rewarded gets done" but "What is reward*ing* gets done."

REWARDING MEDIOCRITY IS COUNTERPRODUCTIVE

As a service, we are too stingy when it comes to personal awards. That said, I feel strongly that we must continue to guard the integrity of the awards process. When Lieutenant General Beydler was the J-5 at Central Command, he was put in the professionally embarrassing position of presiding at an awards ceremony for an obese airman. It left a mark. Later, as the commanding general of II Marine Expeditionary Force, he made it a point to ensure that Marines who were decorated were within standards. Rewarding technical proficiency while ignoring other deficiencies will backfire. If what gets rewarded gets repeated, why would you ever want to reward mediocrity? The commanding general required that height/weight and last physical fitness test scores be included at the bottom of award nominations. Though the stats had little bearing on the award board's calculus, it did serve as an effective bulwark in preserving standards.

Saved Rounds—Some Thoughts and Tips

*   Appreciate to motivate!
*   *An indicator*—does the number of achievement medals awarded match the number of nonjudicial proceedings in a given quarter? In the business world I would ask, Does your incentives program match your HR issues?
*   Never let a call for a service-award nomination go unanswered.
*   Keep a log/journal on your top performers. With a record of tangible and quantifiable examples of merit, you can rapidly put together an award nomination with metrics that matter.
*   An easy place to start when drafting a unit award is the command chronology (the unit's history). This is another reason to stop entrusting the updating of the command chronology to terminal lieutenants marking time on the staff.
*   Require your admin officer (S-1) to include the award nominee's height/weight and physical fitness test score at the bottom of the summary of action.

Recommended Reading

*   *The Leadership Challenge: How to Make Extraordinary Things Happen in Organizations*, by James M. Kouzes and Barry Z. Posner.
*   *The Effective Executive: The Definitive Guide to Getting the Right Things Done*, by Peter F. Drucker.

38

The Best Legal Advice
I Ever Received Was
to Get Good Legal Advice

In 2012, under intense pressure from Congress and the press, the thirty-fifth Commandant of the Marine Corps and the Sergeant Major of the Marine Corps toured Marine bases around the globe to deliver what became known as the "Heritage Brief." The Commandant's remarks focused on purging sexual assault and harassment from the ranks. While well intentioned, his talk was overly blunt and adversely impacted the prosecutions of dozens of Marines charged with sexual assault. During a speech at Camp Pendleton on 23 May the Commandant stated, "My lawyers don't want me to talk about this, but I'm going to anyway. . . . The defense lawyers love when I talk about this, because then they can throw me under the bus later on and complain about unlawful command influence."[1] Just as he had been advised would occur, military judges later determined that the Commandant, with his Corps-wide brief to commanders and potential court-martial members, had exercised unlawful influence in cases that involved them. By defying legal advice, the Commandant did himself and the Marine Corps no favors.

Some of your decisions as a commander will adversely affect Marines. You owe it to each individual to make the right decision. Admittedly, as a junior officer I kept the staff judge advocate (SJA) at a distance. As a commander, however, the best legal advice I ever received was to get good legal advice. Our SJA was always in my inner circle. While the decision was always mine to make, I consulted "the Judge" on every significant issue.

IT'S THE PROCESS

As a commissioned officer in the U.S. Marine Corps, I have sworn to defend the Constitution, and with it the requirement for due process. As discussed in Maxim 26, it is important to maintain a degree (or two) of separation from your disciplinary cases. You must do so to remain neutral and detached as you evaluate the evidence and make successive decisions in the disciplinary process. Your mission is to maintain good order and discipline while ensuring that each Marine receives due process. Focus on the process and listen to your SJA, and you will accomplish your mission.

Commanders with Article 15 authority have been granted by Congress, through the Uniform Code of Military Justice, quasi-judicial powers. During a nonjudicial punishment (NJP) procedure, you objectively analyze all the evidence, some of which may come from the Marine standing in front of you. Do not assume at the outset that the charges laid before you are fully supported by the evidence. Ask the hard questions. For most Marines, being the subject of an NJP hearing is among the most significant events of their lives. Strive to ensure that all who observe the hearing, including the Marine standing front and center, depart with an understanding that the process was fair and just.

To avoid the quagmire of unlawful command influence, you always have the option to pull a matter up to your level if you don't concur with how a subordinate commander is handling it. This, however, was one of the most difficult decisions I made in command. I did so reluctantly, knowing that I was signaling a lack of confidence in a commander. I did so because the commanding officer in question was unable to recognize the cumulative effect that similar cases were having on the climate and good order of the command.

INVESTIGATIONS

Your investigating officers will collect evidence and offer their opinions and recommendations. Before approving an investigation finding, ensure your SJA has reviewed it for completeness. The SJA will often identify procedural issues and lines of questioning the investigating officer has not pursued. As a commander, you cannot send an investigation back because you don't agree with the opinions or recommendations. You can, however, send it back for clarification or to direct the investigator to expand the investigation's scope. Ultimately, the investigation is yours, and you may approve, disapprove, modify, or add to findings, opinions, and recommendations. Your SJA should assist you with your endorsement.

If the investigation involves alleged sexual harassment, discrimination, or an equal-opportunity issue, ensure that the equal-opportunity advisor reviews the investigation before you do. Again, the equal-opportunity representative will identify procedural issues and bring to the surface questions the investigating officer failed to ask. You will want to address those concerns in your endorsement.

PERFORMANCE EVALUATIONS

An area into which until recently I never considered pulling the SJA is adverse performance evaluations. I took no pleasure in submitting an adverse performance evaluation, but having an evaluation redacted or expunged from a Marine's official military personnel file by the Board for Correction of Naval Records because of a procedural error is even more frustrating. With respect to their performance evaluations, Marines are entitled to administrative due process outlined in the

Performance Evaluation System order. Follow the process in the order and have your sergeant major and staff judge advocate review before submission.

GOVERNMENT ETHICS

It would be easy if ethics simply involved matters of right and wrong. If so, adherence to Maxim 4 ("Do Right and Fear No Man") would be all that is required. Unfortunately, ethics in the military also includes abundant and often complex government ethics rules. Your SJA carries the additional title and duty of "ethics counselor" and is available to assist in avoiding "ethics" landmines. Seemingly innocuous events, such as "hail and farewells," gifts, meals, travel, and conferences are shrouded in ethics rules. A call to the SJA will avoid situations like seeing a revered boss censured for accepting a farewell gift because the value exceeded the permissible limit.

If you deploy for an exercise with foreign militaries, you inevitably will find yourself in the awkward position of being offered a gift you are not authorized to accept. Turning down the gift may go well beyond awkward; insulting a foreign host may undo everything the Marines just accomplished. In such circumstances, the SJA will help navigate the bureaucratic rules and enable you to save face without legal jeopardy. You are unlikely to be able to keep the Bahraini falcon made of gold, but the Romanian plaque and Macedonian ceramic lion may be all right.

TRAVEL

While perhaps an issue more in the purview of senior officers, compliance with some of the less obvious restrictions in the *Joint Federal Travel Regulations* has been the subject of recent inspector-general investigations. As the director of operations for Marine Forces Central Command, I had oversight of the Marine operational support (OAS) aircraft (C-12s and UC-35s) assigned to the CENTCOM area of responsibility. Like the ethics rules described above, the regulations governing the use of OAS aircraft are numerous and intentionally restrictive. As a default "yes" guy, I expected the air officer to find a way to support requests we received, but pulling the SJA into the discussion ensured we protected the boss. When I approved (or denied) airlift requests, the SJA ensured I was on solid legal footing.

DOING RIGHT VS. BEING RIGHT

Your SJA will help you determine whether or not a given policy or course of action is legally permissible, but that does not necessarily mean that a measure is wise in a particular situation. Leadership challenges are never clear-cut. Doing the right thing (Maxim 4) entails even more than just being legally compliant. Marines will expect decisions from you, their commander, to be just and wise, not just legally permissible. Here is where your moral compass comes into play. Remember, if it doesn't feel right, it's not right.

Saved Rounds—Some Thoughts and Tips

- "I can't tell you what to do, but you can't do nothing." (General Neller)
- Tell your sergeant major or executive officer to cut the feed if you ever start a speech with "My lawyers told me not to say this, but . . ."
- When conducting nonjudicial punishment (Article 15, for those in the Army or Air Force), stick to the script. This will ensure your Marines receive the process they are due and assure all who observe and review the proceedings that they were fair and just.
- "Get me to 'yes.'" That was my direction to my SJA. It is easy for a lawyer to say "You can't do that," but a good SJA will help you find a legally permissible and ethical route to your objective, even if you have to shift to an alternative course of action to get there.

X

Communication

You Said It, but That Doesn't Mean They Heard It

*The single biggest problem in communication
is the illusion that it has taken place.*
ATTRIBUTED TO GEORGE BERNARD SHAW

"Just because you said it, doesn't mean they heard it." This axiom, along with its corollary, "I know what you said, but let me tell you what they heard," were two sage pieces of wisdom I picked up from SgtMaj Conrad Potts. The lesson for me was to follow up and ensure that the message I intended to send was received by the people whom I intended it to reach. If that sounds simplistic, you never asked a private first class to explain in his own words what the colonel said.

When addressing Marines in formation or other large gatherings, less is more. The more succinctly you can get your point across, the less room there is for misunderstanding. The more senior the speaker, the greater the propensity for the audience to dissect each word in search of an interpretation that best supports their agendas.

Leadership is about making connections. You don't have to be a gifted orator to be a great commander, but you do need to connect with your troops if your message is to resonate with them. In *The 21 Irrefutable Laws of Leadership,* John Maxwell writes, "You are the message," and "Every message is filtered through the leader."[1]

Public-speaking and teaching skills are critical "arrows in the quiver" of leadership. As the director of the Marine Corps Command and Staff College, I found that my public-speaking facility improved with every lesson I taught. Your ability to speak clearly and engage your audience is important in leading effectively. Looking your troops in the eye, reading their facial expressions and physical body language to know when you are getting through, rather than simply talking "at" them, are learned arts. Admittedly, this was an area I was not well attuned to in my early days as a company commander.

LEADERSHIP IS A PERFORMING ART

In order to improve my public-speaking skills, I studied and read the works of great lecturers. I watched Technology, Entertainment, Design (TED) talks to polish my delivery, and I rehearsed my speeches in front of my wife. (If you want honest feedback, ask your wife; if you are really courageous, ask your teenaged kids!) I would watch myself on video with the sound turned off in order to detect nonverbal distracters. For example, thanks to an overly active Irish sweating gene, I have a distracting habit of touching my face when speaking in public.

The best public speakers follow the same format your grade-school English teacher impressed on your writing— "Tell them what you are going to tell them. Tell them. Tell them what you told them." As an Irish guy from Boston, I never had a problem infusing my talks with a high degree of emotion. Later I learned that by tempering my emotions I could drive home a point better. The use of silence—a long, pregnant pause—can signal the importance of the point you are about to make.

I used my time on the Council on Foreign Relations (CFR) in New York City to polish my communication skills. The CFR military fellows received numerous requests to address the council members and other influential groups around the city. I spoke at large investment banks, insurance companies, and executive clubs. When addressing self-identified elites, I routinely employed self-deprecating humor to introduce myself to the audience. People expect Marine Corps officers to display a high degree of confidence, but if you can mix in a degree of humility, you can make a lasting connection. Leadership coach and Pastor Craig Groeschel once said, "We impress people with our strengths and connect with people through our weaknesses." Be yourself, he adds, "People will follow a leader who is always real; not a leader who is always right."[2]

THE EAGLES ARE ALREADY SCREAMING

The Navy fellow on the CFR during my tenure was Capt. Clint Carroll, the former commander of the 3rd Amphibious Group and a former Deputy Commandant at the U.S. Naval Academy. When correcting junior officers, he told me, Clint was ever mindful that long before he opened his mouth, the eagles on his collar were already screaming. As you grow more senior, it is easy to forget that your rank can magnify the tone and tenor of your remarks to junior Marines and sailors. When senior officers raise their voice, the message is amplified more than they may intend. When colonels—or worse, generals—lose their cool, it can paralyze the entire unit. While a little thunder and lightning from a major can get folks moving, the public microburst of a senior officer will send folks running for cover.

LET ME TELL YOU A STORY

It is hard to find a more gifted leader and public speaker than our sixteenth president, Abraham Lincoln. In studying Lincoln's leadership style, I grew to appreciate his use of parables to get his message across, subtly but effectively. Instead of confronting hostile congressmen or disgruntled cabinet members directly, he would tell them a story. Not since Jesus walked the earth has there been a leader with a greater repertoire of allegories. In his book *Lincoln on Leadership*, Donald T. Phillips argues that a well-chosen story or anecdote was Lincoln's chief form of persuasion.[3] As a president elected without a mandate, governing a country engulfed in civil war through a cabinet composed of former political competitors—later characterized as a "Team of Rivals"—Lincoln knew that an autocratic, domineering, top-down approach would not work. Instead he refined his natural democratic style and found it more effective to allow the hearer to distill the message from his stories. Instead of confronting his often self-absorbed generals, like George McClellan, directly he adroitly assuaged their egos by allowing them to infer the president's tacit correction or spur to move out.

The best commanders and staff officers know the most effective way to communicate their message is through not PowerPoint but a good story. As the go-to planner on the MARCENT staff, LtCol Reggie McClam could bring a brief alive by wrapping it in a story. Reggie was charismatic, articulate, and sharp, and his presentations were always novel in their delivery. I would watch in admiration as he found new and unexpected ways to personalize information. Whether or not you were buying what he was selling, Reggie's message was always delivered with clarity and in a manner that you would remember.

Saved Rounds—Some Thoughts and Tips

- The Boston Celtics' esteemed coach Red Auerbach would often say, "It's not what you say, it's what they hear."
- If your executive officer asks the staff to "stand fast" after your staff meetings so he can explain what "the colonel meant to say," you need to work on your communication skills.

- Before saying something to a large group of Marines, ask yourself whether it's something you want your boss (or mom) to see on YouTube (because they may).
- Watch your pronouns (see Maxim 29). The best commanders are great communicators, whose messages are "we-centered" rather than "me-centered."

Recommended Reading

- *The Power of Communication: Skills to Build Trust, Inspire Loyalty, and Lead Effectively*, by Helio Fred Garcia. Garcia is president of the crisis management firm Logos Consulting Group and a perennial favorite at the Commander's Course and Marine Corps media training symposium in New York City. His book is an adaptation of Marine Corps warfighting doctrine (MCDP-1) for strategic communications practitioners.
- *Speak with Impact: How to Command the Room and Influence Others*, by Harvard's Allison Shapira, is full of insightful and practical tips on how to improve your public speaking and presentations of all types.
- *Team of Rivals: The Political Genius of Abraham Lincoln*, by Doris Kearns Goodwin, is full of practical examples of how President Lincoln used persuasive communication.

40

The *E* in "E-mail" Stands for "Evidence"

When a man assumes a public trust,
he should consider himself public property.
THOMAS JEFFERSON[1]

I sent some very unbecoming e-mails over the years. Fortunately, I was never held to account for any of the "Irish
e-mails" I sent as a captain. I did, however, learn from the
misfortune of some other ill-tempered commanders. Today
if I am upset or annoyed by the tone or tenor of an e-mail
or by an ill-conceived task from higher headquarters, I allow
my response to gestate in the Draft folder overnight. If in the
morning, after my blood pressure has returned to a safe level,
I still want to reply, I press send—on a revised e-mail that no
longer looks anything like the initial "hot and bothered" draft.

Today, e-mail is but a single facet of the ever-growing threat
space that defines social media. The old adage "Say it forget it,
write it regret it" is borne out in numerous background checks
and IG investigations. The context or date-and-time stamp of

an errant text or tweet is of little solace. Here is one area in which I am truly concerned for this next generation of officers. If a simple Google search could cause me to be judged for some of the stupid and inappropriate things I said (or did) when I was twenty-two years old, I would not be for long where I am today.

"Character is what you do when no one is watching," said Secretary Gates to a group of newly minted officers. The trouble today, in the age of the iPhone and YouTube, is that someone is always watching. The downside to commanding at the colonel level, overseeing three separate command elements, was the number of investigations into officer and SNCO misconduct that I had to adjudicate. Apparently, the obliviousness of these people to our standards of conduct was equaled only by their ignorance of the electronic trail they left behind. With probable cause, the government's ability to search e-mails, texts, posts, etc., of the accused is extensive— what you hurriedly delete doesn't really go away. The discovery process in many of these cases was disturbing to me. In some it was a betrayed spouse or another Marine in the command who discovered the malfeasance on Google.

"FRIENDING" AND "FOLLOWING" ON SOCIAL MEDIA

I have two Facebook accounts, a personal one and a professional one, as well as a professional Twitter account. Showing my age, I do not have an Instagram or Snapchat account. For those, I rely on my wife to keep me abreast of what our adult children are doing online. As the commander of the headquarters battalion on board Camp Lejeune, Col Dave Bardorf taught me the value of maintaining a professional Facebook account. By doing so he was able to "friend" Marines in his command and join various "groups" while firewalling off his personal Facebook profile. If the "Marines United" scandal and groups like the "Tip of the Spear" have taught the leadership of the Corps anything, it is that you cannot afford not to be on social media. Social media may expose commanders to security threats, identity theft, and anonymous defamation, but abstaining from that world denies commanders crucial feedback and an extensive sensor network. In the future, failure to know of and properly address issues because you decided not to engage in this domain will have severe consequences.

THE FREEDOM OF INFORMATION ACT (FOIA)

The next time you log onto your government computer, reread the banner on the screen saver. Your e-mails are not yours. If the address includes a "~.mil" at the end, it belongs to the government. When prosecution of a social deviant disguised as a field-grade officer was initiated (the MEF commanding general was the convening authority for the court-martial), the disgraced officer (by this time a civilian) made numerous attempts to subpoena all my e-mails in the hope of discovering evidence of undue command influence or other grounds by which to impeach my testimony.

In another example, the U.S. Army lost two prominent and rising general officers after an investigation revealed that they failed to take appropriate action after receiving an e-mail from a friend (and fellow general officer) that included inappropriate comments about a female member of Congress. The e-mail, which they had initially dismissed as social banter, was discovered in connection with an investigation of another brigadier general who was later court-martialed for misconduct. The media and Congress were not quick to overlook his fellow officers' inaction. The Army Chief of Staff was required to apologize, and the generals' letters of resignation were accepted.

Saved Rounds—Some Thoughts and Tips
- Don't send inappropriate e-mails or post stupid things online. Google has a long memory.
- Allow a cooling-off period before you react. This is especially true when corresponding on any "platform" that leaves an electronic audit trail.
- Google yourself and your unit on a regular basis.

XI

_____

Leading through Crisis/Failure

41

The First Report Is Always Wrong

Since 9/11, the only thing I have done outside of command is operations. I served as a watch officer with I Marine Expeditionary Force for the "march up" to Baghdad in 2003, as a branch chief in CENTCOM's Operations Directorate (J3) forward in Qatar, as the current operations officer for III MEF on the Korean Peninsula, and as the Assistant Chief of Staff for Operations (G-3) for 3rd Marine Expeditionary Brigade (MEB) in Japan. My most recent operational experience was as the Assistant Chief of Staff for Operations (MARCENT G-3) for all Marines in the Middle East. I *get* operations.

Trust me when I say that the one thing I can affirm—without caveat or qualification—is that in a crisis the first report you receive is always wrong. Things are never as good or as bad as first reported. More importantly, however, is the fact that how you receive this initial news will determine how, when, or even if you will receive a follow-on report.

GEN John Abizaid knew this maxim well and when he was the commander at USCENTCOM averted professional embarrassment on several occasions by not forwarding reports until they were verified. As a young major, I sat on the Joint Operations Center (JOC) floor during multiple commander's update briefs when his staff erroneously reported that Saddam Hussein—High Value Target (HVT) Number 1, the ace of spades in the notorious deck of cards—had been captured. This debacle was repeated no less than four times before the 4th Infantry Division finally rolled him up on 13 December 2003.

My takeaway from the chaotic environment of the operations floor of a combatant command prosecuting two simultaneous campaigns was that nothing moves faster than bad information. Well-intentioned action officers will often monitor the chat rooms of subordinate and adjacent commands. When they see a report that trips a commander's critical-information requirement, they report it up (ideally with the appropriate caveats). Unfortunately, the first things that drop out in these flash reports are the caveats. In a chaotic and undisciplined environment, information is often passed on before it is verified.

BREATHE THROUGH YOUR NOSE

When you receive a report that something really bad has happened in your area of operations (AO), my advice is to breathe through your nose. The more dreadful the news, the calmer you as the commander must appear. People will gravitate toward a leader who is calm in the storm. As Rudyard Kipling wrote in one of my favorite poems, "If you can keep your head when all about you are losing theirs. . . ."[1]

Defining reality in crisis can be extraordinarily difficult, but it is your first obligation as a commander. In a chaotic environment you can be uncertain, but you cannot be unclear. Andy Stanley once wrote that you can be wrong and people will still follow you. This is not so with clarity. Often in a crisis, the first person to gain a clear grasp of the situation also gains influence.[2]

Businessman and insurance icon Jack Kinder once said, "You are not made in a crisis—you're revealed." Bad things happen to good units. How you respond in those moments will define what kind of leader you are and may define your entire career. This is when the vertical pronoun needs to come out. U.S. Army colonel Rick Ullian, a former task force commander in Afghanistan, advises, "You need to own it from the start." If the staff observes you taking responsibility for an incident even before all the facts are discovered, they and your subordinate commanders are less likely to cover up or "spin" the details. Later, an investigation will determine who was at fault. If an honest mistake was made that resulted in a mishap, the commander may, or may not, be held culpable. Commanders, however, are unlikely to survive even the perception that an incident was covered up, whether negligence or nefarious activity was involved or not.

In Maxim 23 ("A Smart Man Knows When He Is Stupid"), I recommended Nassim Nicholas Taleb's *The Black Swan: The Impact of the Highly Improbable*. Taleb demonstrates how mental bias can dangerously expose the mission to unforeseen risk. In a crisis, we are prone to see only things that confirm our initial assessment. Taleb finds that in a phenomenon he dubs "belief perseverance," the more detailed the information, the more likely people will focus on the noise. Paradoxically, the more information you have, the stronger your original conviction. Taleb argues that the more information we have, the greater our confidence but not necessarily our aptitude.[3] The takeaway here is that the later we form our opinions, the more likely they are to be accurate. In a crisis, snap decisions are often required, but snap decisions are unlikely to be helpful.

Walk before you talk . . . investigate before you initiate . . . just don't be the junior guy holding the secret that "they" should have reported.

In an operational environment defined by a twenty-four-hour news cycle and social media, a commander's ability to develop the situation has been significantly reduced by the advent of the Blackberry, now smartphone. Junior leaders have ever less time to develop the situation before reporting up the chain of command. In this initial report, you must guard against passing along conjecture. In reporting a mishap,

I always prefaced my reports with "This is an initial report." Your bosses will understand what this means and will expect a follow-up report, which they know may be significantly different than what you initially reported. That is okay, but don't be the junior guy holding the secret. Conversations with your boss about bad things that happen on your watch are never pleasant. They are, however, much easier when it's you who initiates the call.

Saved Rounds—Some Thoughts and Tips

- Killing the messenger is poor leadership and counterproductive.
- When initially reporting an incident, always caveat it with, "This is an initial report."

Recommended Reading:

- Rudyard Kipling's poem "If."
- *Lincoln on Leadership: Executive Strategies for Tough Times*, by Donald T. Phillips, breaks down Lincoln's leadership principles under practical historical examples. Lincoln spent countless hours in the telegraph office anxiously awaiting news from the front. The news was often not good, but Lincoln never overreacted or attempted to micromanage his generals. He provided encouragement and strategic direction where required. If the commander failed to heed the president's counsel, he replaced him.

42

Bad Things Can and Will Happen to Good Units

In his book *Good to Great* Jim Collins describes a conversation he had with ADM James Stockdale, Medal of Honor recipient and former prisoner of war (POW), in which the admiral debunks the utility of optimism in a crisis. Collins calls the admiral's counterintuitive view of optimism the "Stockdale Paradox." Quoting Stockdale he writes, " 'You must never confuse faith that you will prevail in the end—which you can never afford to lose—with the discipline to confront the most brutal facts of your current reality, whatever they might be.' "[1]

In the depravity of captivity in the "Hanoi Hilton," the optimists among the prisoners eventually succumbed. Convinced that they would be freed and home by the holidays, the optimists lost hope when another Christmas would come and go. Admiral Stockdale survived, and inspired the other prisoners to endure, by virtue of his fortitude. Stockdale's resiliency didn't rest on hope, it was built on pure grit.

The truth is that bad things can and will happen to good units. Good commanders have the courage to face the realities before them. Max de Pree, American businessman and

writer, once said, "The first responsibility of a leader is to
define reality."[2] When leaders deny or attempt to "spin" an
unfolding disaster, they quickly lose credibility and the confidence of the people they will need to fix the problem. Peter
Drucker said, "A time of turbulence is a dangerous time,
but its greatest danger is a temptation to deny reality."[3] In
a crisis, your people are acutely aware of the dangers before
them. If you attempt to convince them otherwise, you will
come across as Pollyannaish and out of touch.

During the height of the Battle of Britain in World War II,
when England's prospects looked bleak, Winston Churchill
stood up the Statistical Office to ensure he received the unvarnished, brutal facts about England's prospects in the war. He
deliberately set the office outside the military chain of command. This direct access served two purposes—it provided
him the clarity required to make informed decisions and pre-
served his credibility with the British people, who were under
no illusions as to the perils they faced.

In September 2012, under the cover of darkness, fifteen
Taliban insurgents dressed as American soldiers breached the
perimeter of Camp Bastion in Afghanistan, destroyed a squadron of AV8-B fighter attack-aircraft, and killed two Marines,
including the squadron commander, LtCol Christopher K.
Raible. (The last time the Marine Corps had suffered such a
significant loss of aircraft on the ground had been in World
War II in an attack on Wake Island that destroyed seven F4F-3
Wildcats, belonging to VMA-211—sure enough, the same
squadron). In the wake of the attack, I learned much about
crisis management from General Gurganus. Throughout the
disaster and its aftermath, he remained out in front. He was
quick to recognize the gravity of and accept the responsibility for the situation and then decisively address the security
challenges and restore the capacity of the air combat element
(ACE) to support operations. The general knew how fast you
could lose control of the narrative, and therefore he was also
quick to get the truth out and dispel rumors about the attack.

His candor and transparency proved to be bulwarks of confidence and increased credibility.

What you cannot do in a crisis is lose control of your faculties. Leaders like General Zinni and General Gurganus led through trying times using intellect, not emotion. As an operations officer, my operations chief knew to remove from the combat operations center (COC) anyone yelling or screaming. You cannot allow others to lose control in a crisis—it is contagious!

The most important thing to remember when leading in a crisis is that everyone is watching you. Doing the right thing is easy when everything is going well, but when it's not, the temptation to compromise standards or even violate your integrity can grow in direct proportion to the crisis itself. If you do compromise, it will not go unnoticed.

Leading through a crisis requires courage. Courage is the ability to act decisively in the face of uncertainty. Courage, Churchill said, "is rightly esteemed the first of human qualities . . . because it is the quality that guarantees all others."[4] The courage Churchill is espousing is not physical courage but what Napoleon referred to as "two-o'clock-in-the-morning courage." Napoleon believed the courage to endure to be the rarest and yet most essential attribute of combat leadership.

Saved Rounds—Some Thoughts and Tips (in a Crisis)

- Be visible, be real, and be positive. If you cannot be real and positive, don't be visible.
- Empathy communicates that you care but is best saved until after a crisis. You can be sympathetic until that time but do not commiserate.
- Simon Sinek wrote that leaders are not the first to see danger; they are the first to act.[5]
- The best leaders see opportunities in a crisis and never miss a chance to turn a potential negative into a positive. Seize the opportunity to address structural or bureaucratic impediments to progress.

- Remember, you can make progress or excuses—just not both.
- In *Supreme Command*, perhaps the most influential book on civil-military relations since Huntington, Eliot Cohen writes, "In war to see things as they are and not as one would like them to be, to persevere despite disappointment, to know numerous opportunities lost and of perils still ahead, to lead knowing that one's subordinates and colleagues are in some cases inadequate, in others hostile, is the courage of a rarer kind than the willingness to expose oneself to the unlucky bullet or shell. Without it, all others would be in vain."[6]

Recommended Reading

- ADM James Stockdale and his wife Sybil coauthored *In Love and War: The Story of a Family's Ordeal and Sacrifice during the Vietnam Years*. The book not only brings to life the admiral's leadership and determination under captivity but can serve as a superior primer for your next family-readiness training session.
- *Endurance: Shackleton's Incredible Voyage*, by Alfred Lansing, is a classic. Sir Ernest Shackleton's adventure in Antarctica is a worthy study on leadership, grit, and man's ability to endure hardship and disappointment.
- If you enjoy Lansing, *South!* is Shackleton's own firsthand account of his Antarctic expedition. Expertly told, *South!* too is a great primer for leadership in command in the most arduous of circumstances.

43

Failure Is the Tuition We Pay for Success

Failure is an integral part of leadership development. Only in failure do we find the personal and professional growth and increased resiliency we require to lead in today's operational environment. As in working out, it is at the point of failure where the greatest growth occurs. Embedded in my command philosophy—"Do Right and Fear No Man" (Maxim 4)—was an implicit declaration that I would accept "aggressive, faith-filled mistakes." As the Deputy Commandant for Combat Development and Integration, Lieutenant General Flynn concluded that when well-intentioned mistakes are treated as learning experiences, subordinates are more likely to make timely and correct decisions in the future. The key is to foster a climate where subordinates are free to make small mistakes because the leadership has put controls in place to prevent large mishaps. Build them a box and step back.

Unfortunately, we still confuse our junior officers with mixed metaphors. We tell them to swing for the fences but chide them when they miss the ball. What we should be telling them to do is to play "small ball" (read or watch *Money Ball*). Try it—if it works, great. Just get on base! If it doesn't, you'll be up again. If we are to rekindle the innovativeness that defined the Marine Corps between the two world wars, we are going to need to build and sustain a culture where our future leaders are more afraid of missing opportunities than of failing.

A popular refrain in Silicon Valley is "fail fast." In that innovation-infused culture, the goal is to push aggressively to find the faults. I once read a story about Tom Watson, the founder of IBM, and his reaction to a resignation letter from one of his executives who had just cost the company ten million dollars in a failed venture. "Fire you?" Watson retorted. "We just spent ten million dollars educating you!"

NEW AND ORIGINAL MISTAKES

In receiving confirmation briefs from subordinate commanders I'd tasked for deployments or exercises, my first question was always, "Did you pull the after-action report from the last time?" My message was clear—you can make mistakes, but you just can't repeat the last one. LtCol Dave Hyman, the wisest commander I ever served with, would remind his officers that "the burning ship on the horizon aligns the fleet." Frederick the Great is believed to have said, "The smart learn from their mistakes; the wise learn from the mistakes of others." By reviewing after-action reports (AARs) or eight-day briefs (mishap reports), you dissect the failures of others in order to find their root causes and implement proper controls to mitigate them in the future. The eight-day brief process is not designed to be pleasant. It is designed to identify missed warning signs to avert future mishaps and leadership failures.

OWN IT

It has been written that failure is an event, not a person. Yet here lies another paradox. On one hand, if you allow failure to become personal, it will diminish your ability to lead, but on the other, failing to recognize and accept responsibility for a mistake is even more damning. The worst thing you can do when something goes wrong is to attempt to hide it or defend it. It is worth repeating: bad things happen to good units. When something goes awry, do not be the junior guy holding the secret. Own it. When it comes to mishaps, missing equipment, and misbehavior—your boss has seen it all before. You must develop the situation, but don't delay reporting mishaps. If you don't have all the facts, *assume it is your fault*. This is when to use first-person singular pronouns: "Sir, I have a mishap to report. I failed to . . ."

Trying to fix mistakes alone or before reporting them never ends well. A quick read of a relieved commander's career obituary in the *Marine Corps Times* will teach you that the cover-up is always worse than the crime.

Saved Rounds—Some Thoughts and Tips

- Pull the AARs of previous iterations of similar events to inform your operational risk management.
- In reporting a mishap, missing equipment, or misbehavior, I always noted that I had already initiated an investigation. If the event is serious enough, though, it is best to request that your boss assigns an investigating officer from outside your command. This will assuage any concerns of a cover-up or a glossing-over of responsibility. Transparency is the best policy when reacting to a significant incident.

Recommended Reading—*An Army at Dawn: The War in North Africa, 1942–1943*, by Rick Atkinson, is the first volume of the Liberation Trilogy (*The Day of Battle: The War in Sicily and Italy, 1943–1944*, and *The Guns at Last Light: The War in Western Europe, 1944–1945*, are the other two). Atkinson's frank portrayal of how the U.S. Army and the Allied coalition applied the lessons of failure in the North African and Italian campaigns into strategic victory in France and Germany is illustrative of a "learning leadership."

XII

On Character

44

Talent Can Get You to the Top, but Only Character Will Keep You There

Watch your thoughts for they become words,
watch your words for they become actions,
watch your actions, for they become habits,
watch your habits for they become your character,
watch your character for it becomes your destiny.[1]

We have all read the headlines in the *Marine Corps Times* many times—a revered colonel relieved for "loss of confidence." Nine times out of ten, the relief was due not to a lack of proficiency but to a lack of character. The troops will gather and mock how an otherwise stellar career was brought down over a travel claim or a "descending zipper" while on travel. I offer a contrasting perspective—relief is often not the result of a single event but a waypoint on an errant path. The truth is that whenever you read about a "fall from grace," chances are there is more to the story. Whatever professional reputation these officers may have amassed, the façade of a weak character eventually wears away. Nothing exposes a lack of character more quickly than power. "I want" is supplanted with "I deserve," and "I can handle it," and the descent begins. Power, success, and fame are all intoxicants—you make some really poor decisions when you are "drunk."

It has been said that when you have integrity, that is all that matters. Conversely, I would add when you do not have integrity, *that* is all that matters. Craig Groeschel, the lead pastor at one of the largest churches in the nation, once preached that reputation is who people think you are, but character is who you really are. When you lead with integrity, your behavior matches your beliefs, and your values align with your actions. This maxim is not just about the personal consequences of a breach of character. Nothing will destroy the cohesion of an organization faster than a breach of integrity at the top.

In defining leadership up front, I intentionally omitted "character" from the required attributes of a leader. History has shown that character is not essential to leadership. Some very evil and unscrupulous people have been effective leaders. This maxim, however, defines the limits of toxic or character-less leadership.

In *The 21 Irrefutable Laws of Leadership*, John Maxwell discusses in his seventh law, concerning respect, the importance of character. For him, character makes trust possible, and trust makes leadership possible. People, Maxwell reminds us, follow leaders who are stronger than themselves.[2] Your legacy as a leader will be defined by how you led. Leading with integrity is more about how you did it rather than what you did. Being a leader worth following requires character. Andy Stanley has written that leading with character requires the will to do what is right even when it is hard. In fact, it means doing what is right regardless of the cost. The most direct path is rarely the most ethical one, Stanley concludes.[3] My takeaway from Stanley's writings extends well beyond leadership: Andy Stanley reminds us that God's grace is ultimately responsible for our position. If we believe that fact to be true, why then, if we hope to sustain His blessings, would we ever compromise God's standards? If that is too theological, allow me to put it in more practical terms: the moral authority from which our power is derived is remarkably fragile. One bad, amoral decision will crack it.

Combat is the ultimate arbiter of character. A leader's character and the core values he has imprinted upon his unit will be revealed when exposed to continuous contact. In *With the Old Breed,* his visceral description of combat in the South Pacific in World War II, former Marine private first class E. B. Sledge wrote that combat "eroded the veneer of civilization and made savages of us all."[4] Lord Moran, Churchill's friend and physician in World War II, did not agree. Moran was convinced that character must be developed before the trials of combat or its dearth will be magnified there:

> Character is a habit, the daily choice of right instead of wrong; it is a moral quality which grows to maturity in peace and is not suddenly developed on the outbreak of war. For war, in spite of much that we have heard to the contrary, has no power to transform, it merely exaggerates the good and evil that are in us, till it is plain for all to read; it cannot change, it exposes. Man's fate in battle is worked out before war begins.[5]

KNOW THE PATH YOU ARE ON

I have seen some great officers get lost. The thing about losing your way is that you do not know when you are *getting* lost; you just know when you *are* lost. Think about it. You make a series of wrong turns and then, before you know it, you look up and you are lost. The truth is that good men and women, people of integrity, can get lost. But they do not just wake up one morning and intentionally throw it all away. When you do the postmortem, you will often find it was a series of small steps (bad decisions) that led them off the cliff. It has been said that we are where we are in life because of the decisions we made. We chose a path. Once on a path, it is your direction, not your intention, that determines your destination.

The Old Testament story of Sampson and Delilah is really a parable about a strong man who gave it all away, one step at a time. In the book of Proverbs, Solomon writes, "The prudent see danger and take refuge, but the simple keep going and suffer for it."[6] The lesson, as explained to me, is not to evaluate your circumstances by where you are but by where you are going. The wise among us are not without iniquity, they are just sensible enough to see their errors and courageous enough to do something about them. The key is to give up your distractors and change before you are forced to. Do not wait until a personal crisis becomes your catalyst for change.

LYING TO OURSELVES

How much is your integrity worth? According to Dan Ariely, author of *The (Honest) Truth about Dishonesty*, it may be as cheap as a ballpoint pen. Blind to our own dishonesty, Ariely finds, most of us cheat just enough that we can still feel good about ourselves.[7] As a Citadel graduate, proud of the honor code we professed, I was initially offended by this allegation. The more I read, however, the more the author's counterintuitive findings made me pause and do some serious self-reflection. Ariely exposes how we deceive ourselves in the ways in which we cheat. He finds that it is not rational forces that drive dishonest behavior but irrational ones. For example, neither the amount of money we stand to gain nor the chance of getting caught is decisive in whether we cheat. In fact, Ariely proposes that from a strictly rational perspective, people do not cheat enough. The author's "Simple Model of Rational Crime," or SMORC, weigh the cost versus the benefit of an act, not the rights and wrongs. Think of a parking ticket—you are late for a meeting, and there is no available parking. Your decision to park illegally is likely a rational rather than a moral decision. You weigh the benefit of the crime, the probability of getting caught, and the expected punishment before deciding to park illegally. The fact that it is wrong (illegal) does not enter into your calculus.

Fortunately for society, Ariely finds, we don't normally apply this rational model to our daily decisions. Instead, we cheat right up to the level beyond which we can't sustain our self-image as reasonably honest people. The problem, as Ariely discovered, is that one immoral act can make another transgression more likely in other domains. Once you understand your foibles, however, you can do something about them. When you see how this slippery slope works, you will pay more attention to early contraventions and apply the brakes. The first act of dishonesty, Ariely indicates, is the most important one to prevent.[8] Therefore, in order to retain our integrity, we must cut down on these seemingly innocuous acts of dishonesty.

In February 2015, two Army War College professors kicked off a firestorm when they published an inflammatory study entitled *Lying to Ourselves: Dishonesty in the Army Profession.* Untruthfulness, Dr. Leonard Wong and Dr. Stephen J. Gerras argue, is surprisingly common in the U.S. military. In fact, the deception and dishonesty that occur in the profession of arms are actually encouraged and sanctioned by the military institution, while its members remain in perpetual denial.[9] When commanders are required to complete forty hours of instruction within just thirty hours and then to report 100 percent compliance with standards, we have designed a system that weights bureaucratic amenability over integrity. After reading Dan Ariely and Wong and Gerras, I grew acutely aware of my own self-deception. The most concerning aspect of Ariely's findings is that cheating is contagious.[10] In fooling ourselves, we fool others. Specifically, Ariely discovered that the more fatigued you are the more likely you are to cheat, because your willpower is reduced. The implications of his research for our profession could not be more profound.

CALIBRATING THE MORAL COMPASS

As a political science and criminal justice undergraduate in the late 1980s, I studied Kelling's and Wilson's "broken windows" theory and learned how big-city policing reduced crime rates by focusing on minor infractions.[11] When he was police commissioner of New York City, William Bratton and other law-and-order advocates adopted these practices with dramatically positive results. What Kelling and Wilson theorized, and what Bratton and his supporters confirmed, is that ignoring small crimes makes matters worse. The same can be said for ethics and discipline in general. Little lies make big lies easier. Left unchecked, our moral compass can slip a degree or two over time. Unfortunately, you may not realize the cumulative effects until you run onto the rocks.

Dan Ariely holds that religions today have evolved to help society counteract destructive tendencies. All the major religions today—Christianity, Judaism, Islam, Hinduism, and Buddhism —include rituals to reset one's moral compass. By acknowledging and owning our minor transgressions, we recalibrate our internal moral compass. Like the Catholic practice of confession, the key is creating an end point and a new beginning.[12]

Saved Rounds—Some Thoughts and Tips
- Addressing junior leaders in the Corps, General Neller would often close with his four rules for success:
  - o Don't be a drunk or use illegal drugs.
  - o Don't sleep with anyone who is not your spouse.
  - o Don't steal anything.
  - o Don't be an asshole.
- It is not your style of leadership that matters, it is the character of your leadership.
- Though you will never be perfect, strive to be authentic, transparent, and accountable.
- Know what your integrity is worth.
- Know your weaknesses. If you have a compromising habit, change it before you have to.

- The "Protect What You've Earned" (PWYE) campaign works. Dan Ariely's research found that moral reminders are effective. Done properly, the obligatory safety brief has merit after all.

Recommended Reading

- *The (Honest) Truth about Dishonesty: How We Lie to Everyone—Especially Ourselves*, by Dan Ariely.
- *Lying to Ourselves: Dishonesty in the Army Profession*, by Leonard Wong and Stephen J. Gerras.

45

The Disease to Please

Herein lies the paradox: when a junior leader tries to be liked by his subordinates, he invariably winds up losing the respect and admiration of the very people he is trying to court. The desire to be liked is a common trap for junior leaders, but "the disease to please" can afflict leaders at all levels. Like other forms of pride, it can insidiously masquerade, metastasizing every time you compromise in favor of something that does not make the unit better or more ready but instead curries favor with the people you are supposed to be leading.

The truth is, we all want to be liked. As Marine officers, we are taught early that it is better to be respected than liked, but this does not set aside our desire for positive affirmation. Servant leadership, however, requires sacrifice. As previously discussed, the cost of leadership is self-interest. Included in this cost can be your popularity. It is easy to be popular when things are going well. Leading with character, however, requires you to do the right thing, and the right thing is rarely the most popular thing—at least not at first. The temptation to compromise is most enticing when the task is arduous or the conditions deplorable. But as Simon Sinek once tweeted, "Give people what they want and they will like you for now. Give people what they need and they will value you forever."[1]

In his book *Good Leaders Ask Great Questions,* John Maxwell confesses that as a young pastor he was very worried about what others thought of him. This is another symptom of the "disease to please." The cure, Maxwell said, comes from the conviction of purpose. Belief in your cause creates conviction; belief in your vision creates inspiration. In the end, your motivation comes from belief in your people . . . not the other way around.[2]

You can be friendly with Marines without being familiar. You can be hard and demanding and still treat people with dignity and respect. There is a reason why military housing and social clubs segregate the officers from the enlisted, and the senior enlisted from the junior NCOs. The decisions we are required to make as military commanders literally come down to life and death. Many of our military customs and traditions are designed to prevent undue familiarity within the ranks, because when we get too close, difficult decisions are even harder.

YOUR CHEATIN' HEART

In *Altar Ego* Craig Groeschel compares compromise to win favor with subordinates to adultery.[3] When we as leaders compromise to curry favor with subordinates, we violate the trust and confidence the organization has placed upon us. To revive an old Latin expression, our *prima facie* duty is to the mission. John Maxwell put it another way, "When you fail to confront poor performance within an organization because it makes you uncomfortable, it is akin to embezzlement."[4] As officers of Marines, we get paid to make the tough calls. Failing to do the right thing for the wrong reason is cheating, plain and simple.

Over the years, I learned to stop worrying about what others thought about me. I agree with Maxwell on that: "Lead well long enough and people will shift from giving you no credit, to giving you proper credit, to giving you too much credit."[5] Looking back, I have been very lucky, receiving more credit than I've deserved. But it wasn't always that way.

DERELICTION OF DUTY

The disease to please can also infect leaders' relationships with their bosses. GEN H. R. McMaster, U.S. Army (Ret.), a former national security advisor to President Trump, in earlier years turned his dissertation at the University of North Carolina into one of the most important books on civil-military relationships of our generation. In *Dereliction of Duty,* General McMaster clearly points the finger at the Joint Chiefs of Staff for failing to speak truth to power and deliberately misleading Congress in the 1964–65 run-up to the U.S. expansion of the Vietnam War. In reviewing H. R. McMaster's book, Admiral Stavridis wrote, "Nothing is more dangerous than a subordinate who will shade or alter the truth in order to curry favor or impress the boss."[6] Leading with character requires an officer to speak truth to power and do what is right regardless of the career implications.

The politicization of the officer corps was not unique to Vietnam. T. R. Fehrenbach's *This Kind of War* is an essential read on the Korean War and the perils of the postwar period for readiness. During World War II and afterward, generals and admirals received recognition and status of kinds not previously seen. As a result, they became more amenable after the war to making military service more "agreeable." The result, borne out in Korea, was an Army ill prepared to fight just five years after the defeat of Nazi Germany and imperial Japan. Senior leaders had curried favor with their civilian masters and the public with disastrous results. The Marine Corps, conspicuously, didn't have this problem.

Saved Rounds—Some Thoughts and Tips

- Remember the "people-pleasing paradox": when you try to be liked, you end up losing the respect and admiration of the people you want to like you.

- Be cautious about the activities you agree to join in with your Marines. You will become an object of ridicule for trying to be a "regular guy."
- Familiarity breeds contempt!

Recommended Reading

- *Altar Ego: Becoming Who God Says You Are*, by Craig Groeschel; or watch his sermon series by the same name online.
- *Dereliction of Duty: Lyndon Johnson, Robert McNamara, the Joint Chiefs of Staff, and the Lies That Led to Vietnam*, by H. R. McMaster, and *This Kind of War: A Study in Unpreparedness*, by T. R. Fehrenbach, should be required reading for every newly minted field-grade officer.

XIII

———

Some Dos & Don'ts

46

Don't Expect What You Don't Inspect

The master's eye fattens the horse, and his foote the ground.
GEORGE HERBERT[1]

In the civilian sector, leadership and management can be discrete functions. Such distinctions, however, are less applicable in the military. Commanders have to be good leaders and effective managers. Infusing the organization with purpose and clearly defining bold and ambitious goals are leadership functions. Supervising to ensure that these objectives are achieved is managerial. As commanders, we enjoy leading Marines, but we are also responsible for the management of the "things" entrusted to our care. Unfortunately, the study of management at our entry- and career-level schools is viewed as antithetical to leadership. I remember in the early nineties when "total quality management" (TQM) was in style. The Corps had to change the name to "total quality leadership" (TQL) before adopting it.

Many commanders are reluctant to get into details, because they are afraid of being labeled micromanagers. "Checking"

however, is not micromanagement but an obligation on those who assume the authority to lead. Micromanagement is telling people *how* to do something; following up to ensure a task has been completed to standard is not. A commander's propensity to "follow up" and supervise to ensure that things are on track is often the single most determinative factor in his success or failure. In ROTC and boot camp, Marines are taught the six troop-leading steps with the acronym "BAMCIS": begin planning, arrange reconnaissance, make reconnaissance, complete the plan, issue the order, and supervise. The emphasis is always on the *S*. The sixth and, as any Marine will tell you, most important troop-leading step is supervision.

A good way to stay on top of things and to ensure your unit is on track is to establish an internal inspection program. As a new commander, you need to set expectations for your inspections up front. I maintained an aggressive internal inspection program at every command. My primary intent was not to find faults but to catch Marines doing a good job. A good inspection program should be properly scheduled, with adequate notification, and conducted with updated checklists. Done properly, an internal inspection program will avert surprises. Marine master gunnery sergeant Curtis Jefferson, the best maintenance management officer ever to wear the uniform, would rightfully boast that he was never surprised by the results of a big inspection. In order to ensure we knew where the challenges were and that we were never surprised, I had the staff go through the entire inspector general and the material readiness inspection checklists every two years. Back-planning against forecast inspection dates, I had a different functional area reviewed by a subject-matter expert every month. Unless you are the subject-matter expert, inspecting highly technical areas yourself makes little sense. At the colonel level, I demonstrated command interest by personally receiving the outbriefs and asking informed questions.

With the notable exception of security, I am not a fan of "no notice" material readiness inspections. They were popular during my tenure as a group commanding officer. The three-star headquarters (MEF) had a battalion or squadron roll out designated equipment reported as operationally ready to a parking lot across from the command post. These inspections came across as "gotchas" and created an adversarial relationship with the general's staff. When a vehicle failed to start or a dead-lining fault (putting something out of service) was discovered, the perception conveyed to the commanding general was of a unit artificially inflating readiness numbers. Anyone who ever spent time on a tank ramp understands that vehicles go down, and that they are most likely to go down at the worse possible moment. Unlike the programmed and scheduled inspections that were deconflicted against operational requirements and the training schedule, these inspections occurred with little consideration to the operational impact or context of where the unit was in its training cycle. Balanced excellence means that you should not have to stop everything to prepare for an inspection.

Material readiness inspections are best conducted at the battalion and squadron levels. As the commanding officer of 1st Tanks, I inspected two vehicles from each type, model, and series (TAMCN, in Marine Corps parlance) every month. Serial numbers were picked at random. Before picking a unit's vehicles for inspection, the operations and logistics officers would confer. They knew my intent: I wanted these inspections to focus on units preparing for gunnery or Marine expeditionary unit (MEU) workups, not the companies returning from combined-arms or extended training exercises. Here I got dirty. I would show up on the tank ramp in coveralls. I thought the maintenance chief was going to swallow his dip the first time I hit the ramp in coveralls to inspect. However, when he saw me take the lieutenants along under the tanks with me he understood what I was doing. My focus was on operational readiness, not dressing and polish. Details mattered. The battalion maintenance chief provided mechanics for the detailed inspection, and the maintenance management officer followed along to ensure the actual readiness "matched the print" (the recorded material readiness in the system). As discussed in Maxim 8 ("Do Routine Things Routinely"), I incorporated my "daily four" into every inspection. Before departing a vehicle, I would:

1. Find a Marine who had done something well and thank her.
2. Find a problem and fix it.
3. Teach something.
4. Learn something.

Finally, on the tanks and gun trucks in particular, I would search into the deepest crevices in search of spent brass. The pretense was that if I could find brass, I could find ammunition. The truth was I wanted the tank commanders to know I would look deep into the confines of their tanks and expected them to do the same.

What you inspect and how often you inspect it signal to the commanders and the staff what you consider important. As a tanker, material readiness and accountability were important to me. 1st Tank Battalion received the highest score on the new readiness inspection (FSMAO) during my tenure, and in the MEF headquarters group I put the battalion commanders on notice that I expected every unit in the group to pass its assessments. In the communication battalion, under LtCol Derek Lane, my emphasis was perceived as patronizing (8th Communications Battalion did not have to be told by a tanker to maintain its equipment set!). But for such units as the intelligence battalion and the expeditionary operations training group (EOTG), this was a foreign concept and an emotional event.

MICROMANAGEMENT

I began this maxim distinguishing micromanagement from proper supervision, but the line between them should never be fixed; it is very much situation dependent. The degree to which you supervise should fluctuate with the experience of the subordinates assigned the task and your confidence in them. There is nothing wrong with supervising different people differently within your organization. Knowing the capabilities and limitations of your people is a Marine Corps leadership principle. This knowledge informs how you supervise. Further, as Craig Groeschel professes, the degree to which you supervise should change as the organization matures.[2] The degree to which you supervise will naturally change after you have set the tone and established your expectations.

"Good to go":

- ✓ Did you verify the surface danger zone? *Yessir, we are good to go.*
- ✓ Did you check to ensure all the crew-served weapons were properly cleared? *Yessir, we are good to go.*
- ✓ Do we have accountability? *Yessir, we are good to go.*

Whenever I hear those three words uttered in response to a precombat check or a confirmation brief, I am immediately inclined to verify. Perhaps it is the product of thirty years of scar tissue, but I have seen how these three words have supplanted proper supervision. Instead of verifying, leaders have grown accustomed to simply asking if a task is complete. Fearful of being perceived as micromanaging or lacking confidence, junior leaders often mistake trust for proper supervision. The problem is, at what point do leaders actually verify the word of a subordinate?

I have seen this play out too many times to recount. The lieutenant asks the platoon sergeant if a task is complete. The staff sergeant replies, "Yes, sir. We are good to go." The platoon sergeant answers confidently because he asked the squad leaders the same question an hour ago. The squad leaders, knowing the leadership would ask, had confirmed with the fire teams that the task was complete. Unfortunately, it turns out, someone didn't understand the task or what the leadership was asking. Instead of getting clarification, someone along the way had just reported it was "good to go" rather than look stupid or derelict. This "good to go" mindset has been responsible for countless mishaps, injuries, and instances of poor readiness.

MICRO-KNOWLEDGE

Another nuance of effective supervision is proper understanding of the task. In his book *A Passion for Leadership*, Robert Gates defines his proclivity to dwell on the details as "micro-knowledge."[3] When you know the details, you can make informed decisions. More importantly, you can better defend the decisions you make. Spending time learning the details should not be confused with dwelling on inconsequential items such as PowerPoint formatting, fonts, or typos. Doing that signals you have lost the bubble.

I wrote above that I didn't personally conduct detailed inspections as a colonel because I was not the subject-matter expert. Instead, I spent time with the chief warrant officers and senior staff NCOs to learn some of the intricate details that distinguish the professionals from the pedestrians in the field. I would have them explain the results of recent inspections, a safety message, or other areas of concern. Now better informed, I could demonstrate my "micro-knowledge" in questions I posed to the commanders and the staff. By demonstrating I cared about the details, I conveyed that I expected them to do the same. I used the same technique when receiving confirmation briefs.

Saved Rounds—Some Thoughts and Tips
- You can't grade your own homework. To be effective, any inspection program must include external assessments by subject-matter experts.
- Fight to ensure your CGRI, FSMAO, or service-equivalent material readiness assessment occurs on your watch, late in your tenure. It is spineless to

defer the assessment to your replacement's watch. Plus, if you do things right as you go, you should see the evaluation as an opportunity to validate the command's good work.

- Deconflict your internal inspection schedule with the training and exercise schedule (TEEP, in the Marine Corps). Functional areas should be inspected when the most value is added, not when it is most convenient for the inspectors.

- If you find yourself working for micromanagers, a good antidote is to provide them with sufficient information to prevent them from feeling the need to do "exploratory surgery." Here, too much information can be a good thing.

47

Don't Be in a Hurry to Make a Bad Decision

The greatest challenge a leader does is making decisions that affect other people. . . . 95% of decisions leaders make can be made by a reasonably intelligent high school sophomore—leaders get paid for the other 5%.
JOHN MAXWELL[1]

Intuition is what we know for sure without knowing for certain.
WESTON H. AGOR

We are where we are because of the decisions we've made. Our decisions become part of the story of our life. The longer you are in the Marines and the more senior you are, the greater the impact and the consequences of your decisions. Chances are your greatest regret is tied to a bad decision. Unfortunately, we never really know what hangs in the balance of our decisions until after the fact.

SLOW IS SMOOTH, AND SMOOTH IS FAST

The commanding officers of the Armor School at Fort Knox when I was a captain would often say, "Don't be in too much of a hurry to die!" In combat, you can't miss fast enough to save your life: in a tank fight, it's not the first to shoot but the first to place "steel on target" that carries the day. The same is true with a decision in a crisis. Do not be in a hurry to make a bad decision. There are times when a positive, immediate decision is required to restore order or carry the day. These decisions are normally tactical in nature, and their urgency doesn't fully carry over outside of the combat zone.

How you make decisions will change as you climb the chain of command. Situations requiring quick, decisive action are more likely to be met by a company commander than by a battalion or regimental commander. When Lieutenant General Beydler, as the director of plans (J-5), approved decision briefs before they went to the commander, U.S Central Command and later when he made the decisions himself as a Marine expeditionary force commander, he was always acutely aware of whose decision it was to make and how long there was to make it. I learned from the general that you were unlikely to recover if you exceed your authority when making decisions and that having to walk back an ill-informed decision erodes your credibility.

In well-run units, 90 percent of the decisions are made as close to the problem as possible. Ideally, most of the decisions are made at the company-grade officer level. The remaining 10 percent of the decisions must be made by the commander. As I mentioned in the first maxim—"Know Thyself"—I don't get to make the easy decisions anymore. Those are rightfully made at the tactical edge, where subordinate leaders are more familiar with the problem. Instead, I get the ugly ones—the gut-wrenching ones, often from among the least-bad options. A good way to ensure that you are properly delegating to and developing your subordinate

leaders is by making the decisions that only you can make—
and leaving all the others to them.

I am not for bashing the next generation, but I have
found that Generation Z (or I-Gen) folks are particularly
challenged when it comes to making timely decisions. The
reason is threefold. First, they grew up in a world with too
many choices. Barry Schwartz, a psychologist made famous
by a TED talk, "The Paradox of Choice," explains how an
excess of options can become paralyzing.[2] Second, as Craig
Groeschel explains, some millennials are made reluctant to
decide by an illusion of perfection.[3] Continuously exposed to
everyone's "highlights reels" on social media, they lack confidence that their decisions will measure up. Finally, millennials
and Gen Z-ers are the victims of Generation X's "helicopter
parenting." Denied the opportunity to make consequential
decisions as young adults, they often lack the confidence to
make decisions as junior officers.

Though I cannot tell you how always to make good decisions, I can help you avoid some really bad ones. As an Irish
guy from Boston, the first thing I will tell you is that emotions
can get you in trouble when making decisions.

- Avoid anger. When emotions are high, judgment is
  low. I have learned never to make a decision when I am
  pissed off. Whenever making a decision about a legal
  or administrative proceeding that will affect the future
  of a Marine, I always sleep on it. As a colonel, during
  nonjudicial proceedings I built in time for delibera-
  tion. Even if I did not get hot during the proceeding,
  I would clear the room and carefully consider all the
  evidence with my sergeant major and SJA before deciding on a punishment.
- Avoid affinity. You can become too close to a problem. Sometimes you need to draw yourself out of its
  immediate proximity to gain perspective. In such a
  situation, you should ask yourself what a leader you

greatly respect would do. Better yet, ask yourself what your successor would do.

- Avoid self-deception. In the Book of Jeremiah, the prophet writes, "The heart is deceitful above all things."[4] Andy Stanley once preached on this topic, how expert we are at selling ourselves bad ideas. We help ourselves see what we want to see. Ask yourself, "Am I being honest with myself?"

- Avoid "either/or" scenarios. I realize this flies in the face of military and specifically Marine planning processes. However, I have found that it is the exception, not the rule, that general officers choose either course of action A or B as presented to them during decision briefs. Instead, most senior leaders, leveraging their experience, select hybrid approaches that take the best from each course of action. The best leaders expand their options.

- Avoid decision fatigue. A good chief of staff will maintain a "to-do list" for the staff and a "to-decide list" for the commander. A useful technique is to group multiple decisions in executive-decision format early in the morning or immediately after lunch, when the commander is fresh. There is strong research that confirms that our decision-making ability drops when we are tired, hungry, or fatigued. A *New York Times* study on decision fatigue looked at an Israeli parole board over the course of a year and more than 1,100 decisions. The study found that the three-judge panel's decisions were more influenced by the time of day and blood-sugar levels than the merits of cases. If you appeared before the panel first thing in the morning, you had a 70 percent chance of being paroled, as compared to a 10 percent chance if your case was presented after 3:30 p.m.[5]

General Van Riper is a huge fan of Robert E. Lee. In an interview with Malcolm Gladwell, he explained how Lee beat

Joseph Hooker at the battle of Chancellorsville in 1863 despite
being significantly outnumbered and having less information
than his opponent. Hooker was overawed by Lee and had little
expectation of victory. Instead, he hoped that Lee, realizing he
was outnumbered, would retreat and simplify Hooker's life.
But Lee didn't simplify the lives of Union generals. Hooker
had far better intelligence on and knowledge of the Confeder-
ates than they did on him, but, Gladwell submits, Lee's lack
of detailed intelligence was actually an advantage.[6] Not being
inundated with too much information, Lee used his insight,
cunning, and courage to decisive effect.

The best combat leaders are capable of making timely and
accurate decisions despite a lack of complete information,
but *knowing when* something is not as simple or obvious as
it seems is equally valuable. In his book *David and Goliath*,
Malcolm Gladwell finds cognitive-reflection tests a good measure of a leader's ability to recognize when something is more
complex than it appears. For example, consider the following
statements. A bat and a ball cost $1.10 in all. The bat costs a
dollar more than the ball. How much does the ball cost? I'll
give you a hint—it is not ten cents.

Perhaps owing to my poor time-management skills, the
more senior I got, the busier I became. As a component G-3,
I indulged my predilection for compact stories. After reading
The Black Swan, however, I became more aware of the dangers of compressed narratives and the risk of severe inferential
mistakes. I learned how easily I could be fooled by "confirmation" and "organizational" biases.

Simon Sinek's book *Start with Why* taught me how wisdom is built in a part of brain that controls feelings and has
no capacity for language. Instead, our brains communicate
intuition in our gut, giving a literal sense to the term "gut
feelings." That part of your brain is powerful enough to drive
behavior that sometimes contradicts our rational and analytical understanding. Daniel Kahneman explains this through
his "System 1" and "System 2" thesis. System 1 is our intuitive

mode; it operates automatically, with little to no effort and no sense of voluntary control. System 2 is our analytical mode; it allocates attention to complex computations or subjective experiences, like choice.[7] When making decisions, our brains continuously oscillate between Systems 1 and 2.

So, when should you trust your instincts, and when should you carefully think things through? Malcolm Gladwell suggests that in straightforward choices, deliberate analysis is best, but that when there are multiple variables in play, our unconscious (intuitive) process may be superior.[8] The underlining premise of his book *Blink* is that there is actually such a thing as *too much* information when making decisions. Whether the situation is that of an emergency-room doctor attempting to diagnose a heart attack or a group of generals attempting to defeat the opposing force during CENTCOM's Millennium Challenge war game, Gladwell believes that intuition, when combined with experience and fused with other sources of data, is superior to the output of deliberate decision-making processes.[9]

THE COST OF NO DECISION

Now that we've belabored the effects of haste, emotion, fatigue, and bias in making decisions, you, as a commander, are still expected to make them. Failure to make timely and accurate decisions will rapidly erode your credibility as a commander. If you are reluctant to decide, your staff and subordinate commanders will grow frustrated with your timidity and the fleeting opportunities that it costs the command. Too many leaders today are unwilling to make a decision until a crisis necessitates one. They abdicate thereby their responsibilities as leaders and become simply crisis managers. In a crisis, you are always left with only the least-bad options. Remember: you can be wrong and people will still follow you, but the same is not true for being indecisive.

Saved Rounds—Some Thoughts and Tips

- Col Doug Stilwell, a former commander of the 22nd Marine Expeditionary Unit, often used the acronym NDBIT—"No decision before its time"—with the staff. Colonel Stilwell understood that not every decision is urgent—that in fact, most are not.
- Make only the decisions you, specifically, have to make—delegate the rest.
- When framing a decision ask yourself, What must be done first? What must be done differently? What might be possible?
- Emotions are rarely constructive in making decisions. Avoid making decisions when you are angry or too close to a problem.
- As Andy Stanley once said, "You can be uncertain, just not unclear." When it is time to make a decision, be decisive.

Recommended Reading—In studying how to make more-informed decisions, I read extensively about how the brain works and how we actually make decisions. Here again I recommend *Thinking, Fast and Slow*, by Daniel Kahneman; *The Black Swan: The Impact of the Highly Improbable*, by Nassim Nicholas Taleb; and anything by Simon Sinek or Malcolm Gladwell. By learning about the neurology and psychology behind decisions, you become aware of your cognitive biases. It was only after I better appreciated how intuition works that I began to feel comfortable applying it.

Don't Make Enemies, but If You Do, Don't Treat Them Lightly

You have enemies? Good. That means you've
stood up for something sometime in your life.
VICTOR HUGO[1]

"Don't make enemies, but if you do, don't treat them lightly." General Zinni gave us that sage advice at the Joint Forces Staff College in Norfolk in 2005. The general's point was that relationships matter. Your "playground skills"—your ability to work with your higher headquarters and your adjacent units—affect your own unit.

Relationships matter most in a crisis. It has been said that you do not want to exchange business cards in a crisis. By cultivating and expanding professional relationships throughout your career, you assemble a virtual Rolodex of friends you can call on to solve a problem or avert a crisis. The broader your network, the more value you provide to your Marines.

The beauty of professional relationships is that many are transferable. The former commanding officer of 10th Marines, Col Brad Hall, taught me the value of transferable professional relationships. I have never met anyone who ever had a cross word to say about Brad. As an Aggie and as a joint planner in multiple Pentagon and Central Command tours, Brad has the most extensive network of professional relationships of any Marine I know. In my own career I deployed to every geographical combatant command at some point, and I routinely reached back to Brad for advice. He inevitably would put me in contact with the right person, in the right place, at the right time to accomplish the mission.

Fear of, or reluctance to engage in, confrontation was never a problem for me. In fact, as a company-grade officer I was too eager to join in a fight, especially with my higher headquarters staff. Confrontations under such circumstances were rarely constructive; more often than not, they negatively affected my unit. I have come to view criticizing higher headquarters to your Marines as a sign of immaturity and disloyalty. Disagreements with your higher headquarters should be addressed privately. By refraining from public rebuke, you gain influence to modify or change plans in private.

Leadership is about influencing the influencers. Within the vast majority of units in the Corps, the staff noncommissioned officers hold the greatest influence. SNCOs will defer to your rank as a new lieutenant, but you will need to gain their respect and confidence before your influence will be realized. By demonstrating respect for their experience and authority and by indicating a willingness to learn, you will gain their respect. The lieutenant who finds himself in perpetual conflict with the SNCO community is unlikely to make it.

When the Board of Regents of the University of Texas system selected Robert Gates, a former head of the CIA, to serve as the president of Texas A&M over Governor Rick Perry's choice, Perry made his dissatisfaction known to him. The governor put Gates on notice that he was actively looking for a reason to replace him. Gates wrote later, "If a leader is not making at least a few enemies along the way, he must not be doing much. Still, in public or private institutions, overt hostility to elected officials or one's bosses—or disloyalty to them—is an unaffordable luxury."[2]

When personality conflicts occur in the Marine Corps, it is said, the senior has all the personality and the junior has all the conflict. While there are recourses for grievances, as a subordinate you are expected to resolve conflicts with your seniors. If you cannot accommodate them or bring them around to your position and you believe you cannot execute your duty in good conscience, you can resign.

"FEED THE POSITIVE, WEED THE NEGATIVE"

In his book *Training Camp*, Jon Gordon uses the metaphor of a garden to illustrate how to maintain a positive command climate. He advocates "weeding" the negative influencers in the organization and "feeding" the positive ones. In a follow-on book, *The Energy Bus,* Jon addressed how confronting "energy vampires" is a key factor in turning around faltering organizations.[3] As I mentioned in Maxim 26 ("Keep Little People Little"), the loudest dissenters do not necessarily represent the majority.

John Maxwell defined confrontation as "saying something you don't want to say to someone you don't want to speak to."[4] If the subject of such a conversation is in your command, such aversion to discussion can lead to breakdown in accountability. In my quest to build the most cohesive combat-ready units possible, I never shied away from confronting negativity.

Saved Rounds—Some Thoughts and Tips
- "Judge me by the enemies I have made." (Franklin D. Roosevelt)
- "Friends come and go, but enemies accumulate." (Anonymous)
- "If you want to make enemies, change something." (Woodrow Wilson)
- "The best way to destroy an enemy is to make him a friend." (Abraham Lincoln)

- It is not what you know, it is whom you know.
  Professional relationships matter, so expand and
  maintain your professional network.
- The populist has no place in the officer corps.
  Attempting to raise your stock with your Marines by
  disparaging your higher headquarters demonstrates
  a lack of integrity and maturity. While it may be
  popular at first, Marines will eventually see through
  your disloyalty.

Recommended Reading—If you are looking for ways to infuse
positive energy into your organization, read anything by Jon
Gordon. *The Energy Bus: 10 Rules to Fuel Your Life, Work, and
Team with Positive Energy* and *Training Camp: What the Best Do
Better Than Everyone Else* are two favorites of mine.

I Don't Have All the Answers, but I Do Know the Questions

In lieu of attending a war college, I had the privilege of attending the Massachusetts Institute of Technology (MIT) for a year as a national securities fellow. As the Commandant's fellow, I was asked to be the keynote speaker for the Leadership in Global Operations course. During the class, one of the combined MBA-and-engineering graduate students asked me how I gave orders. What appeared on the surface to be a simple question was not. He wasn't asking me to regurgitate the five-paragraph-order format. I knew he was asking me how I led a battalion. In formulating my response, I realized that my leadership had matured to the point that I no longer told people what to do. Instead, I asked questions. As a lieutenant and even as a captain, I never had a problem telling people what to do. But as a battalion commander, and later as a group commander, I understood that if I had to tell people what to do, I was speaking to the wrong people. By my asking and answering questions with the staff, a dialogue ensued that stimulated critical thinking and drew out new ideas. Sometimes I used "bread crumb" questions to lead the staff where I wanted to go, while giving them room to come up with their own solutions, which were often better than what I had envisioned. Whether they arrived at my conclusion or came up with a better way, they had ownership of the idea.

A great read on how to ask the right questions and foster a constructive command climate can be found in Capt. David Marquet's best-selling book *Turn the Ship Around*. After taking command of a nuclear submarine, a poorly performing boat of a class with which he had limited experience, Marquet found himself in an unfamiliar position. Accustomed to being the subject-matter expert, he was now in charge of a boat of which he had very little technical knowledge. Acutely aware of his lack of technical knowledge, Marquet knew that if the crew was waiting on him to tell them what to do, at best nothing would happen and at worst he could cause a catastrophic mishap. To mitigate his lack of knowledge and foster a climate of initiative, he espoused a command philosophy in which he avoided giving any direct orders. Instead, he would provide direction and intent. Submarine crews operate on a system of "positive control": sailors are accustomed to requesting permission before performing a task. Breaking with naval tradition, Marquet replaced the "request permission to" language with "I intend to." The difference was more psychological than legal—Marquet was still accountable. However, he wanted the crew to take ownership of their actions instead of simply carrying out assigned tasks. Marquet wrote that there are only three things he could not delegate as the commanding officer. "I can't delegate my legal responsibilities, I can't delegate my relationships, and I can't delegate my knowledge."[1] He could ask others to take responsibility for everything else.

Prior to assuming command of 1st Tank Battalion in 2008, I had been away from the tank community for over five years. During that time the M1A1 main battle tank received several upgrades with which I was not familiar. Like Captain Marquet, I had an extremely humbling experience the first day I

climbed on board my tank and couldn't figure out how to turn
it on. The tank commander's panel I was accustomed to had
been replaced with a new digital version. The truth is, having
been away from the operational forces in billets outside their
occupational fields (on B-billets, in the Marine Corps), many
commanders lack current knowledge on the latest gadget or
procedure. Some are afraid to ask and show their ignorance.
Admittedly, asking very basic questions may sometimes make
you look like an idiot. I never concerned myself with reinforcing this stereotype. Instead, I found that by asking a lot of
stupid questions, I got great answers. By asking "What is this?,"
"What does the manual say?," "How does this work?," "Why
do we do it this way?," you will learn. You will learn the material, and you will learn about people. You will discover who is
a subject-matter expert, who is not, and who will bullshit you.

Great questions can challenge the status quo and increase
efficiency or effectiveness while at the same time increasing
proficiency. My favorite question from Kouzes and Posner's
The Leadership Challenge is: "What have we done this week
to improve so we are better this week than last?" The authors
describe how asking this question every week created a culture
of innovation and continuous improvement within an organization.[2] I vowed to close every commander and staff meeting
with this question going forward.

Another favorite question is "What do you think?" By
design, this question can draw responses that go in a number of different directions. By asking subordinates what they
think, you may confirm your intuition or challenge your
assumptions. It can be a good metric by which to assess someone's intellect or judgment. The question itself can be a great
lead into a mentorship session in which you can teach the staff
how you think.

In his book *Good Leaders Ask Great Questions*, John Maxwell writes, "You only get answers to the questions you ask."[3]
In other words, there are things you will never know unless
you ask. I get a little incensed when a senior officer takes time

out to answer questions but junior officers become timid and fail to take advantage of the opportunity. I realize that by the time they hit the operating forces, peer norming has taken care of most of the "spring butts," but given the opportunity to ask a three- or a four-star general a question, you should do so and be intentional with your inquiries. If you know a senior officer is coming to speak with your unit, ensure that a few junior officers have an intelligent question or two in the queue.

Saved Rounds—Some Thoughts and Tips

- The following are situation-dependent questions I found useful:
  - Office call (incoming officers)
    - I always ask about their family before I ask anything duty related.
    - What does success look like for you on this tour?
    - What do I need to know?
  - Trooping the lines
    - Who is doing a great job around here whom no one has noticed?
    - If you were me, what would you do?
    - If I were smarter, what question would I ask?
    - What am I missing? (I always assume I'm missing something.)
    - Fill in the blank: "If I had ___, I would ___."
  - Office call (outgoing)
    - If you were me, what would you do differently?
    - What do we need to do better?
    - What are you going to tell me that no one else will?
    - What are we not doing that we should?

- What is the one dumb thing that we should stop doing?
- What are we not doing that we should?
- Remember, when asking questions focus on the "quest." Where do you want the conversation to go?
- General questions rarely lead to specific answers. It often takes three to seven follow-up questions to get to the root of an issue.

Recommended Reading—*Good Leaders Ask Great Questions: Your Foundation for Successful Leadership*, by John C. Maxwell.

XIV

Final Thought

50

If the Boss Is Not Having Fun, No One Is Having Fun!

If you are not having fun and enjoying your time in command, know that your subordinates are not having fun either. Being a Marine is not easy, and leading Marines is the toughest job in the world. Your mission is to build cohesion in your unit and, by extension, to build in a "love of the service." Being a Marine stationed at Twenty-Nine Palms in California or deployed to some austere, inhospitable location is hard enough. Leaders need to find opportunities to make it rewarding.

When I commanded 1st Tank Battalion we worked hard, but we also played hard. Twice a year I did an overnight "professional military education" trip with the officers. Each summer the lieutenants pooled their resources, and instead of throwing separate "wetting downs" we chartered a bus and went to Vegas.[1] In the winter, we rented some cabins on Big Bear Mountain and went skiing. Those weekends were among the most memorable of my entire career. Despite the adage "What happens in Vegas, stays in Vegas," the officers who went on those trips continue to tell those stories today.

THE FAMILY WE WERE BORN INTO AND
THE FAMILY WE ARE SWORN INTO

I have been blessed with a remarkable wife who has been a complete partner throughout my career. In addition to volunteering to be a "Key Wife," Candace was very active in our family-readiness team and took on the other "obligations" associated with being the commanding officer's wife (COW—I didn't make up the acronym). She was a great mentor to young wives in the battalion and group, and she provided comfort to families during horrific tragedies. The Marine Corps provided us some remarkable houses that we made homes. When living in a relatively large house in a "premier location," we felt obliged to share it and so entertained regularly. Inspired by Col Mike and Doreen O'Neil and Col Brent Bailey's "white elephant" Christmas party, Candace and I have thrown similar events for twenty years. In addition to some great parties, we always made it a point to have the sergeant major and his wife over regularly, as well as the staff and subordinate commanders and their families.

On Thanksgiving, Christmas, and Easter, Candace and I loved to open our home to single Marines staying in the barracks over the holiday. This was a special tradition for us, one our children will always remember. When saying grace before the holiday meal, I would give thanks for the "family we were born into and the family we were sworn into." When your Marines view the unit as a family, you have done it right.

MERAKI AND MOTIVATION

I picked up the word *meraki* from Jon Gordon's book *The Energy Bus* and hearing him use it on a podcast. *Meraki* is Greek for doing something with passion and absolute devotion. No matter how difficult the task, meraki requires that it be done with all of your effort and enthusiasm and with complete love. Meraki comes from your heart. It means putting your soul—a piece of yourself—into something. The closest word in the English language I have found is "ardor."

Ardor too means doing something with great passion and a strong feeling of energy and eagerness. The adopted (from the Chinese) Marine Corps concept of "gung ho" (working together) is synonymous with ardor. Col Evans Carlson, the 2nd Raider Battalion commander in World War II, wrote that he expected the officers to "train hard and work together harmoniously."

According to John Hagel's, John Seely Brown's, and Lang Davison's research published in the *Harvard Business Review,* only 20 percent of the respondents to a national survey say they love their jobs.[2] Jon Gordon asserts, however, "If you don't love it, you'll never be great at it."[3] Motivation is a choice. If you are waiting on your leadership to motivate you, you will most likely be disappointed. If you draw your motivation from your mission, your morale will ebb and flow. Despite what the "jodies" (marching cadences) may promise, not every formation in the Marines Corps is a parade and not every meal is a feast. As mentioned, it is rare to have consecutive "good days" in command. If you are not a self-motivated individual, you have picked the wrong profession.

SHARE THE PAIN TO SHARE THE GAIN

Literally, the word "passion" means suffering. Any Marine who ever served can attest there is an ample amount of suffering associated with the profession. When this suffering is shared by the unit, it builds cohesion and esprit. Passion derived from shared suffering can be inspiring. When Marines witness their leaders sharing their discomfort, their commitment and respect for the command grows. However, when leaders order their men to sacrifice while they sit back in comfort, they create cynicism and erode confidence in the command. A leader who "suffers first" gains credibility and a better appreciation and understanding of the situation. As LtCol Brad Tippet, the commander of 3rd Battalion, 1st Marines, once said, "The man who is warm and dry will never understand the man who is cold and wet." Unfortunately, the similar word "compassion" does not often come with Marines as one of the ideal attributes of a leader. I remind lieutenants that its literal meaning is "suffering together." In the Marine Corps, you have to share the pain in order to enjoy the gain.

YOU'LL BE HAPPY WHEN . . .

Marshall Goldsmith concludes his book *What Got You Here Won't Get You There* by exposing the "Great Western Disease" he calls "I Will Be Happy When."[4] Instead of enjoying what they have, too many people today become trapped in the fallacy that material wealth, position, or location will make them happy. If your happiness is based on what you want, you will eventually tire of it once you get it and will need to have something more or something different. "I will be happy when I get that promotion," or "I will be happy if I get those orders." This ritual is a recipe for continued frustration and disappointment.

I have never been stationed in Hawaii, but I have visited the islands many times. On the northern shore of Oahu there is a beach surrounded by majestic cliffs that protect a small bay favored by the local bikers. It is very remote, and you have to know the right person even to get directions there. It is a three-hour drive over the mountains up Route 99 to Route 83, past majestic waterfalls and through lush valleys. There are those who have made the trip only to be disappointed to find a small, deserted beach populated by a small shaved-ice stand. They missed it. Their journey was wasted.

SUCCESS IS NEVER SATISFYING

I think some Marine officers become disillusioned because they are pursuing a fleeting objective they call "success." Those selected to lead Marines today represent the distilled excellence of this great country. I believe today's officers would be successful in any profession they pursued. I have learned, however, that if success is what you are pursuing, you will never be satisfied. During my tenure as a fellow at

MIT, I took a couple of classes at the Sloan School of Management. Though I had never been invited to the Endicott House, I knew its reputation as the primary site of the Sloan School of Management's Senior Executive Program. Every year, the most successful, talented, and intellectual people in the world gather to share their experiences in what has been dubbed the "gathering of the Titans." Simon Sinek, who has attended the event, was intrigued to learn that most of these executives were not happy. Sinek explained why: "There is a difference between being successful and feeling successful."[5] I have discovered myself that if achievement is something you attain, success is a feeling or a state of being. Instead of success, I have chosen to pursue a life of significance. By significance, I mean having a positive impact on others. If success is about *you,* it will never be satisfying. Fulfillment occurs when you have had a significant impact on others—the people you serve.

The reason I am still a Marine today is very different from the reason I joined the Corps thirty-four years ago. At eighteen years old, I had something to prove. I joined the Corps because I wanted to measure myself. I wanted to prove I had what it took to lead the best. At twenty-eight years old, I wanted to change the world. At forty-eight years old, I just wanted to serve Marines. Today, I realize that I cannot change the world but that I can change the small piece I touch. I aspire to serve in order to make a positive impact on Marines.

Saved Rounds—Some Thoughts and Tips

- If you are not having fun, get out.
- "Every man's happiness is his own responsibility." (Abraham Lincoln)
- Contentment comes from within. It is a personal choice.
- Bloom where planted!
- Find opportunities to increase cohesion and morale through social events.

- Don't define your success by rank or position but rather by the impact you had on others.

Recommended Reading—*Meditations,* by Marcus Aurelius. Like leadership, happiness is an inside job.

CONCLUSION

These maxims are not universal laws but situationally dependent techniques designed to put principles into practice. They are tools in the toolbox, techniques that can be applied by leaders regardless of their particular styles. These maxims are neither new nor novel, nor are they ready-made solutions or quick fixes. When it comes to leadership, there are no shortcuts or fixed formulas. To be effective, a leader must first and foremost be competent. Effective leadership requires a high degree of emotional intelligence and an understanding of human nature and basic psychology. Most importantly, leaders need to be authentic, know themselves intimately, and genuinely care for Marines.

Instead of rehashing the Marine Corps' fourteen leadership traits and eleven leadership principles, these maxims focus on character, courage, and will. My definition of leadership as *the ability to inspire others to find the will and the way to accomplish the mission* acknowledges that the best solutions are most often found within an organization, not imposed from above. As a leader, you don't have to be the smartest, fastest, or strongest, but you do have to be the most determined. Others may find a better way, but you must model the will to accomplish the mission regardless of the circumstances. Perseverance, resilience, and will are the hallmarks of a combat leader.

The first maxim—know thyself—is foundational, because self-reflection makes leadership development possible. Admittedly, when I was a captain I thought I knew everything and saw almost everything in absolute terms. Experience, however, has impressed upon me the value of humility. Humility allows you to see what more needs to be done and helps you identify your blind spots. I no longer aspire to be the smartest guy in the room. In fact, I have learned that the best leaders surround themselves with people more gifted than themselves.

Before you can lead them, you have to love them. A leader's respect for the Marines and sailors entrusted to their care is best transmitted through the little things. By taking the time to get to know your people you communicate that you care and increase their sense of self-worth in the process. As a combat leader, there are physical, mental, and spiritual aspects to how you care for Marines' well-being. Doing what is best for Marines has little to do with short-term comfort and is unlikely to be popular at first. As the Commandant reminds us all, the best form of troop welfare is tough and demanding training.

The moral component to leadership is a subtext throughout this compendium. Ethical issues are always entwined in leadership challenges or problems. History has revealed the disastrous consequences that ensue when a leader's ends are detached from the means. Character still counts. As stated throughout this volume, your professional reputation as a leader will rest more on how you accomplished the task than on what you accomplished.

My command philosophy distilled down to a single sentence—do right and fear no man—encapsulates the indispensable leadership qualities of virtue and courage. Your moral courage as an officer of the Marines will be of more value to the institution than your physical bravery. There is a spiritual aspect to my leadership philosophy, and I unapologetically include references to my faith throughout this manuscript. You may not personally share that faith, but navigating the fog of the contemporary operating environment will require an internal moral compass, fixed true.

The essence of effective leadership is credibility. Credibility is derived from competence and character. When there is congruence between a leader's actions and their words, people trust and believe in the organization. To sustain this trust, leaders must stay in touch. By actively listening, they learn what is really going on. Credibility, therefore, is maintained through contact. Leaders who are in touch—without being overly familiar—are perceived as credible.

Your job as a commanding officer is to set a vision, enforce the standards, and increase the will and resiliency of the Marines and sailors assigned. In every organization that I commanded from the platoon through the group level, my primary objective was always to build the most cohesive, combat-ready unit possible. Of the indicators of leadership—discipline, proficiency, morale, and esprit de corps—cohesion is the most powerful. When you focus on cohesion initially, all of the other metrics will be more efficiently and effectively achieved. Most significantly, in combat, unit cohesion inoculates Marines from fear. It is a catalyst for action, governs the behavior of the group, and provides the will and the resilience to carry on in the face of unimaginable adversity.

Leadership is not a process but an art that must be developed. I am proof that leadership can be taught and that the poorest prospects can be developed. Any honest study of leadership will concede that experience is the best teacher. However, through deliberate study and practice, leadership can be learned outside of the "school of hard knocks." Socrates once said that a leader's undeveloped mind is a prisoner of his or her own experiences. Since new lieutenants lack professional experience, they must synthesize the experiences of others through self-study. True disciples of leadership study and model the behavior of great leaders.

As you develop as a leader, your tools will become more precise and more powerful. As a company-grade officer I relied heavily upon competition to build unit cohesion, pride, and purpose. As I matured as a leader, however, my focus changed from "down and in" to "up and out." Instead of relying on competition to build esprit de corps, I strove to create synergy through cooperation. Professional relationships matter here. When you understand how your unit fits into the bigger picture, you can magnify its impact.

As a field-grade officer, you will find that your sins will change from those of commission (doing something stupid) to those of omission (failing to prevent something stupid). The battle against pride and hubris is never-ending. Commanders need to be attuned to how gulfs of perception can form and widen within their organizations. I am forever grateful for the candid advice I received from my senior enlisted advisors and mentors throughout my career. Sergeant Major Potts' sage feedback—"I know what you said, but let me tell you what they heard"—still echoes in my mind. In command, perception is often reality. It is the leader's responsibility to identify and rectify issues of perception wherever discontinuity exists.

In compiling these maxims, I vowed to be candid. In order to identify some traps and barriers to effective leadership, I shared my own mistakes and missteps so the reader can learn from my faults. When highlighting the shortcomings of others, it was never my intent to malign them or impugn their reputations. When providing a negative example of leadership, I attempted to shield the identity of the individual involved, by including only enough information to provide context. The truth is that the "disease to please" and the treacherous sense of hubris are all too common in units throughout the Corps. Many junior leaders fail initially to take ownership of their stumbles, while others blame their predecessors.

Commanding and leading Marines has been the most professionally rewarding experience of my life. Having dedicated myself to a profession of arms, I have found a purpose greater than myself. It has been said that life has meaning only if you're committed to a cause greater than your own comfort. As a Marine officer, you will be asked to forgo wealth, security, and convenience to pursue an ideal. For me, fulfillment is more about significance than success. At some point, the Marine Corps will break everyone's heart. If you stick around long enough, you will be passed over for promotion. Even the Commandant will be told his services are no longer required. My advice, therefore, is not to define your success by a rank or position but by the significance of the impact you had in the lives of Marines.

If you are preparing to take command and are developing your own command philosophy, I hope these maxims will assist you. Know that time is not on your side. Your time in command may be as short as a few months or as long as a couple of years. More important than a philosophy, you need a plan—a leadership strategy—so you don't squander your opportunities. Napoleon once said, admonishing his commanders, "You can ask me for anything else, but don't ask me for time!"

Good luck!

ACKNOWLEDGMENTS

This manuscript is a direct reflection of the lessons I learned from some great leaders and mentors. Some of these maxims are direct lifts from superior leaders I have worked for or in close proximity to. Where appropriate, I did my best to attribute the leadership lessons to the original sources, but some of these axioms are common practice within the Corps.

I shared my initial work with LtCol Stu Lockhart, USMC (Ret.), before it had taken form. Stu is one of the smartest and best-read officers I had the pleasure to serve alongside. He provided the structure throughout and contributed many of the historical references.

Initially, I shared this work only with friends and professional acquaintances who I knew would provide me with straightforward, constructive critiques. Additionally, I shared it with LtCol Derek Lane and LtCol Jon Bradley, because I knew they would keep it honest. LtCol Rob Bodisch's personal example and assistance in proofreading were most helpful. My classmate and screenwriter, Barry Dorsey, helped me translate/remove some of the Marine Corps jargon so this work can benefit a wider audience.

In compliance with Maxim 38 (that the best legal advice I ever received was to get legal advice), I sought the counsel of my favorite staff judge advocate, Col Dave Bligh.

If it were not for the time the Council on Foreign Relations (CFR) made available to me, this book would still be an outline. The research assistants at the CFR, specifically Rachel Brown, Sherry Cho, Gabe Walker, and Jennifer Wilson, are undoubtedly members of the future intellectual elite of this country. They did an incredible job of proofreading and formatting this manuscript. Additionally, I greatly appreciate the time and feedback provided by the CFR's senior and military fellows. BGen Brian Bruckbauer and Col Rick Ullian, in particular, were beneficial.

Finally, I would like to thank my wife, Candace, for the time I should have spent with her while writing this book.

GLOSSARY

Spelled-out terms having "generic" uses—that are not always and necessarily used as, or in, proper (official) names or titles of persons, organizations, or programs—are given in lower case.

AAR	after-action report
ACE	air combat element
ACMC	Assistant Commandant of the Marine Corps
ADSEP	administrative separation
aka	also known as
ALMAR	All Marine (bulletin)
AO	area of operations
BAMCIS	troop-leading procedures: *b*egin planning, *a*rrange reconnaissance, *m*ake reconnaissance, *c*omplete the plan, *i*ssue the order, *s*upervise
BHAG	big hairy audacious goal
CAX	combined-arms exercise
CENTCOM	(U.S.) Central Command
CEO	chief executive officer
CG	commanding general

CGRI	commanding general readiness inspection
CO	commanding officer
COA	course of action
CONGRINT	congressional inquiry
CUB	commanders update brief
CWO	chief warrant officer
DEOMI	Defense Equal Opportunity Management Institute
DI	drill instructor
ELF	eye laser (safe) filter
EPD	extra punitive duty
FOIA	Freedom of Information Act
FRO	family readiness officer
FSMAO	Field Supply Maintenance Analysis Office
G-3	(the assistant chief of staff for operations on a general's staff)
GCE	ground combat element
GEM	general-officer e-mail
HHQ	higher headquarters
HMMWV	High Mobility Multipurpose Wheeled Vehicle
HVT	high-value target
I&I	inspector-instructor
IG	inspector general
IOC	Infantry Officers Course
J-5	(the assistant chief of staff for plans on a joint staff)
JOC	Joint Operations Center

JP-1	Joint Publication 1
JTF	joint task force
LAR	light armored reconnaissance
LOGCOM	Logistics Command
LtGen	Lieutenant General (three-stars, pay grade O-9)
MARCENT	(the Marine component command in U.S. Central Command)
MAW	marine aircraft wing
MCDP	marine corps doctrinal publication
MCMAP	Marine Corps Martial Arts Program
MCPP	Marine Corps Planning Process
MCRD PI	Marine Corps Recruit Depot Parris Island
MEB	Marine expeditionary brigade
MEF	Marine expeditionary force
MGySgt	master gunnery sergeant (pay grade E-9)
MHG	MEF Headquarters Group
MMOA-3	Manpower Management Officer Assignment Office Three
MRS	muzzle reference system
NCO	noncommissioned officer
NJP	nonjudicial punishment (UCMJ article 15)

O-6	(officer pay grade of a colonel or Navy captain)
OCS	Officer Candidate School
OPT	operations planning team
ORM	operational risk management
OSA	operational support aircraft
PCP	praise, correct, praise
PFT	Physical Fitness Test
POA&M	plan of action and milestones
PT	physical training
PTSD	post-traumatic stress disorder
PWYE	"Protect What You Earned"
R4OG	retrograde, redeployment in support of reset and reconstitution operations group
RADBN	radio battalion
ROTC	Reserve Officer Training Corps
SDZ	surface danger zone
SJA	staff judge advocate
SMEAC	(the five-paragraph order format: situation, mission, execution, administration [and logistics], command [and signal])
SNCO	staff noncommissioned officer
SOP	standard operating procedure

TAD	temporary additional duty (TDY in the Army and USAF)
TBS	The Basic School
TEEP	training and exercise employment plan
TMI	"too much information"
T&R	training and readiness
UCMJ	Uniform Code of Military Justice
XO	executive officer

NOTES

PREFACE

1. U.S. Navy Department, *Marine Corps Value: A User's Guide for Discussion Leaders,* Marine Corps Tactical Publication [MCTP] 6-10B (Washington, D.C.: Headquarters U.S. Marine Corps, 2 May 2016), x. This edition replaced Marine Corps Reference Publication (MCRP) 6-11B.
2. John C. Maxwell, *Good Leaders Ask Great Questions* (New York: Center Street, 2014), 124.

LEADERSHIP DEFINED

1. U.S. Navy Department, *Marine Corps Manual* (Washington, D.C.: U.S. Government Printing Office, 1921).
2. Anthony Zinni, *Leading the Charge: Leadership Lessons from the Battlefield to the Boardroom* (New York: St. Martin's, 2009), 46.
3. Christopher D. Kolenda, *Leadership: The Warrior's Art* (Carlisle, Pa.: Army War College Press, 2011), 6.
4. Lord Moran [Charles Wilson, 1st Baron Moran], *The Anatomy of Courage* (London: Constable, 1945), 180.
5. Maxwell, *Good Leaders Ask Great Questions,* 125.
6. Jim Kouzes and Barry Posner, *The Leadership Challenge* (New York: John Wiley & Sons, 2003), 12.
7. Simon Sinek, *Start with Why* (New York: Penguin, 2011), 39.
8. Jim Collins, *Good to Great* (London: Harper Business, 2001), 21.

CHAPTER 1. KNOW THYSELF

1. Sun Tzu, *The Art of War,* trans. Ralph D. Sawyer (New York: Basic Books, 1994), 6.
2. Maxwell, *Good Leaders Ask Great Questions,* 47.
3. Maxwell, 47.
4. Benjamin Franklin, *Poor Richard's Almanack* (Los Angeles, Calif.: U.S.C. Publishing, 1914).

5. Zinni, *Leading the Charge*, 65.

6. John Maxwell, "Failure Is an Inside Job," *John Maxwell's Blog*, page 41, 10 October 2010, last modified January 2012 (accessed August 2020), https://www.goodreads.com/author/show/68 .John_C_Maxwell/blog?page=41.

CHAPTER 2. IT IS NOT ABOUT YOU

1. Gen Joseph F. Dunford, "Meeting Today's Global Security Challenges," speech to the Center for Strategic and International Studies, 29 March 2016.

2. Simon Sinek, *Leaders Eat Last: Why Some Teams Pull Together and Others Don't* (New York: Penguin, 2014), 65.

3. Simon Sinek, "What It Means to Lead," address to the Armed Forces Communications & Electronics Association, ArLaTex chapter, last modified May 2015, https://www.youtube.com /watch?v=dGHWy60VdXw (accessed August 2020).

4. John Maxwell, *The 21 Irrefutable Laws of Leadership* (Nashville, Tenn.: Thomas Nelson, 2007), 223.

5. Rick Warren, *The Purpose Driven Life: What on Earth Am I Here For?* (Grand Rapids, Mich.: Zondervan, 2012), 25.

6. Robert K. Greenleaf, *The Servant as Leader* (South Orange, N.J.: Greenleaf Center for Servant Leadership, 2015).

7. Mark 10:34 [New International Version, hereafter NIV].

8. Sinek, *Leaders Eat Last*, 181.

9. Zig Ziglar, *Zig Ziglar's Secrets of Closing the Sale: For Anyone Who Must Get Others to Say Yes!* (Ada, Mich.: Revell; 2004).

10. Ori Brafman and Rod Beckstrom, *The Starfish and the Spider: The Unstoppable Power of Leaderless Organizations* (London: Penguin, 2006).

11. Robert M. Gates, *A Passion for Leadership* (New York: Knopf Doubleday, 2017), 161.

12. Robert Coram, *Boyd: The Fighter Pilot Who Changed the Art of War* (Boston: Little, Brown, 2002), ix.

13. Coram, 285.

14. Jon Gordon, *Training Camp: What the Best Do Better than Everyone Else* (New York: John Wiley & Sons, 2009), 58.

15. Maxwell, *21 Irrefutable Laws of Leadership*, 148.

16. U.S. Navy Department, *Leading Marines*, Marine Corps Warfighting Publication [MCWP] 6-11 (Washington, D.C.: Headquarters U.S. Marine Corps, 2002), 4.

CHAPTER 3. MARINES DON'T CARE HOW MUCH YOU KNOW BUT WILL KNOW HOW MUCH YOU CARE

1. MCTP 6-10B, chap. 15, 15-2, and app. A, 15-17 to 15-21.

CHAPTER 4. DO RIGHT AND FEAR NO MAN

1. Commandant of the Marine Corps (Director of the Marine Corps Staff), message to All Marine Corps, ALMAR 033/16, date-time group 031813Z October 2016, subject: "Spiritual Fitness."
2. Stanley Milgram, "The Perils of Obedience," *Harper's* 247:1483 (1973), 62–77.
3. Sinek, *Leaders Eat Last,* 101.
4. Kolenda, *Leadership,* 91.
5. Sinek, *Leaders Eat Last,* 74.
6. John Avlon, *Washington's Farewell: The Founding Father's Warning to Future Generals* (New York: Simon & Schuster, 2017), 151.

CHAPTER 5. ORGANIZATIONS MOVE AT THE SPEED OF TRUST

1. Stephen M. R. Covey, *The Speed of Trust* (New York: Free Press, 2006).
2. U.S. Navy Department, *Warfighting,* Marine Corps Doctrinal Publication [MCDP] 1 (Washington, D.C.: Headquarters U.S. Marine Corps, 20 June 1997, with Change 1, 4 April 2018).
3. James Kouzes and Barry Posner, *The Leadership Challenge: How to Make Extraordinary Things Happen in Organizations* (New York: Farrar, Straus and Giroux, 2011), 12.
4. Ash Carter, speech to the Association of the United States Army (AUSA), Republic of Korea, last modified October 2015, https://insidedefense.com/document/carters-ausa-speech (accessed 22 August 2020).
5. Sinek, *Leaders Eat Last,* 20.
6. Andy Stanley, "Trust vs Suspicion," *Leadership,* podcast, 5 April 2013, https://podbay.fm/p/andy-stanley-leadership -podcast/e/1365185340 (accessed 22 August 2020).
7. Stephen R. Covey, *Seven Habits of Highly Effective People,* in *The Stephen R. Covey Interactive Reader* (New York: First Fireside Edition, 1990), 34.
8. Maxwell, *21 Irrefutable Laws of Leadership,* 61.
9. Jack Welch and Suzy Welch, *The Real-Life MBA: Your No-BS Guide to Winning the Game, Building a Team, and Growing Your Career* (New York: HarperCollins, 2015).
10. Sinek, *Start with Why,* 151.
11. Craig Groeschel, "Leadership Podcast: Firing Your Inner Boss," *Life. Church,* 6 June 2017, https://www.life.church/leadershippodcast /fire-your-inner-boss/.

CHAPTER 6. YOUR GREATEST IMPACT WILL BE
ON THE ENDS OF THE BELL CURVE

1. John C. Maxwell, *Developing the Leaders around You: How to Help Others Reach Their Full Potential* (Nashville, TN: Thomas Nelson, 1995), 9.

2. Maxwell, *Developing*, 79.

3. Maxwell, *21 Irrefutable Laws of Leadership*, 249.

4. Maxwell, *21*, 249.

5. Maxwell, *Good Leaders Ask Great Questions*, 188.

CHAPTER 7. IF YOU TREAT THEM LIKE ADULTS,
THEY WILL ACT LIKE ADULTS

1. Maxwell, *Good Leaders Ask Great Questions*, 183.

CHAPTER 8. DO ROUTINE THINGS ROUTINELY

1. Andy Stanley, "Leadership," podcast, 1 December 2016, https://podbay.fm/podcast/290055666 (accessed 7 December 2020).

2. Kouzes and Posner, *Leadership Challenge*, 55.

3. As republished in Geoffrey Ingersoll, "General James 'Mad Dog' Mattis Email about Being 'Too Busy to Read' Is a Must-Read," *Business Insider*, last modified 9 May 2013 (accessed 22 August 2020), http://www.businessinsider.com/viral-james-mattis-email-reading-marines-2013-5.

4. Bryan McCoy, *The Passion of Command: The Moral Imperative of Leadership* (Quantico, Va.: Marine Corps Association Bookstore, 2006), 60.

5. Kolenda, *Leadership*, 25.

6. John Kotter, *Leading Change* (Brighton, Mass.: Harvard Business Review Press, 2012), 187.

CHAPTER 11. THAT POINT WHERE EVERYONE ELSE SUCKS

1. Stanley McChrystal et al., *Team of Teams: New Rules of Engagement for a Complex World* (London: Penguin, 2015), 126.

2. Kolenda, *Leadership*, 58.

3. Lt Col Dave Grossman, *On Killing: The Psychological Cost of Learning to Kill in War and Society* (New York: Open Road Media, 2014), 87.

4. Angela Duckworth, *Grit: The Power of Passion and Perseverance* (New York: Simon & Schuster, 2016), 247.

5. James Kerr, *Legacy: What the All Blacks Can Teach Us about the Business of Life* (London: Constable, 2013), 150.

CHAPTER 12. MAKE WINNING A HABIT

1. Jon Gordon, "Become a Better Version of You," *EntreLeadership*, podcast 161, last modified 21 August 2016, http://entreleader

shippodcast.entreleadership.libsynpro.com/2016 (accessed August 2020).

2. Maxwell, *21 Irrefutable Laws of Leadership,* 197.

3. Duckworth, *Grit,* 262.

4. Duckworth, 262.

5. Tom Ricks, *The Generals: American Military Command from World War II to Today* (London: Penguin, 2012), 78.

6. Kouzes and Posner, *Leadership Challenge,* 154.

CHAPTER 13. TRUE GRIT

1. MCDP 1, 1.

2. Steven Pressfield, *The Warrior Ethos* (New York: Black Irish Entertainment, 2011), 59.

3. *Marine Corps Manual* (1921), 1, para. 1100.

4. Malcolm Gladwell, *Outliers: The Story of Success* (London: Allen Lane, 2008), 32.

5. Duckworth, *Grit,* 15.

6. Duckworth, 189.

7. "Blood, Toil, Tears, and Sweat, May 13, 1940," *International Churchill Society,* https://winstonchurchill.org/resources /speeches/1940-the-finest-hour/blood-toil-tears-and-sweat-2/.

CHAPTER 14. EMBRACE THE SUCK

1. Kouzes and Posner, *Leadership Challenge,* 217.

2. Steven Pressfield, *The Virtues of War: A Novel of Alexander the Great* (New York: Random House, 2005).

3. Daniel Goleman et al., *Primal Leadership: Unleashing the Power of Emotional Intelligence* (Brighton, Mass.: Harvard Business Review Press, 2013), 6.

4. Goleman, 6.

5. "USMC General Lewis B. Chesty Puller Quotes," *Military Quotes,* http://www.military-quotes.com/chesty-puller.htm (accessed 20 August 2020).

CHAPTER 15. THERE CAN BE NO MORALE WITHOUT ATTRITION

1. Kolenda, *Leadership,* xxii.

2. Kolenda, 86.

3. Malcolm Gladwell, "The Talent Myth," *New Yorker,* 22 July 2002.

CHAPTER 16. PRAISE, CORRECT, PRAISE (PCP)

1. Daniel Kahneman, *Thinking, Fast and Slow* (New York: Farrar, Straus, and Giroux, 2011), 175.

2. Maxwell, *Developing the Leaders around You,* 127.

CHAPTER 17. ENFORCE ALL THE STANDARDS ALL THE TIME

1. Arthur S. Collins Jr., *Common Sense Training: A Working Philosophy for Leaders* (Novato, Calif.: Presidio, 2011), 209.
2. Jeff Schogol, "Top Marine: Nude Photo-Sharing Scandal Shows 'We've Got to Change,'" *Marine Corps Times,* March 2014.
3. Jim Frederick, *Black Hearts: One Platoon's Descent into Madness in Iraq's Triangle of Death* (New York: Crown Archetype, 2010).
4. A recent appreciation of the general's famous concept (which he originally published in 1999) is Franklin Annis, "Krulak Revisited: The Three-Block War, Strategic Corporals, and the Future Battlefield," *Modern War Institute at West Point,* 3 February 2020, https://mwi.usma.edu/krulak-revisited-three-block-war-strategic-corporals-future-battlefield/.
5. Bob Scales, *Scales on War: The Future of America's Military at Risk* (Annapolis, Md.: Naval Institute Press, 2016), 105.

CHAPTER 18. PEOPLE DO WHAT PEOPLE SEE

1. Kouzes and Posner, *Leadership Challenge,* 221.
2. Kouzes and Posner, 221.
3. Sinek, *Start with Why,* 17.
4. Rudyard Kipling, "Gunga Din," in *Barrack-Room Ballads* (1890), republished many times, recently in *Selected Verse: Rudyard Kipling* (New York: Pan Macmillan, 2016) and online at *Poetry Foundation,* 2020, https://www.poetryfoundation.org/poems/46783/gunga-din.

CHAPTER 19. BALANCED EXCELLENCE

1. E. D. Swinton, *The Defence of Duffer's Drift: A Few Experiences in Field Defence for Detached Posts Which May Prove Useful in Our Next War* (London: 1904; repr. Middleton, Del.: CreateSpace, 2016).
2. McCoy, *Passion of Command,* 28.

CHAPTER 20. BRILLIANCE IN THE BASICS

1. McCoy, *Passion of Command,* 34.
2. Carl von Clausewitz, *On War,* ed. and trans. M. E. Howard and Peter Paret (Princeton, N.J.: Princeton University Press, 1976), 122.
3. Saul McLeod, "Skinner: Operant Conditioning," *Simply Psychology,* last modified 2018, https://simplypsychology.org/operant-conditioning.html (accessed August 2020).
4. Grossman, *On Killing,* 177.
5. Moran, *Anatomy of Courage,* 173.
6. Kolenda, *Leadership,* 83.
7. Gladwell, *Outliers,* 41.
8. Duckworth, *Grit,* 120.
9. Duckworth, 37.

CHAPTER 21. COMPLACENCY KILLS

1. Marine Corps Intelligence Activity, *Future Operating Environment (FOE) 2015–2025: Implications for Marines* (Quantico, Va., June 2015), 8.
2. Maxwell, *Good Leaders Ask Great Questions,* 237.
3. "Jules Ellinger Quote," *IZQuotes,* last modified October 14, 2005, http://izquotes.com/quote/342161 (accessed August 2020).
4. Craig Groeschel, "Leadership Podcast: Embracing Change, Part 2," *Life.Church,* last modified 6 July 2016, https://www.life.church /leadershippodcast/embracing-change-part-2/ (accessed August 2020).
5. Kotter, *Leading Change,* 16.
6. U.S. Navy Department, *Marine Operating Concept: How an Expeditionary Force Operates in the 21st Century* (Washington, D.C.: Headquarters Marine Corps, September 2016), https://www.mcwl.marines .mil/Portals/34/Images/MarineCorpsOperatingConceptSept2016.pdf (accessed August 2020).

CHAPTER 22. FIND YOUR BLIND SPOTS

1. Marshall Goldsmith and Mark Reiter, *What Got You Here Won't Get You There* (Westport, Conn.: Hyperion. 2007), 35.
2. Goldsmith, 123.
3. Christopher Chabris and Daniel Simons, *The Invisible Gorilla,* video, http://theinvisiblegorilla.com/gorilla_experiment.html.
4. Kahneman, *Thinking, Fast and Slow,* 24.
5. Charles Duhigg, *Smarter, Faster, Better: The Transformative Power of Real Productivity* (Random House, 2016), 88.
6. Goleman, *Primal Leadership,* 108.
7. Goleman, 126.
8. Malcolm Gladwell, *Blink: The Power of Thinking without Thinking* (Boston: Little, Brown, 2007), 84.
9. Gladwell, 85.
10. Micah Zenko, *Red Team: How to Succeed by Thinking Like the Enemy* (New York: Basic Books, 2015), 46.
11. Zenko, 32.
12. Maxwell, *21 Irrefutable Laws of Leadership,* 124.
13. C. S. Lewis, *Mere Christianity: The Case for Christianity, Christian Behaviour, and Beyond Personality* (1943; repr. Westwood, N.J.: Barbour, 1952).

CHAPTER 23. A SMART MAN KNOWS WHEN HE IS STUPID

1. Thomas Jefferson, Batture Pamphlet, *The Proceedings of the Government of the United States, in Maintaining the Public Right to the Beach of the Mississippi, adjacent to New-Orleans, against the Intrusion of Edward Livingston, prepared for the use of Counsel,* 25 February 1812.
2. Covey, *Speed of Trust.*
3. McChrystal, *Team of Teams,* 79.

4. Nassim Nicholas Taleb, *The Black Swan: The Impact of the Highly Improbable*, 2nd ed. (New York: Random House, 2010).

CHAPTER 24. DON'T ALLOW THE URGENT TO DISPLACE THE IMPORTANT

1. Drake Baer, "Dwight Eisenhower Nailed a Major Insight about Productivity," *Business Insider,* last modified 10 April 2014, http://www.businessinsider.com/dwight-eisenhower-nailed-a-major-insight-about-productivity-2014-4 (accessed August 2020).
2. Covey, *Seven Habits of Highly Effective People,* 151.
3. Maxwell, *Developing the Leaders around You,* 79.
4. Jack Welch, "Winning the Game," *EntreLeadership,* podcast, last modified 11 May 2015, http://entreleadershippodcast.entreleadership.libsynpro.com/jack-welch-winning-the-game (accessed August 2020).

CHAPTER 27. IF YOU HAVE TO TELL PEOPLE YOU'RE IN CHARGE, YOU'RE NOT

1. Zinni, *Leading the Charge,* 54.
2. Maxwell, *21 Irrefutable Laws of Leadership,* 13.
3. Maxwell, *Developing the Leaders around You,* 24.
4. Andy Stanley, *Next Generation Leader: Five Essentials for Those Who Will Shape the Future* (New York: Multnomah, 2006), 45.
5. McCoy, *Passion of Command,* 66.
6. McCoy.

CHAPTER 28. WITH GREAT POWER COMES GREAT RESPONSIBILITY

1. *Marine Corps Manual* (1921), para. 1100, sect. 2.d.
2. Matthew 20:26 (NIV).
3. Ryan Hawk, "Simon Sinek: Leadership—It Starts with Why," *Learning Leader Show,* podcast 107, last modified 16 March 2016, https://learningleader.com/episode-107-simon-sinek-leadership-it-starts-with-why/ (accessed August 2020).
4. Kouzes and Posner, *Leadership Challenge,* 185.

CHAPTER 30. THE TWO MOST SCREWED-UP PEOPLE IN THE MARINE CORPS

1. Gates, *Passion for Leadership,* 26.
2. "Walter Lippmann Quote," *IZQuotes,* n.d., http://izquotes.com/quote/330615 (accessed August 2020).
3. Collins, *Good to Great,* 21.
4. Collins, 26.
5. Maxwell, *Good Leaders Ask Great Questions,* 250.
6. Bob Russell and Bryan Bucher, *Transition Plan: 7 Secrets Every Leader Needs to Know* (Peabody, Mass.: Ministers Label, 2010).

CHAPTER 31. MARINES WHO KNOW WHERE THEY ARE GOING ARE EASY TO LEAD

1. Covey, *Seven Habits of Highly Effective People*, 95.
2. Jim Collins and Jerry I. Porras, *Built to Last: Successful Habits of Visionary Companies* (London: Harper Business, 197).
3. Gates, *Passion for Leadership*, 86.
4. Gordon, "Become a Better Version of You."
5. Gates, *Passion for Leadership*, 90.
6. Kotter, *Leading Change*, 127.
7. Kotter, 127.

CHAPTER 32. KNOW AND MEET STANDARDS

1. Maxwell, *Good Leaders Ask Great Questions*, 159.
2. "Expectancy Theory of Motivation," MSG: Management Study Guide, n.d., http://managementstudyguide.com/expectancy-theory-motivation.htm (accessed August 2020).
3. Gates, *Passion for Leadership*, 209.

CHAPTER 34. WHEN IN CHARGE, TAKE CHARGE

1. MCDP-1, 98.
2. MCDP-1, 58.

CHAPTER 35. COMMAND AND FEEDBACK

1. Chairman of the Joint Chiefs of Staff, *Doctrine for the Armed Forces of the United States,* Joint Publication [JP] 1 (Washington, D.C., 2013, incorporating change 1, 12 July 2017), V-1.
2. 2 Samuel 11:1–4 (NIV).
3. 2 Samuel 12:7 (NIV).
4. Anton Myrer, *Once an Eagle* (1968; repr. New York: Harper Perennial, 2013).
5. Goleman, *Primal Leadership*, 192.
6. Gates, *Passion for Leadership*, 118.
7. Gates, 118.
8. Ken Blanchard and Phil Hodges, *The Servant Leader* (Nashville, Tenn.: HarperCollins, 2003), 84.
9. "General Douglas MacArthur's Farewell Speech: Given to the Corps of Cadets at West Point, May 12, 1962," *National Center for Public Policy Research,* http://www.nationalcenter.org/MacArthurFarewell.html (accessed August 2020).
10. Maxwell, *Good Leaders Ask Great Questions*, 49.
11. Maxwell, 53.
12. Stanley, *Next Generation Leader,* 110.
13. Rick Warren, Twitter, 11 April 2017.
14. Stanley, *Next Generation Leader,* 103.

15. Stan McChrystal, "What's Missing with Big Data? Human Filters," *LinkedIn,* last modified 14 December 2015, https://www.linkedin .com/pulse/big-idea-2016-whats-missing-data-human-filters-stan -mcchrystal (accessed 20 August 2020).

16. Craig Groeschel, "Leadership Podcast: Creating an Empowering Culture, Part 1," *Life.Church,* https://open.life.church /training/212-craig-groeschel-leadership-podcast-creating-an -empowering-culture-part-1, n.d. (accessed August 2020).

17. Kolenda, *Leadership,* 93.

CHAPTER 36. SPARTAN SPOUSES

1. Steven Pressfield, *The Gates of Fire* (New York: Random House, 2007).

CHAPTER 37. PIN IT WHERE YOU WIN IT

1. Kouzes and Posner, *Leadership Challenge,* 289.

2. Kouzes and Posner, 275.

3. Kouzes and Posner, 279.

CHAPTER 38. THE BEST LEGAL ADVICE I EVER RECEIVED WAS TO GET GOOD LEGAL ADVICE

1. Michael Doyle, "Tough Talk by Marine Commandant James Amos Complicates Sexual-Assault Cases," *National Review,* 13 September 2012.

CHAPTER 39. YOU SAID IT, BUT THAT DOESN'T MEAN THEY HEARD IT

1. Maxwell, *21 Irrefutable Laws of Leadership,* 172.

2. Craig Groeschel, "Leadership Podcast: Sharpening Your Communication Skills, Part 1," *Life.Church,* n.d., https://www.life.church /leadershippodcast/sharpening-your-communication-skills-part-1/.

3. Donald T. Phillips, *Lincoln on Leadership: Executive Strategies for Tough Times* (New York: Warner Books, 1993), 43.

CHAPTER 40: THE *E* IN "E-MAIL" STANDS FOR "EVIDENCE"

1. Robert C. Baron, *Thomas Jefferson: In His Own Words* (Golden CO, Fulcrum Publishing, 2009), 5.

CHAPTER 41. THE FIRST REPORT IS ALWAYS WRONG

1. Rudyard Kipling, "If," in *Selected Verse: Rudyard Kipling* (New York: Pan Macmillan, 2016).

2. Stanley, *Next Generation Leader,* 79.

3. Taleb, *Black Swan,* 144.

CHAPTER 42. BAD THINGS CAN AND WILL HAPPEN TO GOOD UNITS

1. Collins, *Good to Great*, 85.
2. "Max de Pree Quotes," *Brainy Quote*, n.d., https://www.brainy quote.com/quotes/quotes/m/maxdepree100557.html (accessed August 2020).
3. Maxwell, *Good Leaders Ask Great Questions*, 133.
4. Eliot Cohen, *Supreme Command: Soldiers, Statesmen, and Leadership in Wartime* (New York: Anchor Books, 2003), 224.
5. Sinek, *Leaders Eat Last*, 1.
6. Cohen, *Supreme Command*, 224.

CHAPTER 44. TALENT CAN GET YOU TO THE TOP, BUT ONLY CHARACTER WILL KEEP YOU THERE

1. The epigraph is often attributed to Ralph Emerson. See *Quote Investigator: Tracing Quotations*, http://quoteinvestigator.com/2013/01/10/watch-your-thoughts/ (accessed August 2020).
2. Maxwell, *21 Irrefutable Laws of Leadership*, 64.
3. Stanley, *Next Generation Leader*, 134.
4. E. B. Sledge, *With the Old Breed: At Peleliu and Okinawa* (Novato, Calif.: Presidio. 1981), 63.
5. Moran, *Anatomy of Courage*, 77.
6. Proverbs 27:12 (NIV).
7. Dan Ariely, *The (Honest) Truth about Dishonesty: How We Lie to Everyone—Especially Ourselves* (New York: Harper Perennial, 2013).
8. Ariely, 131.
9. Stephen J. Gerras and Leonard Wong, *Lying to Ourselves: Dishonesty in the Army Profession* (Carlisle, Pa.: U.S. Army War College Press for the Strategic Studies Institute, 2015).
10. Ariely, *(Honest) Truth about Dishonesty*, 206.
11. James Q. Wilson and George L. Kelling, "Broken Windows: The Police and Neighborhood Safety," *Atlantic*, March 1982.
12. Ariely, *(Honest) Truth about Dishonesty*, 253.

CHAPTER 45. THE DISEASE TO PLEASE

1. Simon Sinek, Twitter, 23 January 2017.
2. Maxwell, *Good Leaders Ask Great Questions*, 165.
3. Craig Groeschel, *Altar Ego: Becoming Who God Says You Are* (New York: HarperCollins, 2013).
4. Maxwell, *Good Leaders Ask Great Questions*, 178.
5. Maxwell, 157.
6. James Stavridis and R. Manning Ancell, *The Leader's Bookshelf* (Annapolis, Md.: Naval Institute Press; 2017), 51.

CHAPTER 46. DON'T EXPECT WHAT YOU DON'T INSPECT

1. George Herbert, *Outlandish* [i.e., Foreign] *Proverbs* (1640).
2. Craig Groeschel, "Leadership Podcast: Creating an Empowering Culture, Part 2," *Life.Church,* 1 February 2017, https://www.life.church/leadershippodcast/ (accessed 11 December 2020).
3. Gates, *Passion for Leadership,* 90.

CHAPTER 47. DON'T BE IN A HURRY TO MAKE A BAD DECISION

1. The first epigraph is in Maxwell, *Good Leaders Ask Great Questions,* 127. Maxwell reprints the second as well: by Weston H. Agor (1939–2007), author of several books and articles in the 1980s and '90s on the nature of intuition and its application for executives.
2. Barry Schwartz, "The Paradox of Choice," *TED Talks,* http://www.ted.com/talks/barry_schwartz_on_the_paradox_of_choice (accessed August 2020).
3. Craig Groeschel, "Leadership Podcast: Leading Up When You're Not in Charge," *Life.Church,* 1 September 2016, https://www.life.church/leadershippodcast/ (accessed August 2020). This is an earlier version of the podcast cited in chapter 46.
4. Jeremiah 17:9 (NIV).
5. John Tierney, "Do You Suffer from Decision Fatigue?" *New York Times Magazine,* 17 August 2011.
6. Gladwell, *Blink,* 262.
7. Kahneman, *Thinking, Fast and Slow,* 21.
8. Gladwell, *Blink,* 267.
9. Gladwell, 267.

CHAPTER 48. DON'T MAKE ENEMIES, BUT IF YOU DO, DON'T TREAT THEM LIGHTLY

1. Adapted from Hugo's 1845 essay "Villemain." The phrase is often attributed to Winston Churchill.
2. Gates, *Passion for Leadership,* 36.
3. Jon Gordon, *The Energy Bus: 10 Rules to Fuel Your Life, Work, and Team with Positive Energy* (New York: John Wiley & Sons, 2007), 162.
4. Paul Martinelli and the John Maxwell Team, "Transformational Leader Podcast," *The John Maxwell Team,* 2020, https://johnmaxwellteam.com/podcast/ (accessed August 2020).

CHAPTER 49. I DON'T HAVE ALL THE ANSWERS, BUT I DO KNOW THE QUESTIONS

1. David Marquet, *Turn the Ship Around! A True Story of Turning Followers into Leaders* (New York: Penguin, 2013), 174.
2. Kouzes and Posner, *Leadership Challenge,* 227.
3. Maxwell, *Good Leaders Ask Great Questions,* 49.

CHAPTER 50. IF THE BOSS IS NOT HAVING FUN, NO ONE IS HAVING FUN!

1. "Wetting down" is an old naval tradition that originated in the Royal Navy and has been adopted by the U.S. Navy and Marines. The wetting-down celebration is normally attended by the unit's officers and is always paid for and hosted by the newly promoted officer. It is customary for the increase in the amount of the first paycheck at the new rank to "go on the bar."

2. John Hagel III, John Seely Brown, and Lang Davison, "The Big Shift: Measuring the Forces of Change," *Harvard Business Review* (July–August 2009).

3. Gordon, *The Energy Bus*, 45.

4. Goldsmith and Reiter, *What Got You Here Won't Get You There*, 222.

5. Sinek, *Start with Why*, 181.

BIBLIOGRAPHY

Except where noted, all listed editions are in print format. These are recommended, but some are also available in other editions (possibly with commentary and appendices), and many are available in audio and various electronic formats.

Appleman, Roy. *East of Chosin: Entrapment and Breakout in Korea* (1950). College Station: Texas A&M University Press, 1987.

Ariely, Dan. *The (Honest) Truth about Dishonesty: How We Lie to Everyone—Especially Ourselves*. New York: Harper Perennial, 2013.

Atkinson, Rick. *An Army at Dawn: The War in North Africa, 1942–1943*. The Liberation trilogy, vol. 1. New York: Henry Holt, 2002.

Avalon, John. *Washington's Farewell: The Founding Father's Warning to Future Generations*. New York: Simon & Schuster, 2017.

Blair, Clay. *Ridgway's Paratroopers: The American Airborne in World War II*. New York: Doubleday, 1985.

Blanchard, Ken, and Phil Hodges. *The Servant Leader: Transforming Your Heart, Head, Hands & Habits*. Nashville, Tenn.: HarperCollins, 2003.

Brafman, Ori, and Rod A. Beckstrom. *The Starfish and the Spider: The Unstoppable Power of Leaderless Organizations*. London: Penguin, 2006.

Card, Orson Scott. *Ender's Game*. New York: Tom Doherty Associates, 1977.

Carroll, Pete, Yogi Roth, and Kristoffer A. Garin. *Win Forever: Live, Work, and Play like a Champion*. London: Penguin, 2011.

Catton, Bruce. *Grant Takes Command*. Boston: Little, Brown, 1994.

Clausewitz, Carl von. *On War*, edited and translated by M. E. Howard and Peter Paret. Princeton, N.J.: Princeton University Press, 1979.

Cohen, Eliot. *Supreme Command: Soldiers, Statesmen, and Leadership in Wartime*. New York: Anchor Books, 2003.

Collins, Arthur S., Jr. *Common Sense Training: A Working Philosophy for Leaders*. Novato, Calif.: Presidio, 2011.

Collins, Jim. *Good to Great: Why Some Companies Make the Leap . . . and Others Don't*. London: Harper Business, 2001.

Collins, Jim, and Jerry I. Porras. *Built to Last: Successful Habits of Visionary Companies*. New York: HarperCollins, 1997.

Coram, Robert. *Boyd: The Fighter Pilot Who Changed the Art of War*. Boston: Little, Brown, 2002.

Covey, Stephen M. R. *The Speed of Trust: The One Thing That Changes Everything*. New York: Free Press, 2006.

Covey, Stephen R. *The 7 Habits of Highly Effective People: Powerful Lessons in Personal Change*. London: Mango Media, 2015.

Drucker, Peter F. *The Effective Executive: The Definitive Guide to Getting the Right Things Done*. New York: Harper Business, 2017.

Duckworth, Angela. *Grit: The Power of Passion and Perseverance*. New York: Simon & Schuster, 2016.

Duhigg, Charles. *Smarter Faster Better: The Transformative Power of Real Productivity*. New York: Random House, 2016.

Drury, Bob, and Tom Clavin. *The Last Stand of Fox Company: A True Story of U.S. Marines in Combat*. New York: Grove Atlantic, 2009.

Fehrenbach, T. R. *This Kind of War: A Study in Unpreparedness*. New York: Macmillan, 1963.

Fick, Nathaniel. *One Bullet Away: The Making of a Marine Officer*. Boston: Houghton Mifflin, 2005.

Franklin, Benjamin. *Poor Richard's Almanack*. Waterloo, Iowa: U.S.C., 1914.

Frederick, Jim. *Black Hearts: One Platoon's Descent into Madness in Iraq's Triangle of Death*. New York: Crown Archetype, 2010.

Freeman, Douglas Southall. *Lee's Lieutenants: A Study in Command*. 1943. Reprinted Old Saybrook, Conn.: Konecky & Konecky, 1998.

Garcia, Helio Fred. *The Power of Communication: Skills to Build Trust, Inspire Loyalty, and Lead Effectively*. Upper Saddle River, N.J.: FT Press, 2012.

Gates, Robert M. *A Passion for Leadership: Lessons on Change and Reform from Fifty Years of Public Service*. New York: Knopf Doubleday, 2017.

Gerras, Stephen J., and Leonard Wong. *Lying to Ourselves: Dishonesty in the Army Profession*. Carlisle, Pa.: U.S. Army War College Press for the Strategic Studies Institute, 2015.

Gladwell, Malcolm. *Blink: The Power of Thinking without Thinking.* Boston: Little, Brown, 2007.

———. *David and Goliath: Underdogs, Misfits, and the Art of Battling Giants.* Boston: Little, Brown, 2013.

———. *Outliers: The Story of Success.* London: Allen Lane, 2008.

———. "The Talent Myth." *New Yorker,* 22 July 2002. http://www.newyorker.com/magazine/2002/07/22/the-talent-myth.

Goldsmith, Marshall, and Mark Reiter. *What Got You Here Won't Get You There: How Successful People Become Even More Successful.* Westport, Conn.: Hyperion. 2007.

Goleman, Daniel, et al. *Primal Leadership: Unleashing the Power of Emotional Intelligence.* Brighton, Mass.: Harvard Business Review Press, 2013.

Goodwin, Doris Kearns. *Team of Rivals: The Political Genius of Abraham Lincoln.* New York: Simon & Schuster, 2006.

Gordon, Jon. *The Energy Bus: 10 Rules to Fuel Your Life, Work, and Team with Positive Energy.* New York: John Wiley & Sons, 2007.

———. *Training Camp: What the Best Do Better Than Everyone Else.* New York: John Wiley & Sons, 2009.

Groeschel, Craig. *Altar Ego: Becoming Who God Says You Are.* New York: HarperCollins, 2013.

Grossman, LtCol Dave. *On Killing: The Psychological Cost of Learning to Kill in War and Society.* New York: Open Road Media, 2014.

Kahneman, Daniel. *Thinking, Fast and Slow.* New York: Farrar, Straus and Giroux, 2011.

Keegan, John. *The Mask of Command.* London: Penguin, 1987.

Kennedy, John F. *Profiles in Courage.* New York: Harper and Row. 1961.

Kerr, James. *Legacy: What the All Blacks Can Teach Us about the Business of Life.* London: Constable, 2013.

Kipling, Rudyard. *Selected Verse: Rudyard Kipling.* New York: Pan Macmillan, 2016.

Kolenda, Christopher D. *Leadership: The Warrior's Art.* Carlisle, Pa.: Army War College Press, 2001.

Kotter, John P. *Leading Change.* Brighton, Mass.: Harvard Business Review Press, 1996.

Kouzes, James M., and Barry Z. Posner. *Credibility: How Leaders Gain and Lose It, Why People Demand It.* Revised edition. New York: John Wiley & Sons, 2011.

Kouzes, Jim, and Barry Posner. *The Leadership Challenge: How to Make Extraordinary Things Happen in Organizations, 3rd Edition.* New York: John Wiley & Sons, 2003.

Krulak, Victor. *First to Fight: An Inside View of the U.S. Marine Corps.* Annapolis, Md.: Naval Institute Press, 1984.

Lewis, C. S. *Mere Christianity: The Case for Christianity, Christian Behaviour, and Beyond Personality.* 1943. Reprint Westwood, N.J.: Barbour, 1952.

Manchester, William, and Paul Reid. *The Last Lion: Winston Spencer Churchill.* Volume 3, *Defender of the Realm, 1940–1965.* New York: Bantam Books, 2013.

Marquet, L. David. *Turn the Ship Around! A True Story of Turning Followers into Leaders.* New York: Penguin, 2013.

Maxwell, John C. *Developing the Leaders around You: How to Help Others Reach Their Full Potential.* Nashville, Tenn.: Thomas Nelson, 1995.

———. *Good Leaders Ask Great Questions: Your Foundation for Successful Leadership.* New York: Center Street, 2014.

———. *The 21 Irrefutable Laws of Leadership: Follow Them and People Will Follow You.* Nashville, Tenn.: Thomas Nelson, 2007.

McChrystal, Stanley, et al. *Team of Teams: New Rules of Engagement for a Complex World.* London: Penguin, 2015.

McCoy, Bryan. *The Passion of Command: The Moral Imperative of Leadership.* Quantico, Va.: Marine Corps Association Bookstore, 2006.

McDonough, James R. *The Defense of Hill 781: An Allegory of Modern Mechanized Combat.* Novato, Calif.: Presidio Press. 1988.

McLeod, Saul. "The Milgram Experiment." *Simply Psychology* (2007). https://www.simplypsychology.org/milgram.html.

———. "Skinner: Operant Conditioning," *Simply Psychology,* last modified 2018, https://simplypsychology.org/operant-conditioning.html (accessed August 2020).

Milgrim, Stanley. "The Perils of Obedience." *Harper's* 247:1483 (1973), 62–77.

Moran, Lord [Charles Wilson, 1st Baron Moran]. *The Anatomy of Courage.* London: Constable, 1945.

Myrer, Anton. *Once an Eagle.* 1968. Reprinted New York: Harper Perennial, 2013.

Phillips, Donald T. *Lincoln on Leadership: Executive Strategies for Tough Times.* New York: Warner Books, 1993.

Pressfield, Steven. *Gates of Fire.* New York: Random House, 2007.

———. *The Virtues of War.* New York: Random House, 2005.

———. *The Warrior Ethos.* New York: Black Irish Entertainment, 2011.

Restak, Richard. *Mozart's Brain and the Fighter Pilot: Unleashing Your Brain's Potential.* New York: Three Rivers, 2001.

Ricks, Thomas. *The Generals: American Military Command from World War II to Today.* London: Penguin, 2012.

Ridgway, Matthew B., and Harold H. Martin. *Soldier: The Memoirs of Matthew B. Ridgway.* New York: Harper & Brothers, 1956.

Russell, Bob, and Bryan Bucher. *Transition Plan: 7 Secrets Every Leader Needs to Know.* Peabody, Mass.: Ministers Label, 2010.

Scales, Bob. *Scales on War: The Future of America's Military at Risk.* Annapolis, Md.: Naval Institute Press, 2016.

Shapira, Allison. *Speak with Impact: How to Command the Room and Influence Others.* Nashville, Tenn.: HarperCollins Leadership, 2018.

Sinek, Simon. *Leaders Eat Last: Why Some Teams Pull Together and Others Don't.* New York: Penguin, 2014.

———. *Start with Why: How Great Leaders Inspire Everyone to Take Action.* New York: Penguin, 2011.

Sledge, E. B. *With the Old Breed: At Peleliu and Okinawa.* Novato, Calif.: Presidio, 1981.

Stanley, Andy. *The Next Generation Leader: Five Essentials for Those Who Will Shape the Future.* New York: Multnomah, 2006.

Stavridis, James, and R. Manning Ancell. *The Leader's Bookshelf.* Annapolis, Md.: Naval Institute Press, 2017.

Sullivan, Gordon R., and Michael V. Harper. *Hope Is Not a Method: What Business Leaders Can Learn from America's Army.* New York: Broadway Books, 1996.

Sun Tzu. *The Art of War.* Translated by Ralph D. Sawyer. New York: Basic Books, 1994.

Taleb, Nassim Nicholas. *The Black Swan: The Impact of the Highly Improbable.* 2nd edition. New York: Random House, 2010.

Warren, Rick. *The Purpose Driven Life: What on Earth Am I Here For?* Grand Rapids, Mich.: Zondervan, 2012.

Welch, Jack, and Suzy Welch. *The Real-Life MBA: Your No-BS Guide to Winning the Game, Building a Team, and Growing Your Career.* New York: HarperCollins, 2015.

Zenko, Micah. *Red Team: How to Succeed by Thinking Like the Enemy.* New York: Basic Books, 2015.

Zinni, Tony. *Leading the Charge: Leadership Lessons from the Battlefield to the Boardroom.* New York: St. Martin's, 2009.

INDEX

Abizzaid, John, 229–30

absence of leadership, xx

administrative separation process (ADSEP), 88–89

adults, treating like and acting like, 38–40

Afghanistan: breakdown in small-unit discipline in, 98–99; Camp Bastion attack, 234–35; Camp Leatherneck R4OG organization, 11–12

alcohol policies, 39–40

Alexander the Great, 82, 103, 134

Allen, Terry de la Mesa "Terrible Terry," 71

Alphas, leading, 163–64

Altar Ego, The (Groeschel), 251, 253

ammo can, filling a, 145

Amos, James, 135

analytical decisions (System 2), 131, 137, 268–69

Anatomy of Courage (Moran), 28, 118

ardor, 284–85

Ariely, Dan, 137, 246–47, 248, 249

Army at Dawn, An (Atkinson), 239

arrogance, 13, 134

ass, showing, 107–8

Athenians, 88

Atkinson, Rick, 239

attributes of leaders: authenticity, xvi, 4, 11, 18, 46–47, 83, 104, 289; caring about Marines whom you serve, xvi, 8–22; exclusion of

character as, 244; inspiring others to find the will to accomplish the mission, xx–xxi, xxii, xxiii; lifelong learning and capacity to implement organizational change, 45; love as fifteenth leadership trait, 17–22, 290; skills and personality traits, xxii, 162, 173–74, 235, 289–93

Auerbach, Red, 222

authority: command relationships and, 189, 191; delegation of authority, 163; establishment and limitations of, 157–58; fear, intimidation, and authoritarian leaders, 24–25, 51–53; great power comes with great responsibility, 161–65; levels of leadership and, 158–59; moral authority, 158–59; power and not being in charge if you have to tell people you're in charge, 157–60; when in charge, take charge, 56, 187–91

Avlon, John, 28–29

awards, medals, and citations, 208–11

Bad Leaders Drive Out Good Ones, 54–57

Bad Things Can and Will Happen to Good Units, 230–31, 233–36

Bahnsen, John C. "Doc," 106–7, 109

323

ABOUT THE AUTHOR

Col Thomas J. Gordon, USMC (Ret.), is a career Marine with thirty years of executive leadership experience commanding diverse organizations in the most demanding environments. His final assignment as director of the Command and Staff College was a fitting capstone to a career spent developing principled centered leaders and returning men and women of virtue and character back to society.

The Naval Institute Press is the book-publishing arm of the U.S. Naval Institute, a private, nonprofit, membership society for sea service professionals and others who share an interest in naval and maritime affairs. Established in 1873 at the U.S. Naval Academy in Annapolis, Maryland, where its offices remain today, the Naval Institute has members worldwide.

Members of the Naval Institute support the education programs of the society and receive the influential monthly magazine *Proceedings* or the colorful bimonthly magazine *Naval History* and discounts on fine nautical prints and on ship and aircraft photos. They also have access to the transcripts of the Institute's Oral History Program and get discounted admission to any of the Institute-sponsored seminars offered around the country.

The Naval Institute's book-publishing program, begun in 1898 with basic guides to naval practices, has broadened its scope to include books of more general interest. Now the Naval Institute Press publishes about seventy titles each year, ranging from how-to books on boating and navigation to battle histories, biographies, ship and aircraft guides, and novels. Institute members receive significant discounts on the Press' more than eight hundred books in print.

Full-time students are eligible for special half-price membership rates. Life memberships are also available.

For a free catalog describing Naval Institute Press books currently available, and for further information about joining the U.S. Naval Institute, please write to:

Member Services
U.S. Naval Institute
291 Wood Road
Annapolis, MD 21402-5034
Telephone: (800) 233-8764
Fax: (410) 571-1703
Web address: www.usni.org